CREATIVE HOMEOWNER®

ULTIMATE GUIDE TO

Kitchens

PLAN ▪ REMODEL ▪ BUILD

CREATIVE HOMEOWNER® Upper Saddle River, New Jersey

COPYRIGHT © 1991, 1996, 2002, 2007

CRE**A**TIVE
HOMEOWNER®

A Division of Federal Marketing Corp.
Upper Saddle River, NJ

ULTIMATE GUIDE TO KITCHENS

MANAGING EDITOR Fran Donegan
SENIOR GRAPHIC DESIGN COORDINATOR Glee Barre
GRAPHIC DESIGNER Kathryn Wityk
PHOTO RESEARCHER Robyn Poplasky
EDITORIAL ASSISTANT Nora Grace
INDEXER Schroeder Indexing Services
COVER DESIGN David Geer, Kathryn Wityk
ILLUSTRATIONS Ian Warpole, Vincent Babak, Clarke Barre
FRONT COVER PHOTOGRAPHY Anne Gummerson
BACK COVER PHOTOGRAPHY *top* www.davidduncanlivingston.com; *bottom row left to right* John Parsekian/CH; Eric Roth; John Parsekian/CH

CREATIVE HOMEOWNER

VICE PRESIDENT AND PUBLISHER Timothy O. Bakke
PRODUCTION DIRECTOR Kimberly H. Vivas
ART DIRECTOR David Geer
MANAGING EDITOR Fran J. Donegan

Current Printing (last digit)
10 9 8 7 6 5 4 3 2 1

Ultimate Guide to Kitchens, Fourth Edition
Library of Congress Control Number: 2006934265
ISBN-10: 1-58011-340-0
ISBN-13: 978-1-58011-340-3

CREATIVE HOMEOWNER®
A Division of Federal Marketing Corp.
24 Park Way
Upper Saddle River, NJ 07458
www.creativehomeowner.com

safety

Although the methods in this book have been reviewed for safety, it is not possible to overstate the importance of using the safest methods you can. What follows are reminders—some do's and don'ts of work safety—to use along with your common sense.

▌ Always use caution, care, and good judgment when following the procedures described in this book.

▌ Always be sure that the electrical setup is safe, that no circuit is overloaded, and that all power tools and outlets are properly grounded. Do not use power tools in wet locations.

▌ Always read container labels on paints, solvents, and other products; provide ventilation; and observe all other warnings.

▌ Always read the manufacturer's instructions for using a tool, especially the warnings.

▌ Use hold-downs and push sticks whenever possible when working on a table saw. Avoid working short pieces if you can.

▌ Always remove the key from any drill chuck (portable or press) before starting the drill.

▌ Always pay deliberate attention to how a tool works so that you can avoid being injured.

▌ Always know the limitations of your tools. Do not try to force them to do what they were not designed to do.

▌ Always make sure that any adjustment is locked before proceeding. For example, always check the rip fence on a table saw or the bevel adjustment on a portable saw before starting to work.

▌ Always clamp small pieces to a bench or other work surface when using a power tool.

▌ Always wear the appropriate rubber gloves or work gloves when handling chemicals, moving or stacking lumber, working with concrete, or doing heavy construction.

▌ Always wear a disposable face mask when you create dust by sawing or sanding. Use a special filtering respirator when working with toxic substances and solvents.

▌ Always wear eye protection, especially when using power tools or striking metal on metal or concrete; a chip can fly off, for example, when chiseling concrete.

▌ Never work while wearing loose clothing, open cuffs, or jewelry; tie back long hair.

▌ Always be aware that there is seldom enough time for your body's reflexes to save you from injury from a power tool in a dangerous situation; everything happens too fast. Be alert!

▌ Always keep your hands away from the business ends of blades, cutters, and bits.

▌ Always hold a circular saw firmly, usually with both hands.

▌ Always use a drill with an auxiliary handle to control the torque when using large-size bits.

▌ Always check your local building codes when planning new construction. The codes are intended to protect public safety and should be observed to the letter.

▌ Never work with power tools when you are tired or when under the influence of alcohol or drugs.

▌ Never cut tiny pieces of wood or pipe using a power saw. When you need a small piece, saw it from a securely clamped longer piece.

▌ Never change a saw blade or a drill or router bit unless the power cord is unplugged. Do not depend on the switch being off. You might accidentally hit it.

▌ Never work in insufficient lighting.

▌ Never work with dull tools. Have them sharpened, or learn how to sharpen them yourself.

▌ Never use a power tool on a workpiece—large or small—that is not firmly supported.

▌ Never saw a workpiece that spans a large distance between horses without close support on each side of the cut; the piece can bend, closing on and jamming the blade, causing saw kickback.

▌ When sawing, never support a workpiece from underneath with your leg or other part of your body.

▌ Never carry sharp or pointed tools, such as utility knives, awls, or chisels, in your pocket. If you want to carry any of these tools, use a special-purpose tool belt that has leather pockets and holders.

contents

dreams and schemes

Planning a new kitchen is a challenging, exhilarating, and exhausting task. But it's well worth the effort. Although remodeling a kitchen is one of the most costly home improvements, it's also one of the most rewarding. You gain a new kitchen that is more efficient and attractive than the old one, and a new kitchen is also a strong selling point should you sell your house.

BEGIN BY DECIDING WHAT YOU WANT

Many people know exactly what they want in their new kitchen. But if your plan isn't clear in your mind, ask yourself the following questions. Your answers will get you started on planning your new kitchen.

▌ What do you like about your existing kitchen?

▌ What do you want to change?

▌ What do you do in your kitchen apart from fixing meals?

▌ Who does the cooking in your house?

▌ How do family members interact when they cook?

▌ Is a typical meal heat and serve? Full-course from scratch? Something else?

▌ How do you entertain?

▌ Is your kitchen a family and company gathering place?

▌ What other tasks would you like to do in the kitchen? Pay bills? Homework? Use a computer? Do laundry?

▌ What decorating style do you want in your new kitchen?

Organize Information

To keep track of all the decisions and details involved in planning and remodeling your kitchen, set up a scrapbook, folder, or file box. Keep kitchen photos clipped from magazines and newspapers, product brochures, articles about new trends or products, physical samples and color swatches of surface materials, notes from visits to showrooms, and all of your ideas and sketches.

Paperwork. You should be able to put your hands on what you need:

- Calendar for scheduling and keeping a record of progress.
- Shopping lists with prices, warranties, serial numbers, receipts, and the like.
- Telephone directory of all subcontractors, suppliers, and service representatives.
- Contracts, permits, and inspection approvals.

Layout and Traffic Patterns. The arrangement of work spaces and appliances, and the flow of traffic through the kitchen greatly influence how tasks are performed.

Appliances. Choose among a number of appliance styles and features. Appliances should be placed so that they function most efficiently and conveniently, so the choices you make will affect the entire plan.

Storage. You need enough of the right kind of storage to provide a place for dry goods, perishables, dishes, pots and utensils, cleaning supplies, recyclables, and anything else you want to keep in the kitchen.

Lighting. Plan on providing good overall lighting in the room, as well as task lighting that illuminates specific work areas.

Surfaces. Colors and textures help define your style. A kitchen's walls, floor, and countertops should be attractive, functional, and easy to clean.

LEFT Remodeling a kitchen is certainly an enormous task, but it is also one of the most rewarding home improvement projects.

ABOVE Create a layout that suits your lifestyle and will help you prepare meals efficiently and safely.

BELOW Reproduction fixtures and distinctive crown molding give this kitchen a traditional look.

HOW TO USE THIS BOOK

Remodeling your kitchen may seem daunting at first, but the project will begin to appear more manageable when you realize that it consists of a series of smaller projects. *Ultimate Guide to Kitchens: Plan, Remodel, Build* is intended to guide you through the entire process. The book will help you:

▌ Analyze your existing kitchen and set your sights on the kitchen you would like to have.

▌ Choose the right materials, products, and appliances for your needs.

▌ Plan a layout that suits your lifestyle and the space available.

▌ Complete the most popular do-it-yourself projects to get the kitchen of your dreams.

▌ Decide what you can handle yourself, and where you might need the services of a professional.

The organization of the book allows you to plan and remodel an entire kitchen yourself. Or you can pick the sections that apply to your own situation.

ABOVE Clean lines and uncluttered work surfaces are the hallmarks of contemporary design.

The Chapters

The *Ultimate Guide to Kitchens* will help you plan, design, and build your new kitchen. The information is presented in such a way that you can pick the level of involvement with which you are most comfortable. Each chapter covers a specific area of kitchen remodeling—from removing your old cabinets and appliances to touching up the final paint job. In between you will find information on cabinets, countertops, sinks and faucets, appliances, lighting, flooring, walls and ceilings, and ways to pay for the project.

In addition to chapters that will help you come up with a design and layout for your new kitchen, the heart of the book is in the 70 step-by-step projects that will help you attain professional-quality results. The list includes the most popular projects in kitchen remodeling. You can use the information to complete the entire project yourself—each project contains a skill-level guide to keep you from getting in over your head, shown at right—or just tackle the projects that interest you and have a professional do the rest.

GUIDE TO SKILL LEVEL

 Easy.
Even for beginners.

 Challenging.
Can be done by beginners who have the patience and willingness to learn.

 Difficult.
Can be handled by most experienced do-it-yourselfers who have mastered basic construction skills. Consider consulting a specialist.

ABOVE Many different skills are needed for a kitchen remodeling. Decide what you want to do yourself, and seek help for the rest.

1 construction basics

Your plans are set. Appliances, cabinets, and other components are on order. Now it's time to tear out your old kitchen and get ready for the new one. You'll have to live with dust, noise, and disorder for some time. And your normal kitchen routine will be disrupted for the duration. Of course, you can eat out every night. But rather than go hungry or go broke from restaurants, try setting up a temporary kitchen—in the dining room, for example. Move the refrigerator there, and organize a cooking station with a microwave and a toaster oven. Use a nearby bathroom as a water supply, and don't forget to adjust your menu accordingly. Now this makeshift kitchen won't be exactly homey, but remember, the inconvenience you experience now will turn into a distant memory once you finish your new kitchen.

TAKING APART YOUR OLD KITCHEN

Kitchen demolition is a misnomer for the job. Dismantling the room is a more suitable term because it's easier and safer than wielding sledgehammers and wrecking bars. Begin by removing everything from the room that isn't nailed or screwed down, including the refrigerator and stove. Then remove the faucet and sink, and the dishwasher. The countertop is next, followed by the base cabinets and the wall cabinets.

TOOLS & MATERIALS
- Screwdriver ▮ Basin wrench ▮ Putty knife
- Groove-joint pliers ▮ Drill with screwdriving attachment (optional)
- Reciprocating saw for tile counters
- Carpet scrap ▮ Hand truck (optional)

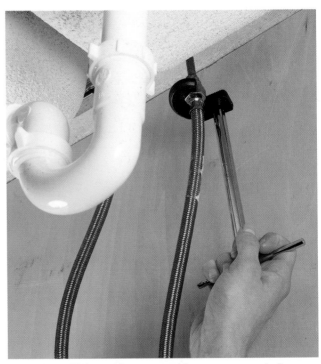

1 Shut off the cold-water and hot-water supply lines to the sink. Then take the supply lines off the bottom of the faucet. Space under the sink is tight, so a basin wrench is generally required. Also disconnect the drainpipe.

4 Carefully pull the dishwasher from under the countertop. To protect the flooring, slide a piece of carpeting under the front legs or get someone to help you keep the front elevated as you pull the unit out.

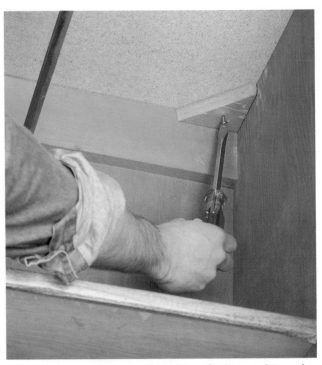

5 Countertops are usually held to the base cabinets by screws driven up through cabinet corner blocks into the underside of the top. Back out the screws and lift up the top with a pry bar.

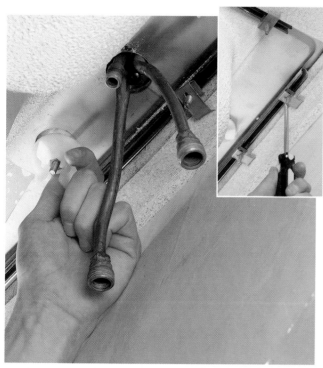

2 To remove the faucet, unscrew the nuts that hold the assembly to the sink. Then remove the sink. Many sinks are held to the countertop with clips (inset). Remove these using a screwdriver.

3 To remove a dishwasher, begin by disconnecting the power and water lines to the bottom of the unit. Then back out the screws on the underside of the countertop that hold the dishwasher in place.

6 Working with a helper, lift off the countertop and remove it from the kitchen. If you don't damage it when taking it out, you can cut it to size and use it in the laundry room as a folding table or in the garage as a workbench.

7 Base cabinets are usually attached to the wall and to each other with screws, the latter driven through the cabinet stiles. Remove all of these screws, and pull out the cabinets.

REMOVING WALLS

project

Think twice before you tear into a wall or ceiling. The job almost always adds up to more than you planned on. The dust and debris somehow find their way into all corners of the house—even if you take serious measures to contain the mess. But if you are committed to the idea, then protect yourself and the house on a couple of fronts. First, make sure to wear gloves, eye and hearing protection, and a heavy-duty dust mask. Keep the room closed off with polyethylene sheeting taped over the doorway. Also try to locate a dumpster just below the kitchen window so you don't have to haul debris through the house.

Begin by shutting off the power and water to the room to prevent a dangerous situation if you inadvertently cut into a water pipe or electrical line. Remove all the trim work. If you want to reuse the molding, be sure to take care when prying it from the walls. Knock a hole in the wall, or cut along the studs to start removing the drywall. Pull off wall sections using a flat pry bar, and remove the nails or screws from the edge of all the framing members using pliers.

TOOLS & MATERIALS
▌ Basic carpentry tools
▌ Reciprocating saw
▌ Pry bar
▌ Masonry chisel (for plaster)
▌ Goggles and dust mask

caution
WALLS AND CEILINGS MAY CONTAIN PIPES, WIRING, OR DUCTS, SO CHECK THESE AREAS CAREFULLY BEFORE WORKING ON THEM. ALSO, COVER HEATING REGISTERS AND EXPOSED DRAINS TO KEEP THEM FREE OF DEBRIS DURING DEMOLITION.

1 Begin the demolition by removing the wall and ceiling trim. If you don't plan to reuse these pieces, then just pull them off with a wrecking bar. But if you want to reuse them, carefully take them off using a flat pry bar. Once the molding is removed, pull out the nails from the backside using locking pliers.

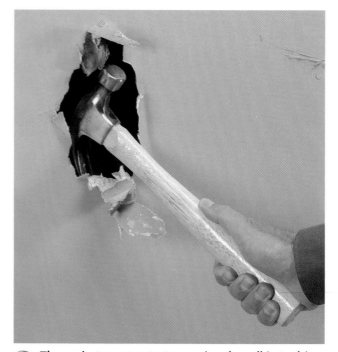

2 The easiest way to start removing drywall is to drive a hammer into the wall. Once a hole is made, you can use a wrecking bar, a flat bar, or the claw on the hammerhead to pull off the drywall. Be sure to wear eye and breathing protection while you work.

DEALING WITH DUST

You probably can't stop the dust generated during demolition from penetrating into other areas of your home, but you can keep the mess to a minimum. Before you begin any demolition, close off the kitchen from other rooms by hanging plastic sheeting over doorways and pass-throughs, and covering heating and cooling registers. Seal the edges of the sheet with heavy duct tape. Overlap two sheets to create a flap in the door you will use to get into and out of the room. You may find it helpful to place a small fan blowing out in a kitchen window. This will help keep any dust generated from migrating to the rest of the house.

3 Remove drywall in large pieces by cutting out wall sections with a reciprocating saw. Use a short blade that cuts just through the drywall.

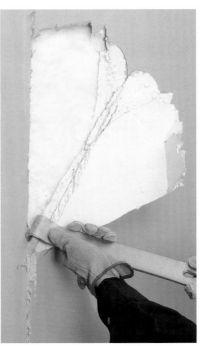

4 Use a pry bar to pull the drywall sections from the wall. If you cut along the sides of the studs, it should be easy to remove large sections at a time.

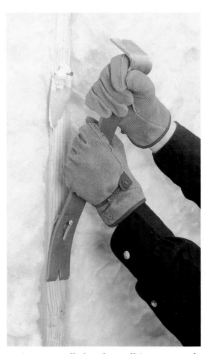

5 Once all the drywall is removed, pull the nails along each stud using a pry bar or nail puller. If screws were used, remove these using a drill-driver.

REMOVING A NONBEARING WALL

project

A nonbearing wall is usually called a partition and supports only the wall covering attached to it. It does not support any weight above it. As such, these walls can usually be removed without having any structural impact on your house. To do this, just strip off the wallcovering; then remove the studs by prying them loose from the top and bottom plates. Finish up by removing the bottom and top plates from the floor and ceiling.

TOOLS & MATERIALS
- Basic carpentry tools
- Sledgehammer
- Reciprocating saw
- Pry bar

1 Once the drywall and any pipe and electrical cable are removed, start dismantling the wall. Use a sledgehammer to loosen one stud at a time. Work carefully, and you'll be able to reuse the lumber for other projects.

2 When the bottom of the stud is loose, twist the top of it away from the top plate. While working, be careful not to step on the bottom wall plate that has nails from the studs sticking up.

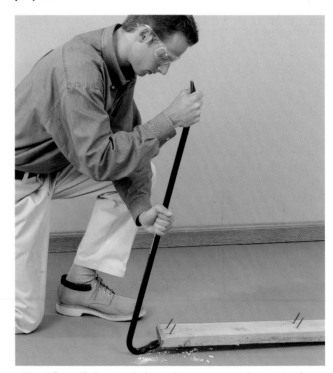

3 After all the studs have been removed, pry up the bottom plate using a wrecking bar. As soon as the plate is free, drive the nails back through the board and pull them out. Pry off the top plate, and remove its nails in the same way.

BUILDING A WALL IN PLACE

If space is tight in your kitchen and you need only a couple of short partitions, then building them in place instead of prefabricating them on the floor and tilting them up is a good approach. (See page 18.) Start by nailing the bottom plate onto the floor, and use it to establish the location of the top plate. Install the top plate; then nail the studs and corner posts between the two.

TOOLS & MATERIALS
- Basic carpentry tools ▮ Framing square
- Chalk line ▮ Framing lumber
- Circular or power-miter saw
- 10d (3 inch), 12d (3¼ inch), 16d (3½ inch) nails
- 4-foot level

1 Begin by establishing the location of the wall on the floor. Lay out these walls so that they are square to the existing walls and to each other. Snap chalk lines on the floor to keep the plates straight; then nail them to the floor.

2 Use a plumb line to establish the location of the top plates so that they align perfectly with the bottom plates. Then begin installing the wall studs. Make sure the studs against the existing walls are plumb before you nail them in place.

3 Fabricate an outside corner post from two studs with ¾-in.-thick spacer boards in between. Then lift it up and drive it between the bottom and top plates. Toenail it in place.

BUILDING A TIP-UP WALL

Most partition walls are built with 2x4 lumber. But if plumbing waste lines will be running through the wall, using 2x6 stock is the better idea. Start by laying out their positions on the floor using a framing square and chalk lines. Then lay out the bottom and top plates at the same time; cut the studs to length; and nail them between the plates. Stand the wall up; make sure it's plumb; and nail it in place.

TOOLS & MATERIALS

■ Basic carpentry tools
■ Framing square
■ Chalk line ■ Framing lumber
■ Circular or power miter saw
■ 16d (3½ inch) nails
■ 4-foot level

1 Lay out the position of the new walls using a chalk line and a framing square. Make sure the new walls are square to the existing walls and to each other. Account for the extra thickness if using 2x6 lumber.

2 Lay out the top and bottom plates together using a framing square or a combination square. Mark the location of the studs on 16-in. centers along the length of the wall.

3 Determine the length of the studs by measuring the distance between the floor and the ceiling, then subtracting 3¼ in. This matches the thickness of two plates (3 in.) and ¼ in. of tip-up room. Cut the studs and nail them between the plates.

JOINING EXISTING WALLS

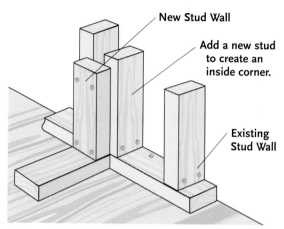

New Stud Wall

Add a new stud to create an inside corner.

Existing Stud Wall

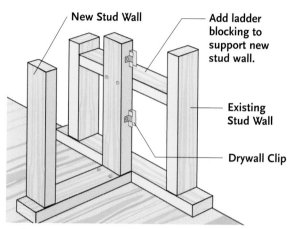

New Stud Wall

Add ladder blocking to support new stud wall.

Existing Stud Wall

Drywall Clip

Joining a new partition to an existing wall will require some work on the old wall. Open up the wall, and install additional studs as shown.

Other options include installing a 2x6 nailer in the adjoining wall cavity or nailing up ladder blocking between existing studs as shown above.

4 Carefully lift up the framed wall, and slide it under the ceiling. Make sure the bottom plate is aligned with the chalk line on the floor, and nail it in place. For walls over 4 or 5 feet long, get some help lifting and holding the wall.

5 Insert wood shimming shingles between the top of the wall and the ceiling to hold the wall in place. Then use a level to check for plumb. Attach the wall by driving nails up through the top plate and into the floor framing above.

construction options

ABOVE Removing a wall not only opens up the room, it also allows you to install a distinctive architectural feature, such as an arch.

LEFT If extra floor space is impossible to find, consider removing part of the wall to visually open the room to the adjoining space.

CLOCKWISE FROM ABOVE Great rooms can consist of the kitchen and an eating area or a kitchen and a family room, above. They are often created by removing the wall between the two rooms, below. Half walls provide both a boundary and a connection between spaces, left.

project

Drywall, also called wallboard, has a gypsum plaster core that is sandwiched between two layers of heavy paper. It usually comes in sheets that are 4 feet wide and from 8 to 16 feet long in 2-foot increments. Common thicknesses are 1/4, 3/8, 1/2, and 5/8 inches.

You can install these panels either horizontally or vertically. Horizontal installations are easier, particularly during the finishing stages. But vertical installations are easier if you are working alone. To prevent cracks, avoid making joints next to doors and windows.

Cutting And Hanging Drywall

Begin by cutting though the surface paper using a sharp utility knife and a straightedge guide. Break the panel against your knee or over a scrap board placed on the floor. Bend back the broken panel, and cut the back paper with a utility knife. Smooth cuts with a file or sandpaper. Then cut any openings needed for electrical outlets or other obstructions. Nail or screw the panels in place, spaced every 6 inches around the edge and every 12 inches in the panel field. To butt one panel tightly against one above, lift panels with a site-made lever made of scrap lumber.

TOOLS & MATERIALS
- Basic carpentry tools
- Drywall panels
- Drywall saw
- 48-inch aluminum drywall T-square (or straightedge)
- Utility knife
- Power drill with drywall screw clutch
- Drywall hammer
- Drywall nails or galvanized drywall screws long enough to penetrate at least one inch into the framing
- Panel lifter

1 To make straight cuts on a drywall panel, first mark the sheet to proper size. Then score the surface paper using a utility knife and a metal straightedge. Always use a sharp blade in the knife and cut only through the paper. Use a drywall saw to make jogged or curved cuts.

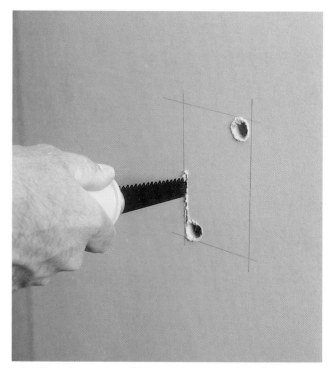

4 To make a cutout for a receptacle or switch box, lay out the box position on the panel. Then drill a hole at opposing corners and cut along the layout lines with a drywall or keyhole saw.

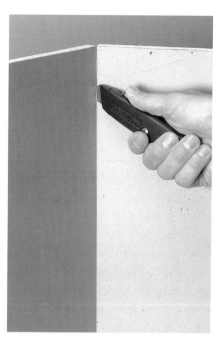

3 After the panel is snapped, stand it on its edge and bend it slightly at the break. Then cut through the paper backing using a sharp utility knife. If the cut edge is too rough to fit, don't recut the panel. Just sand down the edge with coarse sandpaper.

2 Once the paper is scored, the panels are easy to break. Just put your knee behind the cut on the back of the panel, and pull both sides toward you. Or place a piece of scrap lumber under the cut, and push down on one side until the panel snaps.

NAILS OR SCREWS?

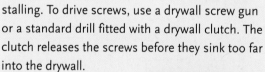

Drywall screws hold better than nails, but for small jobs and patches nails will suffice. Use 1⅝-inch ring-shank drywall nails for ½-inch drywall and 1⅞-inch nails for ⅝-inch drywall. Drywall screws should be at least ¾ inch longer than the thickness of the panel you are installing. To drive screws, use a drywall screw gun or a standard drill fitted with a drywall clutch. The clutch releases the screws before they sink too far into the drywall.

5 When you need to lift a panel off the floor so it fits tight to the one above, use a simple site-made lever. Put a wide board under the panel, then another smaller board under the wide board. Step on the end of the lever, and the panel will move up.

TAPING DRYWALL

If you plan to paint your finished walls, the quality of your drywall finishing job is crucial. The smallest dents and ridges will show through paint, especially high-gloss products. Wallpaper hides more, and ceramic tile or wood paneling require only one coat of compound and tape on the drywall.

For a top-notch job, begin by filling the screw and nail dimples with joint compound. Then start taping the joints between panels. There are two types of drywall tape: paper tape and self-sticking fiberglass mesh tape. Generally speaking, fiberglass tape works well on tapered joints (along the long edges of the panels) but doesn't work as well in corners and butt joints (across the ends of the panels). If you want to keep things simple, just use paper tape for everything.

First apply a thin coat of compound across a joint; embed a piece of tape in this compound; smooth the tape in place; and cover it with another thin coat of compound. Use tape on inside corners and metal corner bead on outside corners. When joints are dry, sand them smooth and apply the last two coats of compound.

TOOLS & MATERIALS
▌ Utility knife
▌ 6-inch-wide drywall knife
▌ 12-inch-wide drywall knife
▌ Sanding block
▌ Tin snips (if you need to cut metal corner bead)
▌ Ready-mix joint compound
▌ Perforated paper tape or fiberglass mesh tape
▌ Metal corner bead (only if outside corners are present)
▌ Pole sander with swivel head and 120-grit sandpaper inserts or sanding screen (optional)
▌ Dust mask

1 Begin the finishing process by filling the nail and screw dimples with joint compound. Use premixed compound instead of the type you mix yourself. And use a 6-in.-wide flexible taping knife. A flexible knife works better for pressing the compound into the depressions.

5 On outside corners, nail metal corner bead to the wall framing. Then apply joint compound to both sides of the bead, using the raised corner as a guide.

2 All joints must be covered with compound and tape. First, spread a thin coat of compound across the joint. Then embed a piece of tape.

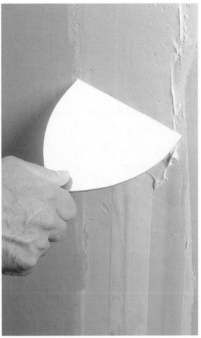

3 Once the tape is smooth, cover it with a thin coat of joint compound. Smooth the surface and remove extra compound using a 6-in. knife.

4 On inside corners, apply compound to both sides of the corner. Then place a folded piece of paper tape over the joint, and embed it in the compound.

6 Once the first coats of compound and tape are dry, sand all joints with a pole sander and 120-grit sandpaper. Smooth the rough spots, and feather the edges. Make sure to wear eye protection and a heavy-duty dust mask.

7 Plan on applying at least two additional coats of compound, with each coat covering a wider area than the one before. Use a 10- or 12-in.-wide taping knife for the final coat. The smoother you apply the compound, the less sanding you'll need to do later.

WINDOWS & DOORS

Sunlight brings cheer and sparkle to any kitchen. All you have to do is welcome it inside with windows, glass doors, or a skylight. When you shop for window and door units, make energy conservation a prime consideration. Double glazing is now standard, but most manufacturers offer windows with low-emissivity (low-e) glazing. These windows have films that reflect heat but let in light. The film also blocks ultraviolet light that can fade fabrics. Look for energy ratings that reflect the entire window unit, not just the glazing. You can also add exterior awnings to shade the windows from unwanted heat gain. Because a house loses more heat at night than during the day, drapes can provide privacy and minimize nighttime heat losses from windows.

ENERGY-EFFICIENT WINDOWS & DOORS

Choose windows, doors, and skylights based on your local climate. Products that meet the following requirements earn the Department of Energy's Energy Star Label. Look for windows, doors, and skylights tested by the National Fenestration Rating Council, an independent testing group.

Northern States
▌ Windows and doors must have a U-factor* of 0.35 or below.
▌ Skylights must have a U-factor* of 0.45 or below.

Middle States
▌ Windows and doors must have a U-factor* of 0.40 or below and an SHGC** rating of 0.55 or below.
▌ Skylights must have a U-factor* of 0.45 or below and an SHGC** of 0.55 or below.

Southern States
▌ Windows, doors, and skylights must have a U-factor* rating of 0.75 or below and an SHGC** of 0.40 or below.

* U-factor is a measurement of heat loss. The lower the number, the less heat lost.
** SHGC stands for Solar Heat Gain Coefficient and is a measurement of how well a product blocks heat caused by sunlight. It is a number between 0 and 1. The lower the number the more heat the product blocks.

Window Types

Before you decide that your kitchen needs more or bigger windows, take down the curtains from your existing windows—the change in light levels may amaze you. If that's not the answer, consider adding or enlarging the windows. Place them wherever they work best. Sometimes

an above-cabinet soffit space provides an excellent site for awning-type windows. Or you may install traditional-style windows. These needn't be the same width as the old ones, but they usually look better if the top edges line up with other windows in the room.

If you want a window to provide natural task lighting for a kitchen sink or work surface, its sill should be 3 to 6 inches above the countertop. For safety reasons, most building codes don't permit windows over ranges or cooktops.

Don't overlook style when selecting a window. If your house is a colonial, for example, stick with a traditional double-hung window instead of the contemporary casement type that may not blend with your home's overall architecture. Also check for other desirable features. A tilt-in unit, for instance, makes cleaning easier. Optional grilles simply pop in and let you create a divided-light window.

For purists, manufacturers fabricate true divided-light windows in standard sizes. There are five common types of windows. They can be used individually, or combined in various ways.

LEFT AND BELOW Counter-to-ceiling windows will maximize natural light but take up cabinet space, left. Speciality windows add a dramatic touch, below.

Fixed Windows. Fixed windows are the simplest type of window because they do not open. A fixed window is simply glass installed in a frame that is attached to the house. Fixed windows are the least expensive, admit the most light, and come in the greatest variety of shapes and sizes. However, they can't be used to provide ventilation.

Double-Hung Windows. Perhaps the most common kind used in houses, double-hung windows consist of two framed glass panels, called sash, that slide vertically on a metal, wood, or plastic track. The glass can be a single pane of glazing or divided into smaller panes, called lites. One variation, called a single-hung window, is made using an upper panel that cannot slide and a lower, sliding panel.

Casement Windows. Casements are hinged at the side and swing outward from the window opening as you turn a small crank. Better casement windows can be opened to a 90-degree angle, providing maximum ventilation.

Sliding Windows. Sliders are similar to double-hung windows turned on their side. The glass panels slide horizontally and are often used where there is need for a window opening that is wider than it is tall.

Awning Windows. Awning windows swing outward like a casement window, but are hinged at the top. Awning windows can be left opened slightly for air even when it rains.

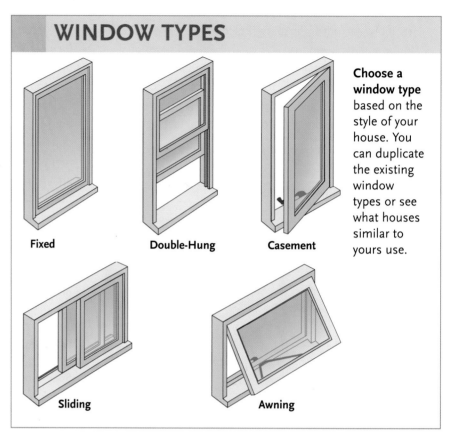

WINDOW TYPES

Fixed

Double-Hung

Casement

Sliding

Awning

Choose a window type based on the style of your house. You can duplicate the existing window types or see what houses similar to yours use.

RIGHT Windows let in light, but they can also make the view part of the design.

WHICH WAY SHOULD WINDOWS & SKYLIGHTS FACE?

Orient a door, window, or skylight to take best advantage of breezes and seasonal sunlight. Also take into account trees, neighboring structures, and the potential view.

• **South light** will pour into windows with a southern exposure in winter because the sun's path is low in the sky. But in the summer, when it rides high in the sky, the sun will beat down on the southern roof instead. Southern exposure is an ideal placement for a window because it gains heat through the window in winter but not in summer, especially if it's shielded by a deep overhang. A skylight on a southern or western exposure will capture solar heat during the winter— and the summer, too. Be careful about this placement.

• **East light** brightens the morning yet rarely heats up the room. Skylights on north- and east-facing roofs lessen heat gain in the summer.

• **West light** subjects a kitchen to the hot, direct rays of late-afternoon sun, which can make a room uncomfortable until far into the night. If a west-facing window is your only option, shade it with overhangs, awnings, sun-stopping blinds, or broad-leaf plantings.

• **North light** has an almost consistent brightness throughout the day. Because it's from an open sky, without direct sun, the light doesn't create glaring hot spots or deep shadows in work areas. North light lacks the drama of other exposures, but kitchen design and colors can compensate for that.

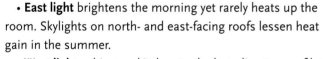

Winter Sun

Summer Sun

W N
S E

Replacement Windows

When buying new windows you'll have two important concerns: the type of window to install and the type of installation.

Replacement Installations. You can install your own windows, of course, or buy the units and hire someone to install them. Or you can shop at one of the increasing number of retailers who offer package deals including installation. If you don't do the job, watch out for the common problem of downsizing, or installing windows that are much smaller than your originals. Downsizing windows by excessively packing out the old frame can

change the scale of the facade and create clumsy-looking trim details inside and out.

There are a few installation methods available. For double-hung windows, you can remove and replace the sash while leaving the window frame in place. It's a good option for replacing damaged or inefficient sash if the overall frame is still in good condition.

Complete replacement is much like installing windows in new construction. But you have the extra work of removing the old units to start with, and after the windows are in, you need to piece-in siding and drywall, and reinstall trim.

Skylights. In a single-story house or one with a vaulted ceiling, a properly planned and located skylight can provide five times more natural light than a window of equal size located in a wall. It's important to plan for the seasonal angle and path of the sun to avoid unwelcome heat gains and losses from skylights. It's usually better to locate a skylight on a north- or east-facing surface, for example, to prevent overheating and provide diffuse light. Venting models, placed near the roof ridge, can also greatly improve natural ventilation. Seek advice from an architect or designer if you're not sure how a skylight will affect your kitchen's climate.

Door Types

Interior and exterior doors are offered in dozens of shapes, sizes, and materials. Most units are made of wood or wood by-products, but many are made of metal and stamped or embossed to look like wood. Exterior doors often incorporate glass panels. French and sliding patio doors are almost all glass. Most interior wood-based doors are fabricated in one of three ways: as individual panels set in a frame, as a hardboard facing molded to look like a panel door and secured to a frame, or as a thin sheet of plywood secured to each side of a wood framework.

Panel and Panel-Look Doors. Panel door styles offer a variety of choices. They can be constructed with as few as three to as many as ten or more solid panels, in all sorts of shapes and size combinations. Sometimes the bottom is made of wood and the top panels are glass.

Flush Doors. Generally less expensive, flush doors come in a more limited range of variations. You can enhance their simple looks with wood molding for a traditional appeal.

Sliders. Sliding doors consist of a large panel of glass framed with wood or metal. Usually one of the doors is stationary while the other slides. Replacing an existing wood door with one that's all or mostly glass can double its natural lighting potential. For safety and security, be sure that the new door has tempered glass and has a secure locking mechanism. Enlarge an existing door or window opening, or cut a new one, to gain access to a deck

TOP AND BOTTOM Skylights allow in five times more light than windows. Used over a sink, top, they provide task lighting. Set near the ridge of a roof, bottom, they provide general lighting to the room.

or patio outside. The frame may be wood, aluminum, or wood covered with aluminum or vinyl.

French Doors. Traditional French doors are framed-glass panels with either true divided lights or pop-in dividers; usually both doors open. Manufacturers also offer units that look like traditional hinged doors but operate

ABOVE Doors with lots of glazing provide natural light, and they help connect the kitchen to the outdoors.

like sliders. If space is limited, consider out-swing patio doors. These units open outward rather than inward like other doors. So you can open them without taking up valuable floor space.

Dutch Doors. Made in two parts, Dutch doors have independently operating sections, top and bottom. Locked together, the two halves open and close as a unit. Or you can open just the top section for ventilation.

Sunrooms, Greenhouses, and Bays

If a full-scale kitchen addition just does not make sense for your house, you might wish to enhance your existing kitchen, at less cost, with a "mini-addition," in the form of a sunroom or greenhouse-like bump out.

Prefabricated Sunrooms. Prefabs usually have double- or triple-glazed glass panels and come in prefit pieces that can be assembled by amateur carpenters, although this isn't a simple project by any means. For a sunroom, you'll need a foundation, which is usually a concrete slab with an insulated perimeter that goes below the frostline.

A sunroom should face within 20 degrees of due south to take greatest advantage of solar heating in colder climates.

Window Greenhouses. Also called box windows, these units provide a site for year-round kitchen gardening. All you need to do is remove a window and hang a prefabricated unit or a home-built greenhouse outside. Fill it with flowering plants or greenery, grow herbs or vegetables, or use it to give your outdoor garden a jump on spring. This window treatment is also an excellent way to replace a poor outside view with your indoor garden, while keeping the window open to light.

As with sunrooms, window greenhouses work best with southern exposures. You might also have sufficient light from an eastern or western exposure if no trees, buildings, or other obstructions cast shadows. You might as well rule out a northern exposure; a north-facing greenhouse loses great amounts of heat in winter, and many plants don't grow well in northern light.

Bay Windows. Bay units allow you to add a foot or two of sunny space without having to construct a foundation. In this case, you would cantilever the bay window from your home's floor joists. Most window manufacturers sell bays in a variety of widths and configurations, ranging from simple boxes to gentle bows. Installing one is a job best left to a skilled carpenter.

ENLARGING WINDOWS

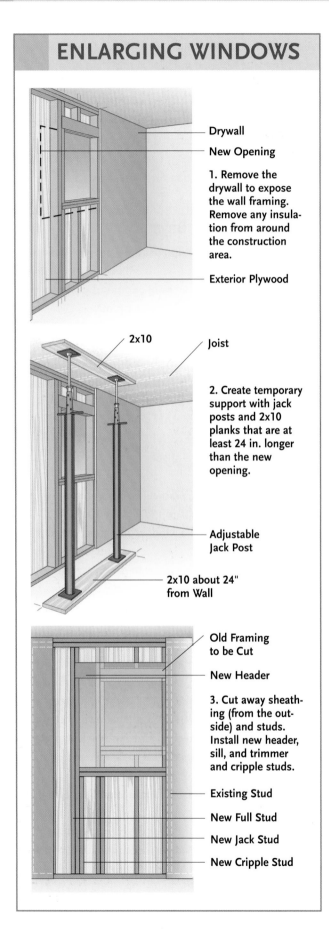

Drywall

New Opening

1. Remove the drywall to expose the wall framing. Remove any insulation from around the construction area.

Exterior Plywood

2x10

Joist

2. Create temporary support with jack posts and 2x10 planks that are at least 24 in. longer than the new opening.

Adjustable Jack Post

2x10 about 24" from Wall

Old Framing to be Cut

New Header

3. Cut away sheathing (from the outside) and studs. Install new header, sill, and trimmer and cripple studs.

Existing Stud

New Full Stud

New Jack Stud

New Cripple Stud

INSTALLING NEW WINDOWS

project

A major kitchen remodel is a good time to increase the size of typically small kitchen windows. But care must be taken to support the ceiling above when enlarging any window opening. Basically, you will need to create temporary supports to carry the load from above until you can install a permanent window header. (See "Enlarging Windows," left.)

Once the opening is ready to go, slide the new window into the opening from the outside of the house. Center the window in the opening, and make it level and plumb using shims driven between the window unit and the surrounding framing. When satisfied with the window position, nail the flange to the sheathing. Then nail the exterior casing boards over the nailing flange. Finish up the outside chores by caulking around the perimeter of the window and the trim with exterior-grade caulk. Clean up any excess caulk, and touch up the paint as required.

Move inside and fill the gap between the window unit and the rough opening with fiberglass batts or low-expanding foam insulation. Don't over fill the gap, or you risk distorting the side jambs and making the sashes difficult to operate.

TOOLS & MATERIALS
▌Window unit
▌Pry bar
▌Shims
▌Level
▌Hammer
▌Roofing nails
▌Exterior casing
▌Casing nails
▌Caulk
▌Fiberglass insulation or low-expanding foam insulation
▌Work gloves
▌Interior casing

1 Once the opening is prepared, slide the new window in place from outside. Have an inside helper center the unit from side to side; then check that the unit is level and plumb. Wedge shims between the window and the framing to keep the window properly aligned.

2 Most new windows have a flange that's nailed to the wall with galvanized roofing nails. Drive these nails every 4 or 5 in. on the sides and top. The bottom of the window usually has flexible flashing instead of a nailing flange.

3 Cut trim boards to fit the space between the window frame and the siding on all four sides. Nail them using galvanized casing nails.

4 Once the casing boards are installed, caulk the perimeter of the window frame and the casing boards with exterior caulk.

5 Move to the inside, and fill the space between the window and the framing with fiberglass or low-expanding foam insulation. Don't overfill with foam.

33

INSTALLING ROOF WINDOWS AND SKYLIGHTS

Installing a roof window or skylight is possible for some do-it-yourselfers, but before deciding to go ahead, be sure you are up to the task.

You'll need to do some of the work inside a cramped attic and part of it crawling around on the roof. If you build a light shaft between the roof and ceiling, you're in for measuring and cutting framing and finishing materials that have tricky angles.

When you have selected your skylight or roof window, read and follow the manufacturer's instructions. Your first job will be to locate the window location on the ceiling of the kitchen.

Planning the Location

First, use a keyhole saw or a saber saw to cut out a piece of the ceiling drywall about 2 feet square, somewhere near the center of where you want the shaft opening to be. Standing on a stepladder and armed with a flashlight, look through the test hole, and inspect the roof and ceiling framing to determine the final location for the opening. Although where you want the sunlight to fall is an important factor, you should also locate the ceiling opening to minimize reworking the framing.

Most skylights and roof windows are designed to fit between two rafters (or three rafters with the middle one cut out). You will need to orient the ceiling opening in the same manner as the roof opening, ideally with joists for its sides. You can make the ceiling opening somewhat larger than the roof opening by adding a light shaft with angled walls. The end of the skylight opening nearest the eaves is usually directly underneath the skylight, and the end nearest the roof's ridge flares out to allow in more light. (See "Framing the Opening" on page 37.)

Cutting the Ceiling Opening

When you have decided where the skylight will go, re-move the insulation at that spot in the attic, and mark the final opening of the bottom of your light shaft on the ceiling drywall. Cut along the outline with a keyhole saw or reciprocating saw, and remove the ceiling drywall or plaster. (See the photo on page 37, under "Cutting a Roof Open.") If there is a joist in the middle of the opening, don't cut it until you're ready to frame the new opening. You will need to add headers to carry the weight.

---

project

INSTALLING A SKYLIGHT

Begin by marking the location of the light shaft opening on the ceiling and driving a nail through the ceiling at each corner. Then go up into the attic; remove the insulation from above this area; and transfer the location of the four nails to the rafters above using a plumb line.

Reinforce the rafters by nailing 2x4 braces across them, above and below the opening. Then, layout the position of the headers at the bottom and top of the opening using a sliding T-bevel. Cut the hole in the roof as shown on page 37, and install the window. Remember, all roof openings need to be flashed. For skylights and roof windows, this usually means weaving aluminum-step flashing between each course of roofing shingles.

Lay out the position of the ceiling headers using a 2x4; then cut out any ceiling joists that are in the way and install the headers. Cut out the ceiling drywall, and then frame the light shaft opening. Begin with the 2x4s that form the ceiling; then fill in the sidewall studs. Cover this framing with drywall; and add insulation between all the framing members.

TOOLS & MATERIALS
- Basic carpentry tools
- Electric drill ▌ Goggles
- Roofing compound
- Chalk-line box ▌ Sliding T-bevel
- Framing lumber (as needed)
- Framing anchors
- 12d (3¼-inch) and 16d (3½-inch) common nails
- Roofing cement ▌ Trowel
- Circular saw with carbide-tipped blade
- Keyhole saw (or reciprocating saw)
- Skylight
- Aluminum step flashing (usually comes in bundles of 100)

1 Lay out the light shaft hole on the ceiling, and drive a nail through the drywall at each corner. Then transfer the location of these nails to the roof rafters using a plumb line. Connect these marks with heavy lines drawn on the sheathing.

2 Reinforce the rafters by nailing 2x4s across the rafters above and below the marked opening. Then establish the four corners of the opening by driving nails up from each corner so that they poke through the top surface of the roof.

3 Cut away the roof shingles and sheathing as shown on page 37. Then mark the location of the support headers at the bottom and top of the opening.

4 Cut out any rafters that fall within the opening, and install headers above and below to carry the load of the missing rafters.

5 Install the window unit according the manufacturer's instructions. Make sure that any mounting hardware is securely screwed to the roof.

(continued on page 36)

(continued from page 35)

6 The window has to be properly flashed to prevent leaks. Different manufacturers have different approaches. But usually step flashing, above, is installed between every layer of shingles.

7 Use 2x4s to frame the light shaft. Hold a straight one between the two openings to mark the location of both headers that support any ceiling joist that was removed.

8 Cut and nail headers to both ends of the ceiling opening to carry the weight of the missing joists. Once the headers are installed, cut out the ceiling drywall and screw the drywall to the perimeter of the opening using drywall screws.

9 Build a frame around the opening using 2x4s. Install the angled members first, then the short studs. Once the framing is done, install drywall on the inside surface. Add insulation between the framing members on the attic side of the light shaft.

CUTTING A ROOF OPENING

If you've left the nails that you drove in at the corners of the roof opening, described in Step 2 on page 35, that makes it easier to snap a chalk line on the shingles to mark the opening. Cut asphalt shingles along this line using a utility knife and straightedge to bare the roof sheathing below. Drill a test hole to gauge the depth of your roof sheathing; you want to set your circular saw blade at that depth so that you don't damage the rafters underneath.

Use the circular saw to cut the opening through the roof sheathing. If you need to cut through wood shingles, place a board below the saw. By doing this, you can ease the saw forward without bumping into the bottoms of the shingles. When cutting through the roof sheathing, keep in mind that you will probably hit nails, so use a carbide-tipped blade.

smart tip

CONTROLLING ENERGY COSTS

THE BIGGEST FACTOR IN THE ENERGY PERFORMANCE OF A SKYLIGHT OR A ROOF WINDOW IS ITS ORIENTATION TO THE SUN. UNITS PLACED ON A SOUTHERN ROOF WILL GAIN MORE HEAT THAN THOSE INSTALLED ON A NORTH-FACING ROOF, WHICH MEANS ALSO THAT THOSE ON THE NORTH WILL LOOSE MORE HEAT THAN THOSE ON THE SOUTH. IN COLD CLIMATES, PURCHASE WINDOWS WITH A LOW-E GLAZING. AND UNITS WITH U-VALUES BELOW 0.35 ARE CONSIDERED EXTREMELY ENERGY EFFICIENT. TO COMBAT OVERHEATING, MAKE USE OF OPERABLE SHADES OR BLINDS.

FRAMING THE OPENING

A skylight requires that you build two new rough openings—one in the roof rafters and one in the ceiling joists—as well as a light shaft, which will run through the attic.

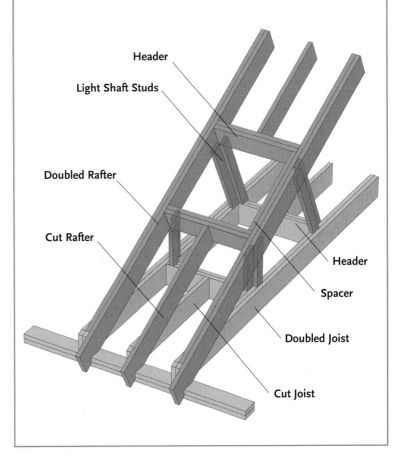

Header
Light Shaft Studs
Doubled Rafter
Cut Rafter
Header
Spacer
Doubled Joist
Cut Joist

2 creating a design

Any work you do on your kitchen, whether it be renovation or new construction, should be based on a well-thought-out plan or design. The design will take into consideration the types of cabinets you want, the layout of the room, the appliances, the countertop material, and the finishes on walls and floor. The trick is to blend all of these elements into a cohesive whole that is both efficient and attractive. This chapter will get you started in creating your design. You will find information on the different types of architectural design and using color and texture in the room. Much of the chapter is devoted to creating a layout that suits the dimensions of the room and the way you and your family use the kitchen. There are 40 layouts shown. Use them as a starting point for creating your own design.

DEVELOPING A STYLE

No matter what your taste—country, traditional, contemporary, or eclectic—as you work on your basic layout you should think about the details that will make your new kitchen suit your way of life.

Architectural Style

A kitchen's design is distinguished more than anything by the style of the cabinets. Assisted by decorative details like the wall and floor treatments, window style, and accessories, the door fronts of the cabinets will put a face on the kitchen's architecture. There are many variations on the following three themes, but most of the differences are in the details.

Traditional. Today's traditional style incorporates elements of English and American eighteenth- and early-nineteenth-century design. Marked by symmetry and balance and enhanced by the look of fine-crafted details, it is dignified, rich, and formal.

Choose wood cabinetry finished with a cherry or mahogany stain or painted white, with details like fluted panels, beaded trim, bull's-eye corner blocks, and dentil and crown molding. For the door style, a raised cathedral panel (top slightly arched) is typical. An elegant countertop fabricated from marble or a plastic laminate faux version fits well into this setting, as do hand-painted tiles. Polished-brass hardware and fittings will add a distinctive touch.

Colors to consider include classic Wedgewood blue or deep jewel tones. Windows and French doors with true divided lights or double-hung units with pop-in muntins have great traditional style appeal. Use formal curtain panels or swags as window treatments.

Furnish this kitchen with an antique or reproduction hutch, where you can display formal china, and a table and chairs in traditional Windsor or Queen Anne style.

smart tip

YOU MAY NOT NEED TO REPLACE YOUR KITCHEN CABINETRY TO GET FINE-FURNITURE QUALITY DETAILS. TRY ADDING CROWN MOLDING TO THE TOP OF EXISTING CABINETS AND REPLACING THE HARDWARE WITH REPRODUCTION POLISHED-BRASS DOOR AND DRAWER PULLS TO ACHIEVE A TRADITIONAL LOOK.

LEFT Cherry-stained cabinets and crown molding place this kitchen squarely in the traditional category. Note the upholstered stools and the traditional light fixtures.

Contemporary. Sleek and unadorned, contemporary-style cabinets consist of plain panel doors and hardware that's hidden or unobtrusive. Contemporary kitchens make extensive use of materials like chrome, glass, and stone. Indeed, its roots are at the turn of the last century, when architects and designers rejected the exaggerated artificial embellishments of the Victorians by turning to natural products and pared-down designs.

Today, contemporary style is taking a softer turn, even in the kitchen, a place where hard edges, cool reflective surfaces, and cutting-edge technology abound. It's not unusual to see updated versions of traditional fixtures and fittings or new uses for natural materials in a contemporary kitchen, especially as improved finishes make these products more durable and easier to maintain. And although black and white are classic mainstays in a contemporary room, many people prefer warmer shades of white.

When selecting cabinets for your contemporary kitchen, pair a frameless door with a wood finish. Laminate cabinetry is still compatible with this style, but for an updated look, wood is a better choice. Although a contemporary room is often monochromatic or neutral, don't be afraid to use color or mix several materials or finishes, such as wood and metal. Combinations of wood and various metals—stainless steel, chrome, copper, brass, and pewter on surfaces like cabinet doors, countertops, and floors—make strong statements, as do stone and glass. Creative combinations like these keep the overall appearance of the room sleek but not sterile. For more visual interest, apply a glazed or textured finish to neutral-colored walls. And bring as much of the outdoors into this room as possible. Install casement style windows, skylights, or roof windows to blend with contemporary architecture. Easy access to adjoining outdoor living spaces, such as decks, patios, or open-air kitchens, is highly desirable. For window treatments, Roman shades or vertical blinds offer a crisp, tailored look.

Stay with metals for lighting fixtures and hardware. Chrome, pewter, or nickel would work well. Keep your eye on function, not frills. The contemporary kitchen tends to be pared down to the essentials of the room.

ABOVE AND BELOW Traditional-style cabinets usually have panel doors and decorative molding, above. Contemporary cabinets rely on sleek designs styles, below.

ABOVE Stainless-steel appliances, here matched to a stainless-steel table, are a mainstay of contemporary design.

Furnishings for a contemporary kitchen tend to have a sleek architectural look, too. In fact, much of what is considered classic contemporary furniture has been designed by well-known twentieth-century architects. Chair and table legs are typically straight, with no turnings or ornamentation. For a sophisticated look, mix complementary materials; for example, pair a glass table with upholstered chairs or a metal table with wood chairs. Display contemporary pottery on a shelf or inside a glass cabinet.

Country. A simple door style, a light stain or distressed-color finish, and unpretentious wooden or ceramic knobs and handles on drawers and doors pull the country look together.

Whether you call it American, French, English, Italian, or Scandinavian, this style is always a favorite because of its basic, casual, relaxed feeling. In fact, every country has

its own version. "Country" implies a deeper connection to the outdoors and the simple life than other styles and uses an abundance of natural elements. Start off with plain wood cabinetry stained a light maple, or add a distressed, crackled, or pickled finish. This is the perfect kitchen for mixing different finishes because unmatched pieces underpin the informal feel of a country room. Cabinet door styles are typically framed, sometimes with a raised panel. Bead-board cabinets are a typical American country choice. Or leave the doors off, allowing colorful dishes and canned and boxed goods to become part of the decor. For the countertop, install butcher block or hand-painted or silk-screened tiles. Another option is a colorful or patterned countertop fabricated from inlaid solid-surfacing material. A working fireplace will definitely add charm to your country kitchen, but a simple potted herb garden on the windowsill will do so, too.

Wood floors are a natural choice in a country setting, although terra-cotta tiles are an attractive accent to a European-inspired setting. Be sure to add throw rugs, preferably braided or woven rag, in front of the sink and range for added comfort underfoot.

For a custom touch, add a stenciled backsplash or wall border. If you want a truly individual look, try a faux finish like sponging, ragging, combing, or rubbed-back plaster. These techniques are easy and add texture to your walls, providing a richer, warmer feeling. Use the space in the soffit area or above a window to hang herbs for drying.

Install double-hung windows. (Standard casement windows look too contemporary in this setting.) Finish them with full trim, and top them with simple cotton curtains, or just install valances. Don't overdress them.

Other Styles. The styles discussed here are really only the tip of the iceberg of styles and looks possible for your kitchen. Others you have probably heard of include Art Deco, Arts and Crafts, and Shaker style. You can also combine styles. Find common elements in different styles that will make them work together. Good examples of compatible looks include country and traditional or Shaker.

ABOVE AND BELOW Elements of country design include such items as bead-board wall and ceiling treatments, above, to the farmhouse table and color scheme and the connection to the outdoors, below.

COLOR BASICS

Of all the ways to personalize a kitchen, color is the most versatile. In fact, the dominant color of a room can actually affect the mood of those within. Red is stimulating, and in its vibrant forms is usually reserved for accents. Yellow and orange are welcoming and happy, but when used over large areas, these colors can promote subtle feelings of unrest; pastel creams, peaches, and corals are good alternatives for large expanses. Blues and greens are restful and calming. Warm up blue with a touch of yellow or coral, and mix almost any color with green, the background color of nature. The brightness of your kitchen colors should be measured against the intensity of natural and artificial light in the room.

Color Schemes. Color can be used in many ways. The method of choosing colors to convey a desired overall effect is called creating a color scheme.

Monochromatic color schemes vary a single hue. You might use only shades of blue or a range of greens, for example. Some beautiful kitchens have been done in one shade of one color, with variety supplied by the gleam of stainless steel or the texture of tile or marble.

Related, or analogous, schemes consist of a range of colors in the same family—all of the tones of autumn leaves, for example, or the various green shades of spring, lightened with touches of yellow. (For more on selecting colors, see "Color Wheel Combinations," page 46.)

RIGHT Bright backsplashes add vitality to the simplest color schemes. Consider colorful counter inlays and flooring.

ABOVE Painted-finish cabinets aren't for everyone, but they do add personality to a kitchen design.

Complementary color schemes use opposites on the color wheel, such as reds and greens or blues and yellows.

Neutral colors such as gray, white, and black mix well with most colors or work well on their own.

Adding white to any color lightens its value, so white added to red produces pink. Black darkens its value, so black added to red produces a shade of maroon. Remember this point when you devise complementary or monochromatic schemes: once you establish your color scheme, different intensities of the same color will serve to vary and fortify the effect.

Color and Space. Color can expand or contract the perceived size of a room. A general principle is that dark colors make a room look smaller; light ones do the opposite. Strong contrasts, such as light cabinets and dark wallpaper, visually take up more space than if these two elements were of the same color and intensity.

Color Trends. Keep in mind that the cabinets, tiles, countertops, and appliances you select will be with you for a while, and trendy colors can become dated quickly. There are certain limitations, too, on the colors you can choose: most appliances come only in white and a limited range of neutral hues. One way to cope with both the dat-

smart tip

THE TYPE OF LIGHT IN A ROOM WILL AFFECT HOW A COLOR LOOKS. PLACE LARGE SWATCHES OF THE COLORS YOU ARE THINKING ABOUT USING THROUGHOUT YOUR KITCHEN TO SEE HOW THEY REACT TO MORNING, AFTERNOON, EVENING, AND ARTIFICIAL LIGHT.

COLOR WHEEL COMBINATIONS

The color wheel is the designer's most useful tool for pairing colors. Basically, it presents the spectrum of pigment hues as a circle. The primary colors (yellow, blue, and red) are combined in the remaining hues (orange, green, and purple). The following are the most often used configurations for creating color schemes.

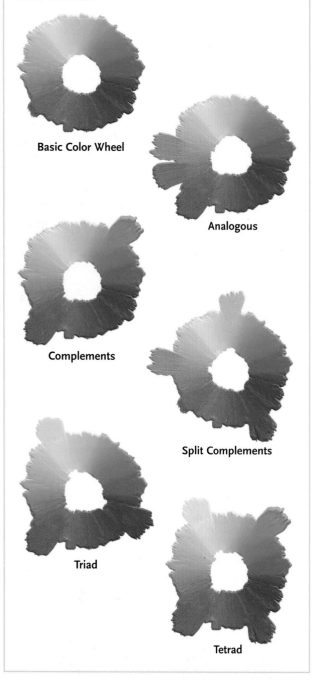

Basic Color Wheel

Analogous

Complements

Split Complements

Triad

Tetrad

ing and color-matching problems is to select appliances with changeable front panel inserts. You simply remove a piece of trim from the door, slip in the color panel of your choice, and replace the trim. Another option is to go with appliances that accept external door panels that match your cabinetry. Lastly, a time-honored and economical solution is to stick with neutral, white, or stainless-steel finishes for appliances—and introduce color on wall, floor, and countertop surfaces that can be replaced or changed inexpensively whenever you wish.

Texture

Brick, vinyl, slate, wood, stone, tile, fabric, and other materials add texture to your kitchen. A glossy plastic laminate countertop, for example, has a shine quite different from the gleam of a satiny stainless-steel sink. By varying textures you can enhance your color scheme.

Say It with Details

You might want to express your individual style using design elements like tile backsplashes with scenes of nature, refrigerator panels of punched tin, burnished-copper range hoods, brick-faced cooking alcoves, exposed ceiling beams, or crown moldings. Maybe you have a treasured plate collection you want to mount in a soffit or display on wall-hung shelves. Perhaps you'll create an interesting vignette with a hand-painted motif or spice up the room with a wallpaper border or stenciled design. The shape and color of your kitchen gains depth and distinction from the details that reflect your individual tastes.

CLOCKWISE FROM TOP LEFT Mosaic tiles combine with sleek stainless steel, top left. The articles on the shelves provide interest, below. The painted tiles on the backsplash complement the rustic cabinetry, bottom left.

REVISING A LAYOUT

What if your existing kitchen is critically cramped, and no amount of rearranging is going to make it much better? Should you dig deep into your finances, call in an architect or remodeling contractor, and plan a kitchen addition? The answer is a qualified "maybe." Full-scale additions almost always cost more per square foot than new construction, so you should realistically expect to recover only part of your remodeling investment— say 75 to 90 percent—when you sell your home. The common alternatives for gaining space are:

- Conversion
- Annexation
- Transposition
- Addition

conversion

One option is to convert a covered porch or entryway into kitchen space. If it's constructed on good footings and has a roof that's in good shape, you may be able to enclose, wire, and insulate the space for considerably less than the cost of a full addition. Since sunrooms and porches often have foundations already in place, it is usually a good idea to try to incorporate these areas into a new kitchen design.

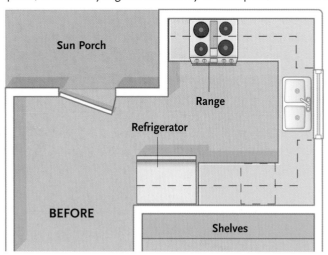

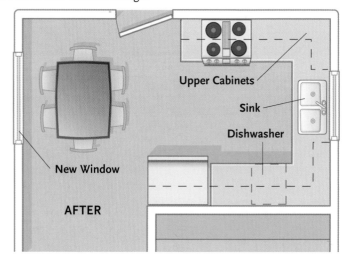

annexation

Look to adjacent areas for a few square feet you might annex. Often, it's as simple as relocating a closet or removing a nonbearing wall. An existing closet, part of a hallway, and even a seldom-used room are good candidates for providing extra space for your kitchen.

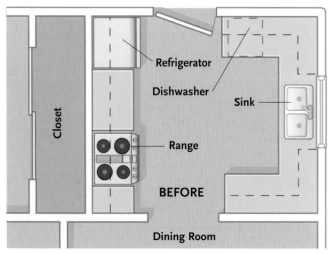

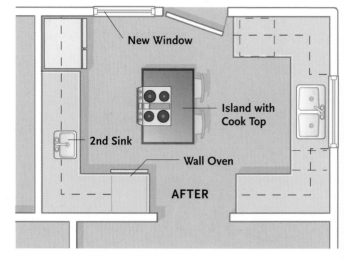

transposition

Transposition. If your kitchen is not only too small but also inconveniently located, you might be able to switch it with another room, such as a bedroom or dining room. You aren't stuck with the layout of your house. Take a look at your kitchen's present location and see if it would work better somewhere else.

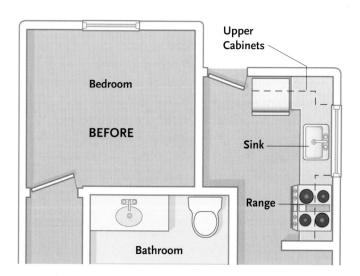

addition

If none of the mini-addition ideas will solve the space problem, there are good reasons to go ahead with an addition:

- Besides providing the larger kitchen you want, an addition can provide you with a family room, expanded dining facilities, a sunroom, deck, or other living space.
- If your kitchen is not only too small but also inconveniently located, an addition may enable you to move it and convert the existing space to some other use.
- A skillfully designed addition may also improve your home's exterior appearance, as well as its views and outdoor living areas.

Planning a kitchen addition starts the same way as any remodeling plan—with graph paper, appliance and cabinet templates, and so forth. But before you break ground, check out your ideas with a knowledge-able contractor, architect, or designer. He or she can tell you whether your scheme is feasible and what building permits you may need. Brand new living space will probably cost more than the other options, but it will give you the most flexibility when it comes time to plan the kitchen.

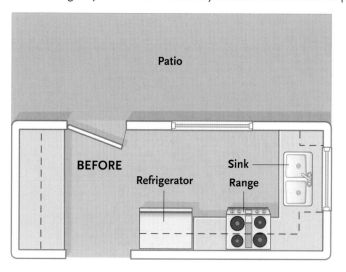

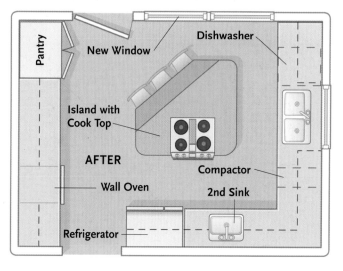

Work Triangle

The so-called work triangle has been a staple of good kitchen design for years. There's a good reason for this. Kitchen efficiency experts have determined that the kitchen's three necessities—sink, range, and refrigerator—should be arranged in a triangular pattern whose three sides total 12 to 26 feet. The minimum and maximum distances conserve walking distance from point to point without sacrificing adequate counter space between work stations. However, many designers see the simple triangle as evolving as lifestyles change. They believe that the lone triangle needs to expand to include more activities. Some families may need multiple triangles in order to encompass all of the activities that take place in their kitchen.

Traffic Patterns

Pay special attention to the way traffic moves through and in your existing kitchen and any new layout you may be considering. You should be able to move easily from one place to another in the kitchen and from the kitchen to other rooms in the house, as well as outdoors.

It's also important that through traffic doesn't interfere with the work areas. Otherwise, carrying a hot pot from the range to the sink could put you on a collision course with youngsters heading for the back door.

Often, you can cure a faulty traffic pattern simply by moving a door or removing a short section of wall. If you have the space, you can add an island or peninsula to redirect traffic. Another way to improve the way a kitchen functions is to experiment with basic layouts.

ABOVE The work triangle connects the range, refrigerator, and sink. It is designed to save steps while cooking.

DIRECTING TRAFFIC

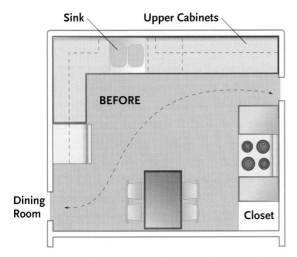
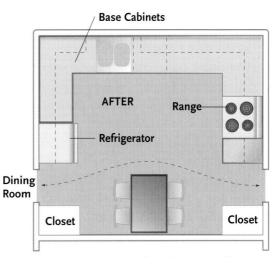

Doors at opposite corners of a room force traffic to cut through the working area of the kitchen (left). Moving the doorways (right) allows traffic to bypass the work triangle.

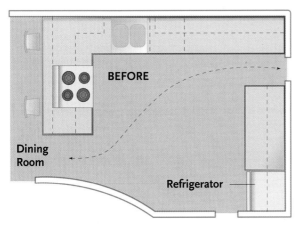
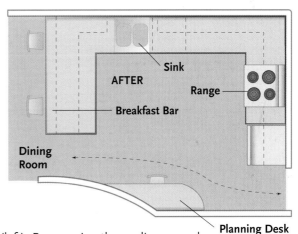

An extended work triangle cuts across the traffic flow (left). Rearranging the appliances and creating a new doorway creates a tighter work triangle with plenty of room for through traffic.

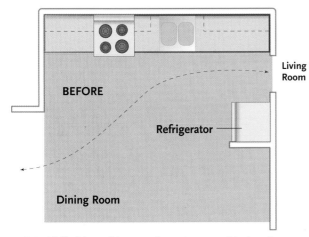
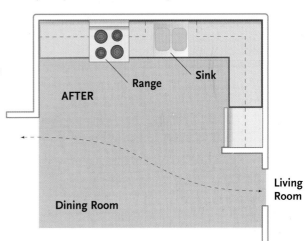

An old-fashioned layout does not provide landing space near the refrigerator (left). Moving the doorway and installing new cabinets solves the problem and redirects through traffic as well.

CREATING LAYOUTS

This section will help you think about the layout of your new kitchen. We've taken what designers and kitchen professionals consider the basic kitchen shapes—one-wall, galley (corridor), L-shaped, U-shaped—and with the help of the National Kitchen and Bath Association (NKBA), we have picked layouts that show how more-complex designs evolve from these simple layouts.

Professionals rely on the basic shapes because the layouts lend themselves to efficient interpretations of the work triangle. Real-life designs become more complex because each kitchen should address the unique needs of the individual homeowners. As you will see, the basic shapes are starting points for creating the layout that best suits your needs.

One-Wall Kitchen

A one-wall kitchen lines up all its cabinets, counter space, and equipment along one wall. This arrangement flattens the work triangle to a straight line. Try to locate the sink between the range and refrigerator for maximum accessibility.

One-wall kitchens make the most sense in tiny single-room apartments or in a narrow space. They are some-times used in a larger multifunctional area to minimize the kitchen's importance and maximize the room's open space. In this context, the kitchen wall could be closed off from the rest of the room with sliding doors, screens, or shutters when it is not in use.

If you are starting with a one-wall kitchen and are able to acquire even a small amount of additional space, there are many options open to you.

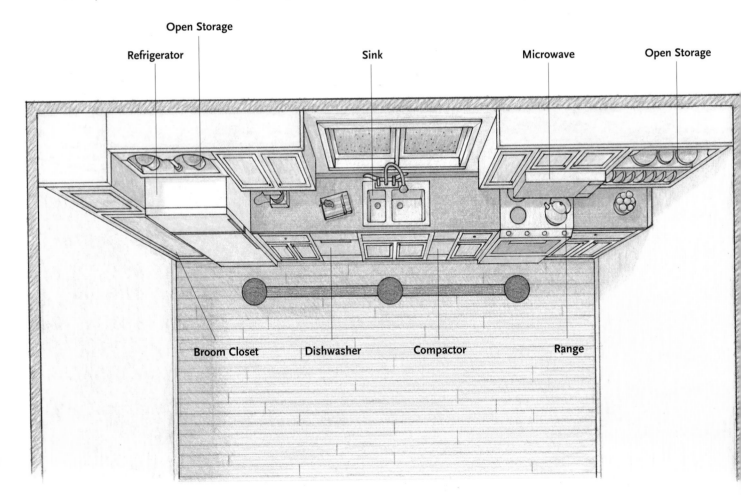

Open Storage

Refrigerator   Sink   Microwave   Open Storage

Broom Closet   Dishwasher   Compactor   Range

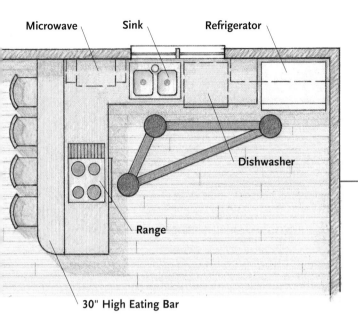

Microwave   Sink   Refrigerator

Dishwasher

Range

30" High Eating Bar

Variation 1

Adding a peninsula to a straight run of cabinets will allow you to open up the work triangle and create what is really an L-shaped room. The peninsula need not be as large as this one, but if you do add a range as shown here, be sure to allow adequate clearances on each side. The NKBA recommends 15 in. on one side and at least 9 in. on the other.

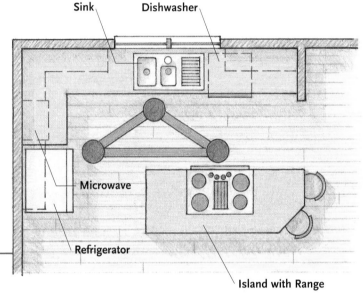

Sink   Dishwasher

Microwave

Refrigerator

Island with Range

Variation 2

Start with the L-shape, add an island, and you've created a well-organized work center. This version adds a full-height wall, but you could leave the eating counter peninsula as shown above as well. This design assumes the kitchen is open to a larger room; the angles on the edge of the island create interest.

LEFT Start with one wall and add a distinctive island, and you've not only created an eye-catching design, you've increased the usable work area as well.

Galley Kitchen

A galley, or corridor, kitchen places appliances, cabinets, and counters along opposite walls. This scheme enables you to establish a good work triangle, but it usually does not leave enough room for multiple cooks. The simple layout works best as a one-cook kitchen.

Try to allow a 48-inch-wide aisle between the facing base cabinets. This makes it possible to open cabinet and appliance doors easily, with space left over for an adult to maneuver around them. Base cabinets are 24 inches deep, so you need a minimum width of 8 feet for a galley kitchen. If space is really tight, you can cut down the aisle to a bare minimum of 36 inches—but watch that appliance doors don't collide with each other when they're opened. Think twice, too, about a corridor arrangement that has doorways at both ends. This pro-motes traffic from outside passing through the work tri-angle.

To ease as many traffic problems as possible, place the refrigerator near the end of a galley kitchen. This will keep people who want something from the refrigerator from interfering with the cook. Another option is to in-stall the primary refrigerator in the food-preparation area and a small model for soft drinks or snacks close to the doorway.

Storage is a real challenge in this compact layout. One solution is to install tall cabinets that extend to the ceil-ing. You'll have to keep a stepladder handy for gaining ac-cess to what's on top, so reserve that space for items that you don't use as often. Another solution, the one chosen in the kitchen below, is to fill the room with cabi-nets and place seldom-used items elsewhere.

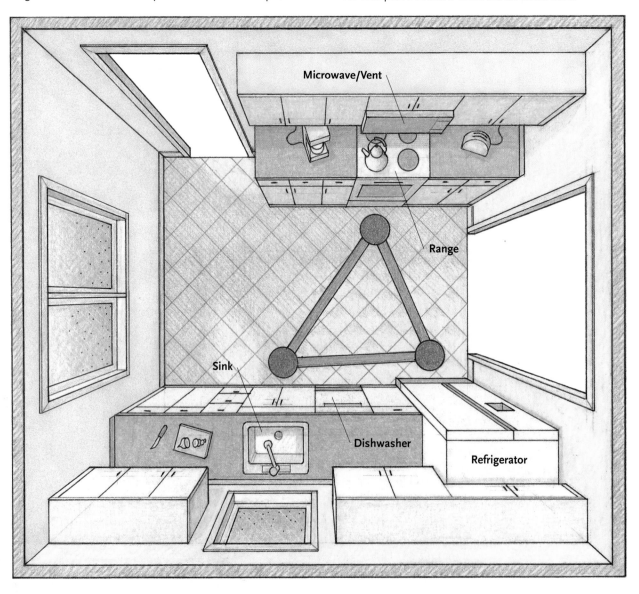

Microwave/Vent

Range

Sink

Dishwasher

Refrigerator

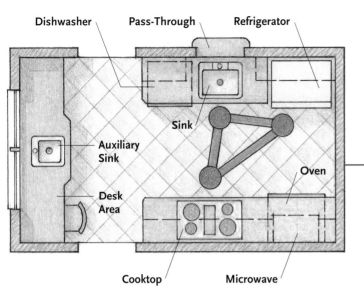

Dishwasher · Pass-Through · Refrigerator

Sink

Auxiliary Sink

Desk Area

Cooktop · Microwave · Oven

Variation 1

Although slightly larger than the basic layout shown on the opposite page, this design shows what moving doors can accomplish. Through traffic does not need to intrude on the main work space, and the new layout provides room for a small desk and a second sink as well.

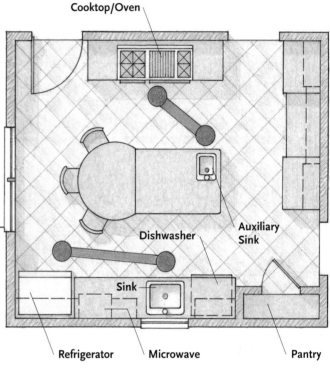

Cooktop/Oven

Dishwasher · Auxiliary Sink

Sink

Refrigerator · Microwave · Pantry

Variation 2

Sometimes a design element that is important to you will interfere with a basic rule. In this case, the eating area cuts off the straight line between the cooktop and the refrigerator. The small detour is acceptable.

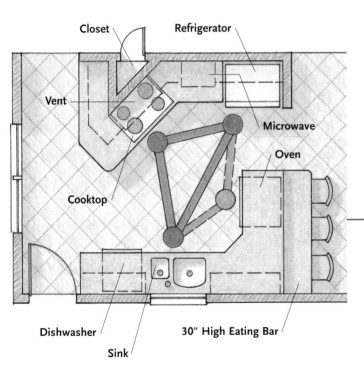

Closet · Refrigerator

Vent

Microwave

Oven

Cooktop

Dishwasher · 30" High Eating Bar

Sink

Variation 3

Two cooks can function efficiently in this layout. The angle that holds the cooktop creates visual interest, and it provides more counter space than does a straight run.

RIGHT The classic galley is small, but it can be appealing. To solve the storage problem, try running available wall cabinets all the way to the ceiling.

L-Shaped Kitchen

An L-shaped kitchen lays out the work centers along two adjacent walls. L-shaped layouts typically have one long and one short leg, creating large amounts of continuous counter space. Although L- shapes require more space than galleys, they permit an efficient work triangle that discourages through traffic. Try to place the main sink at the center of the work triangle, ideally under a window.

One advantage of an L-shaped layout is that you can often fit a kitchen table or booth into the corner diagonally opposite the L. Planned with care, an L-shaped kitchen can accommodate two cooks with ease. One can prepare food on counters adjacent to the sink while the other works at the range.

L-shaped kitchens are also natural candidates for incorporating a snack counter into the design. If the short leg of the L opens up to a family room or living room, a counter is a good transition to an open floor plan. This arrangement will, however, deprive you of wall space for cabinets. So be sure to plan out your storage needs carefully before deciding on the counter.

Another advantage to this layout is the opportunity for incorporating an island into the floor plan, if space allows. (Attach a peninsula to one leg of the design, and you've created a U-shaped space.) If you do include an island or peninsula in an L-shaped kitchen, plan the clearances carefully. Walkways should be at least 36 inches wide. If the walkway is also a work aisle, increase the clearance to 42 inches. A 36-inch clearance is fine for counter seating, unless traffic goes behind it. In that case, clearance should be 65 inches.

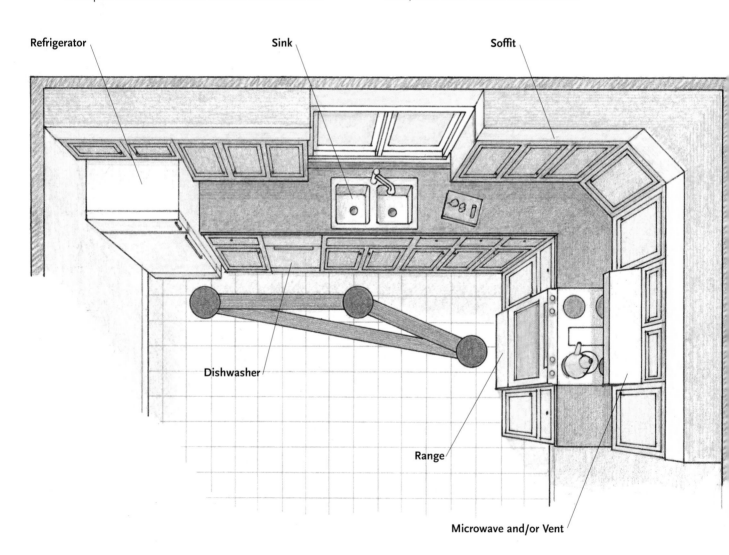

Refrigerator Sink Soffit

Dishwasher

Range

Microwave and/or Vent

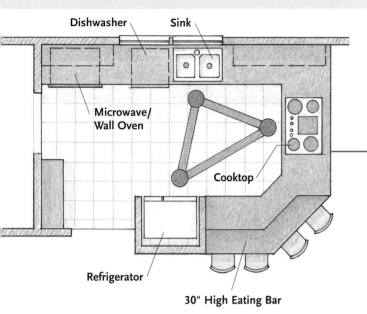

Dishwasher

Sink

Microwave/Wall Oven

Cooktop

Refrigerator

30" High Eating Bar

Variation 1

Adding a peninsula to the basic L-shaped kitchen creates a U-shaped layout. From a cook's viewpoint, this is an extremely efficient shape because of the compact work area. The U-shape is actually considered one of the basic kitchen shapes and is covered more thoroughly on the next page.

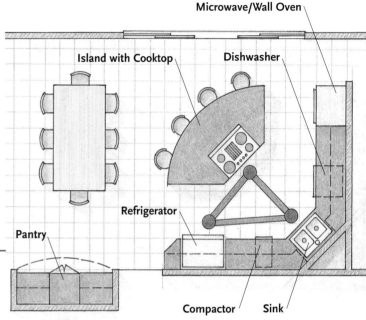

Microwave/Wall Oven

Island with Cooktop

Dishwasher

Refrigerator

Pantry

Compactor

Sink

Variation 2

A new island allows you to move one of the major appliances off the L. This design is for a large kitchen, but even in half the space, the L plus island creates an efficient layout. Counter seating on the island is a bonus.

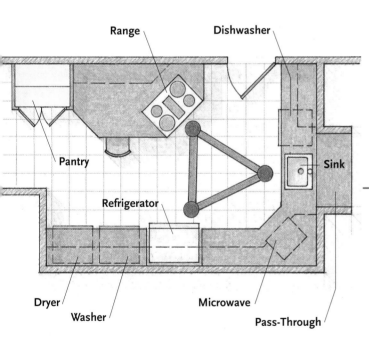

Range

Dishwasher

Pantry

Refrigerator

Dryer

Washer

Microwave

Pass-Through

Sink

Variation 3

This kitchen is a little less than 10 ft. wide, but it shows how good design can make even a small space efficient. The doorway into the work area is not the most ideal situation, but sometimes it can't be avoided.

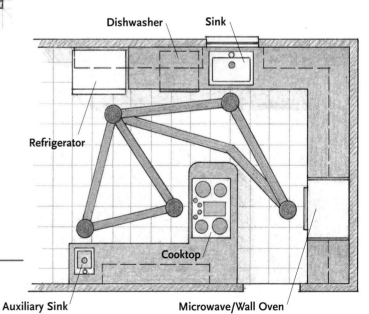

Dishwasher

Sink

Refrigerator

Cooktop

Auxiliary Sink

Microwave/Wall Oven

Variation 4

A double L-shaped layout provides plenty of work space for a second cook. Notice how the second sink and the refrigerator are placed so that non-cooks can use them without interfering in the work areas.

U-Shaped Kitchen

A U-shaped kitchen arranges cabinets, counters, and appliances along three walls, making it highly effective. Some plans open up one or more walls to an adjacent area like a family room or informal dining space. An extra dividend is freedom from through-traffic.

A U-shaped plan incorporates a logical sequence of work centers with minimal distances between them. The sink often goes at the base of the U, with the refrigerator and range on the side walls opposite each other. The U-shape takes up lots of space, at least 8 feet along both the length and width of the kitchen. Corners are a problem, too, because access to storage can be a challenge. Lazy Susan shelving helps make use of this otherwise dead space.

As with the other basic shapes, U-shaped layouts need not be absolute. Extending one of the walls with a peninsula creates a G-shaped kitchen. This layout is so common that many designers think of the G-shape as one of the basic kitchen designs.

A G-shaped plan is ideal for providing room for two cooks to operate independently or in concert without interfering with each other. The plan defines two separate work triangles that usually, but not always, share the refrigerator.

Often there's a second sink and separate cooktop and oven areas. With this arrangement, one cook moves between the refrigerator, sink, and cooktop while the other moves between the refrigerator, second sink, and oven. Sometimes both work triangles can share two points, like the sink and refrigerator, and diverge at the cooktop and ovens.

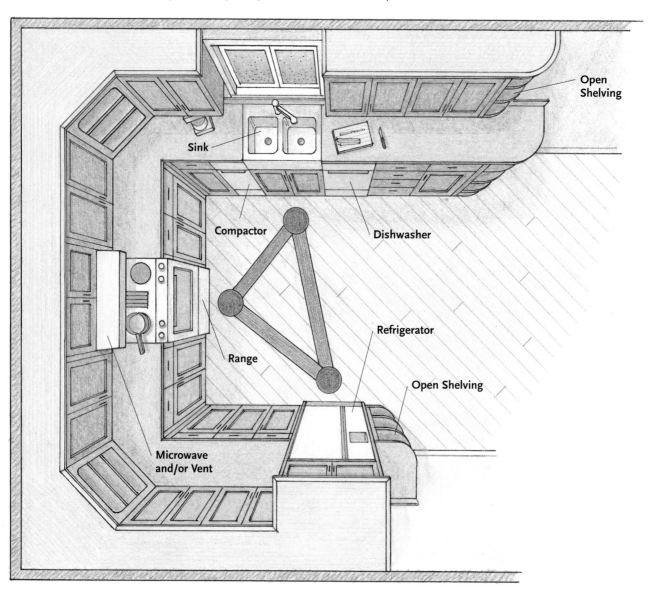

Open Shelving

Sink

Compactor

Dishwasher

Range

Refrigerator

Open Shelving

Microwave and/or Vent

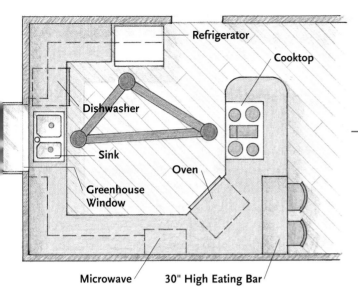

Refrigerator

Cooktop

Dishwasher

Sink

Oven

Greenhouse
Window

Microwave   30" High Eating Bar

Variation 1

Many designers consider the G-shaped layout a basic kitchen shape. It is formed by adding a peninsula to the end of the basic U-shape. This layout makes it easy for multiple cooks to work together. Adding a second sink and modular refrigeration to this design would make it even more efficient.

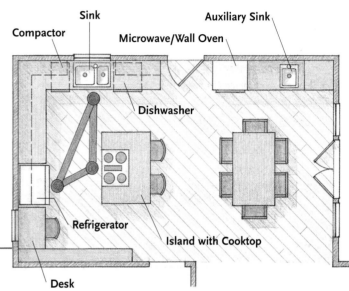

Sink

Compactor

Auxiliary Sink

Microwave/Wall Oven

Dishwasher

Refrigerator

Island with Cooktop

Desk

Variation 2

Adding an island to a U-shaped kitchen makes the space more functional. In large spaces, it allows you to create two areas without sacrificing a compact work area. The area near the table is a good location for a microwave for reheating leftovers.

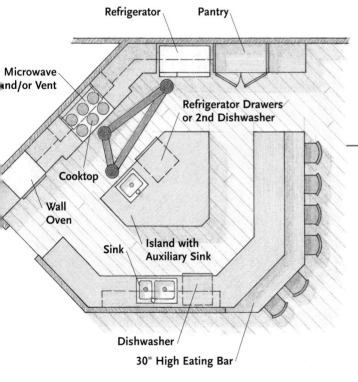

Refrigerator   Pantry

Microwave
and/or Vent

Refrigerator Drawers
or 2nd Dishwasher

Cooktop

Wall
Oven

Sink   Island with
Auxiliary Sink

Dishwasher

30" High Eating Bar

Variation 3

Having a large space with which to work allows for layouts that truly fit the way you function in the kitchen. The turn in the snack counter permits diners to face one another, making that area more appealing.

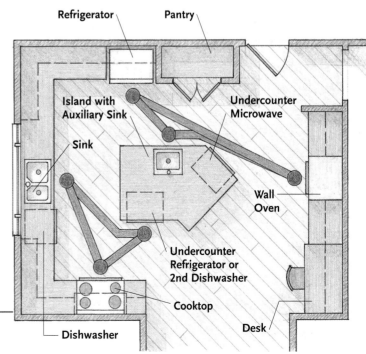

Refrigerator   Pantry

Island with
Auxiliary Sink

Undercounter
Microwave

Sink

Undercounter
Refrigerator or
2nd Dishwasher

Wall
Oven

Cooktop

Dishwasher

Desk

Variation 4

One of the strong points of the U-shape is the way through traffic need not interfere with the work areas. This kitchen has three doorways, yet most of the work areas are located out of the flow of traffic.

Off-the-Wall Space

If you've run out of wall space but have floor space to spare, consider improving your kitchen's efficiency with a peninsula or island.

Peninsulas. Properly sized and properly placed, peninsulas cut down on steps and increase counter space. Peninsulas also offer flexible storage because you can design them for access from either side. The peninsula base and ceiling-hung cabinets become convenient places to keep tableware and other dining-area supplies.

To prevent doors from colliding, allow a minimum of 48 inches of floor space between a peninsula and the counter opposite it. If plumbing and ventilation hookups permit, you might choose to place the range or sink in the kitchen side of a peninsula. On the other side you might choose to install an elevated eating counter.

Islands. In a big L- or U-shaped kitchen, you can shorten the distance between the sink, range, and refrigerator with a center island. This arrangement works especially well in the large kitchen of an older home, visually breaking up open floor space, increasing efficiency, and sometimes providing eating space.

Some homeowners choose to install a range or cooktop in the island; others use it for the sink and dishwasher. Either way, allow for adequate counter space on either side of the sink or cooking unit. As with a peninsula, make sure you'll have at least 48 inches of space between an island and any other counter. Consider using a different surface here, too, such as butcher block for chopping or marble for rolling pastry dough.

ABOVE A built-in table added to a run of counter and cabinets forms a peninsula that becomes a sunny breakfast nook.

ABOVE AND RIGHT Island fixtures help create multiple work areas and provide locations for additional storage, above. Fitted with a cooktop or range, they become ideal locations for eating bars, right.

MEASUREMENTS FOR PLANNING

With a pencil, graph paper, measuring tape, ruler, eraser, and scissors, you can draw an outline of the space you have and try out different arrangements of appliances, counters, and cabinets. You can also buy commercial planning kits that have a floor-plan grid and cutouts of standard-size cabinets, appliances, tables, and the like.

Careful Measuring

Start by making a rough floor plan of your existing kitchen. Include doors and windows, obstructions, breaks in the wall, outlets and switches, and any other pertinent information.

Measure accurately, all in inches, so you don't confuse 5'3" with 53"—a significant difference. Write measurements on the rough sketch as you go. Start at any corner of the room, and measure to the first break or obstruction—a window or range, for instance. Note this measurement on your sketch. Measure from that point to the next break or obstruction, and so on around the room. Also measure the height of doorways and windows from the floor up and from the ceiling down.

Measure the vertical and horizontal location of electrical outlets, light switches, and lighting fixtures. Show the rough locations of gas and plumbing lines, as well as ducts and vents.

Measure around the room at two or three heights: floor level above the baseboard, counter height (36 inches), and with arms stretched high (6 or 7 feet). Add up the measurements recorded along the walls for overall measurements. Now measure the overall length and width of your kitchen at the floor, and note this on your sketch. These should equal the corresponding overall measurements. If there's a significant difference in the measurements at different heights, your room is out of square, and it may be tricky to get a snug fit for your cabinets, which are square.

If the difference is too great to be masked by molding and caulk, say ½ to ¾ inch, you may need the help of a professional.

ABOVE Great results begin with careful planning and measuring. Cabinets are available in several sizes to fit most spaces.

USING GRAPH PAPER AND CUTOUTS

Begin planning by carefully measuring your existing kitchen (left). Record all dimensions in inches to avoid confusion. Transfer the drawing to graph paper (right), and use cutouts to create new layouts.

Scale Drawings

You can use each square of ¼-inch graph paper to represent 6 inches of actual floor space. Lay out the room's four walls to scale, referring to your rough sketch. Draw all irregularities on your scaled plan, being sure to account for the thickness of any walls that project into the room. Draw the existing doors and windows to exact scale, even if you expect to change them when you remodel. Also indicate existing utility lines and electrical connections.

Don't bother with appliances, cabinets, counters, or any other elements you plan to rearrange. These are best dealt with by cutting scaled templates from graph paper. Then, you can move the templates around to experiment with any layout that occurs to you.

Cabinets. Assembling a run of kitchen cabinets and appliances requires fitting a series of standard-size components into a space that's probably not an exact multiple of any dimension. The job isn't difficult because custom and stock cabinet widths progress in increments of 3 inches. By juggling sizes you can usually put together a series of cabinets that ends up just shy of the total distance from one wall to another. You'll make up the difference with filler strips at one or both ends.

The drawings on page 64 depict typical cabinet dimensions, but if you're taller or shorter than average, you may want to alter the heights at which your cabinets will be installed. You also may mix and match installation heights to create specialized work sites. Most base cabinets are 30½ inches high. Toe space and the base on which they rest bring them up to 34½ inches. Add another 1½ inches for the countertop, and the total counter height comes to 36 inches.

Adjusting Heights. Some studies indicate that the standard 36-inch counter height is too low for most people and that 37½ inches is better. If you want to elevate your counters an inch or so, increase the height of the toe space.

The distance between the countertop and the bottom of the wall cabinets typically measures 15 to 18 inches. The 18-inch height allows room for tall appliances on the counter or for a microwave oven installed under the wall cabinets. The 15-inch height makes upper shelves in the wall cabinets more accessible to shorter people.

63

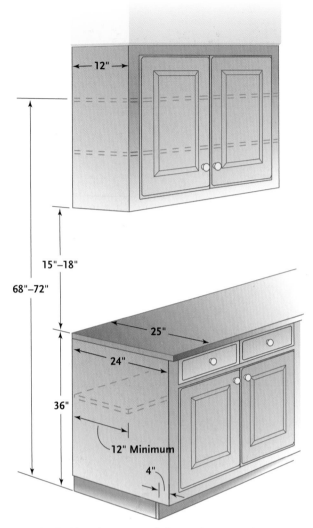

Preparing Your Plan. Use the dimensions for cabinets, appliances, and sinks in the table "Typical Kitchen Dimensions," opposite, when you draw and cut out templates for your scaled kitchen plan. There's not much you can do about appliance dimensions, of course, but most manufacturers can modify stock or semi-custom cabinets to your order for special equipment or space needs.

Corners. One of the trickiest parts of planning a run of cabinets and appliances comes when you arrive at a corner. Storage here tends to be inefficient, especially in the deeper recesses of base cabinets, where things sneak out of sight, out of reach, and soon out of mind as well. There are a variety of alternatives, however, thanks to specialty cabinets.

The two most popular ways to turn a corner are with blind bases, straight units that have a door on only one side and overlap the beginning of the next run, and corner bases, which integrate two cabinets into a single L-shaped unit. With blind bases you usually need a filler so that doors will clear each other. Wall cabinets also come in blind and corner units. When ordering blind cabinets, you must specify whether you want a left-hand or a right-hand version.

Another way to negotiate a turn is to situate a sink, refrigerator, or range there. Corner sinks may arrange basins at right angles to each other and fit into a standard corner base. Be sure to allow adequate counter space on either side of a sink or appliance. Use the small triangle of counter space in the corner to hold useful or decorative items, or make it a raised platform for plants.

A peninsula offers an excellent opportunity to take advantage of dead corner space inside cabinets. Items that can't be easily reached from the kitchen side can be stowed on the opposite side. Like blind bases, peninsula corner cabinets come in left- and right-hand configurations.

ABOVE Alter these typical dimensions to suit your needs. For example, tall people are more comfortable working at a higher-than-standard counter.

ABOVE For a sink base cabinet, a dummy drawer covers the bowl. Wide doors provide access to plumbing.

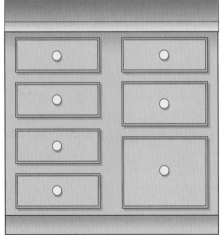

ABOVE In a drawer base cabinet, storage drawers come in a variety of sizes. Plan storage needs carefully before ordering.

ABOVE Base-cabinet widths are available up to 48 in. Combine base cabinets with efficient add-on storage options.

ABOVE Corner appliances make efficient use of this normally wasted space. Be sure to allow for landing space on the counter.

smart tip

DRAW UP YOUR KITCHEN PLAN IN THIS ORDER: SINK, RANGE, REFRIGERATOR. ONCE YOU HAVE THE BASIC TRIANGLE LOCATED, ADD THE OTHER APPLIANCES, SUCH AS WALL OVENS AND A DISHWASHER, AND THEN THE CABINETS, COUNTERS, AND EAT- ING AREAS.

● TYPICAL KITCHEN DIMENSIONS

Cabinet Dimensions (in inches; ranges in 3-in. increments)

Cabinet	Width	Height	Depth
Base unit	9–48	34½	24
Drawer base	15–21	34½	24
Sink base	30, 36, 48	34½	24
Blind corner base	24 (not usable)	34½	24
Corner base	36–48	34½	24
Corner carousel	33, 36, 39 (diameter)	X	X
Drop-in range base	30, 36	12–15	24
Wall unit	9–48	12–18, 24, 30	12, 13
Tall cabinet (oven, pantry, broom)	18–36	84, 90, 96	12–24

Appliance Dimensions (in inches)

Appliance	Width	Depth	Height
Cooktop	15, 30, 36, 42, 46 (with grill)	22	X
Wall oven	24, 27, 30	24	24–52
Range	24, 30, 36	24, 27	36, 72 (oven above)
Professional range	36–68	30–36	35–37
Vent hood	30, 36	18–20	7–9
Refrigerator	28–36	28–32, 24 (built-in)	58–72
Modular refrig./freezer	27	24	34½, 80
Upright freezer	28–36	28–32	58–72
Chest freezer	40–45	28–32	35–36
Dishwasher	18, 24	24	34½
Compactor	15, 18	24	34½
Washer and dryer	27–30	27–30	36, 72 (stacked)
Grill	18–36	21–22	X
Microwave oven	18–30	12–16	10–18

Sink Dimensions (in inches)

Sink Type	Width	Front to Rear	Basin Depth
Single-bowl	25	21–22	8–9
Double-bowl	33, 36	21–22	8–9
Side-disposal	33	21–22	8–9, 7
Triple-bowl	43	21–22	8, 6, 10
Corner	17–18 (each way)	21–11	8–9
Bar	15–25	15	5½–6

CREATING CUSTOM FLOOR PLANS

There are many ways to revise the floor plan of an existing kitchen. The room's peculiarities, combined with the special desires of the homeowners, lead to solutions that other remodelers might never consider.

So why bother to study how others might do things? With a little inspiration from one project here, a clever idea from another there, you'll be attuned to the possibilities that exist in your own remodeling project. To acquaint you with some possibilities, we've prepared floor plans for four existing kitchens, then redesigned them to better suit the families that live there.

ANNEXING A PANTRY

This typical early-twentieth-century kitchen contained few built-in components. The original kitchen supplemented meager counter and storage space with an adjacent "butler's pantry," not a bad feature if you happen to have a butler. Meals, even breakfast, were prepared in the kitchen and pantry by servants and then carried to a formal dining room to the left.

The typical modern family of four has no servants and would much rather eat light meals in the kitchen. To make space for a table and four chairs, we removed the wall between the kitchen and pantry. Then, to create an efficient work triangle, we also relocated the door to the dining room and arranged cabinets, counters, and appliances in a more efficient U-shaped layout.

An angled range with an overhead vent hood occupies dead corner space, with a microwave oven and tall storage cabinet to the left. There wouldn't have been enough space for a sink under the original window to the right of the range's new location, so we closed up that window—in the old pantry—moved the sink a couple of feet, and installed a greenhouse bay behind it. Now the refrigerator ends the run of cabinets and counters.

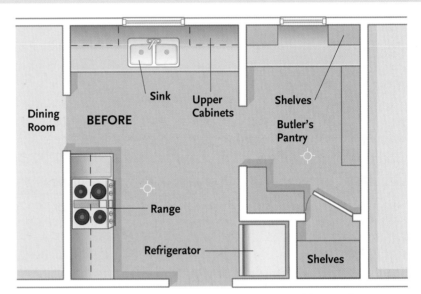

An inefficient layout was only one of this kitchen's problems. There was no counter space and most of the available storage was in another room.

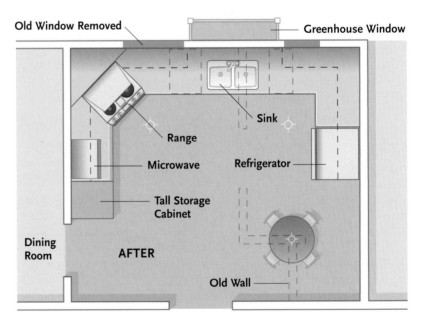

Removing a wall and moving a doorway opens up the space to allow for a classic U-shaped layout and a much more efficient work triangle.

REORGANIZING WASTED SPACE

The builder of this family-style kitchen meant well but failed to achieve a layout that worked smoothly. Lack of floor space is no problem here. In fact there seems to be way too much of it. Imagine repeatedly taking a dozen or more steps back and forth from the refrigerator to the sink or carrying hot, heaping plates to a table stranded in the middle of nowhere.

Counter space is also poorly allocated. There's too much next to the refrigerator and none at all to the right of the burner top. Also, every time the wall-oven door is opened it blocks traffic from the adjacent doorway.

Shrinking the Kitchen. The redesign cuts the working and dining areas down to size and adds some new angles. We moved the sink to an angled penin-

sula, making room for a compactor to the left of the sink. At the end of the peninsula, a custom-made, movable octagonal table is within easy reach of the refrigerator and cleanup center. Pull the table away from the peninsula, and it can seat up to eight.

The angles of a new china cabinet and the counter space next to the relocated refrigerator parallel those of the table and peninsula. Now the refrigerator has a handy "landing" counter, where groceries can rest on their way from store to storage, either in the refrigerator or the new pantry next to it. Moving the cooktop to the sink's former site provides generous counter space to the left and right of the burners. This also makes it possible to bring the wall oven closer to the other appliances, out of the through-traffic lane.

Wide-open spaces aren't always a good thing. Here, there are too many steps between the major appliances, as well as a critical shortage of counter space.

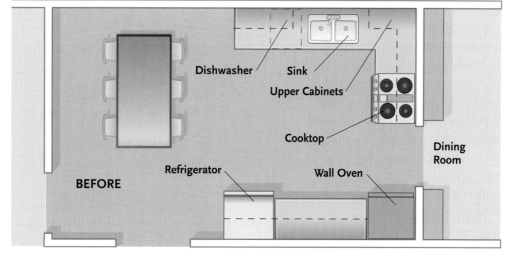

BEFORE

Dishwasher · Sink · Upper Cabinets · Cooktop · Refrigerator · Wall Oven · Dining Room

Adding a peninsula and table cuts the kitchen to a manageable size. It also allows for shifting the locations of the sink and cooktop, creating a more efficient work triangle.

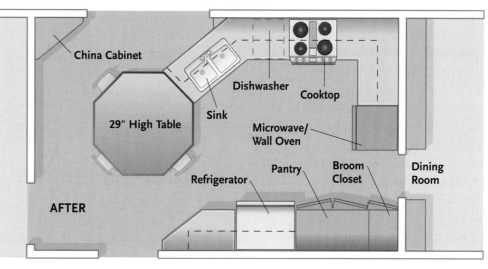

AFTER

China Cabinet · 29" High Table · Sink · Dishwasher · Cooktop · Microwave/Wall Oven · Refrigerator · Pantry · Broom Closet · Dining Room

REVAMPING AN OUTDATED KITCHEN

As old kitchens go, this one worked reasonably well. The range was a long hike from the sink, but otherwise the L-shaped layout defined a manageable work triangle and there was space left over for a table, chairs, and extra storage.

Fine-Tuning. Besides suffering from a somewhat awkward work triangle, this kitchen lacked counter space for today's common counter-top appliances.

In the first tune-up redesign, moving the range to the corner helps solve both problems: the triangle's legs are shorter, and the counter space next to the refrigerator is in-creased by more than a foot. Adding a peninsula next to the sink further increases usable counter and cabi-net space. With more storage in the kitchen proper, we decided to replace the extra floor-to-ceiling cabinets at the left with a planning center. Wall-hung cabinets and a built-in desk make a handy new place to conduct family business.

Splurging. Now look what could happen to the ho-hum kitchen if the homeowners spend a bit more. The second redesign moves the sink, not the range. A triangular peninsula accommodates the sink, dishwasher, a planter, and a planning desk.

To further tighten the work trian-gle, we have angled the refrigerator slightly. This move cramped the space formerly occupied by the table and chairs, so they were replaced by a piano-shaped table jutting out from the wall. Lastly, the space next to the dining room has become a hospitality center, complete with a bar sink.

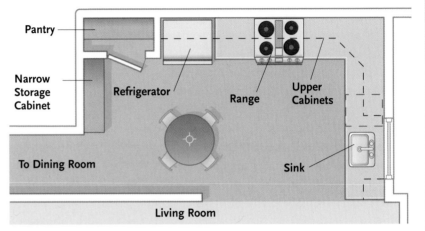

Before. This L-shaped layout put the refrigerator a long way from the sink and lacked an adequate amount of available storage space.

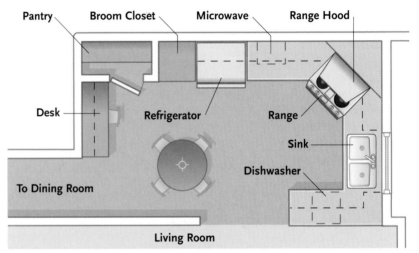

Fine Tuning. Moving the appliances tightens the work triangle. A new peninsula by the sink increases the work and storage space.

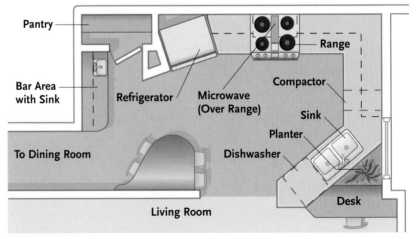

Splurging. Angling the refrigerator and sink, and adding a distinctive table add interest to the design. Moving the desk creates room for a wet bar.

STRETCHING INTO A PORCH

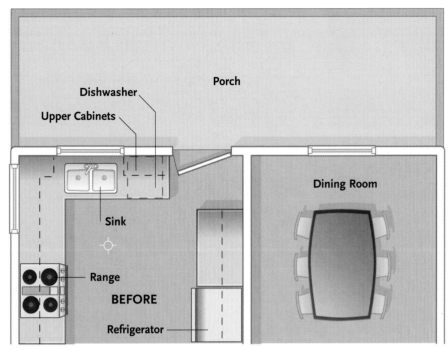

Porch

Dishwasher

Upper Cabinets

Dining Room

Sink

Range

BEFORE

Refrigerator

This tiny kitchen has a lot of potential. The existing, little-used porch offers the potential space the owners need to open up the space.

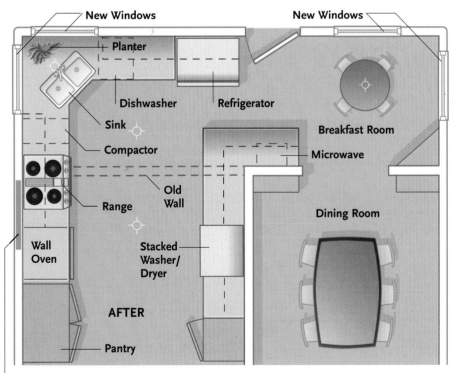

New Windows

New Windows

Planter

Dishwasher   **Refrigerator**

Sink

Compactor

Breakfast Room

Microwave

Old Wall

Range

Dining Room

Wall Oven

Stacked Washer/ Dryer

AFTER

Pantry

The kitchen doubled in size and now has a much more efficient design. It also has a sunny, informal eating area that the family can enjoy all year round.

Old Window Removed

Older homes often have kitchens that are tiny by today's standards, but many open to a side or back porch that begs to be brought in from the cold. Enclosing a porch is an obvious way to add kitchen space.

Case Study. This small kitchen stranded a range at one end of a compact L and positioned the refrigerator at the other end. Using the porch's existing roof and floor enabled the owners to triple their kitchen space, at a fraction of what an all-new addition would have cost.

A kitchen eating area was one priority, so about half of the old porch now provides a place for family meals. Converting the dining room window into a doorway provides access to the eating area and back door without passing through the work zone.

In the kitchen area, elongating the old L more than doubles cabinet and counter space. Baking, cooking, and cleanup centers are well defined but still convenient to each other. A new sink fits into dead corner space.

Now the refrigerator stands against the new back wall, handy to the eating area. In the refrigerator's old location the owners have stacked a washer and dryer, with adjacent counter space for sorting and folding laundry and a broom closet.

69

3 plumbing and wiring

The more complex your kitchen remodeling plans, the more likely you will need to alter or improve the plumbing and wiring systems. This may be as easy as installing a new faucet or switching out an old light fixture for a newer model, or your plans may be more ambitious and involve installing new plumbing fixtures where none exist or running a new electrical circuit from the panel box to your kitchen. In any case, you will need to know the basics of both plumbing and wiring, including joining different types of pipe, making simple wiring connections, and installing fixtures and appliances. A do-it-your-selfer should be able to handle the projects shown in this chapter. Just remember that maintaining safe working conditions and using the proper tools and materials are the keys to a successful project.

PLUMBING BASICS

Compared with the systems of pipes that carry water to and from a bathroom, a kitchen's plumbing needs are relatively simple: hot- and cold-water supply lines, a drain-pipe, and the necessary venting where you plan to install the sink. If you'll be installing a gas range, the gas line routed to its location is also considered plumbing. All of your kitchen's other water users—waste-disposal unit, dishwasher, water purifier, ice maker—tie into the same lines that serve the sink.

With luck, you already have supply and drain lines at or near the place where you'll put the sink. If not and you plan to move the sink more than a couple of feet, prepare to move supply lines, drains, and venting. The same holds true if you plan on adding a second sink to your new kitchen.

Explaining all the plumbing materials and skills needed to do your own plumbing work is beyond the

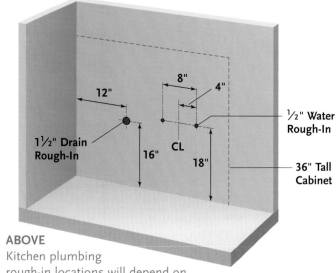

ABOVE
Kitchen plumbing rough-in locations will depend on where you want to place the sink. The standard height for water pipes exiting a wall is 18 in. Kitchen faucets have 8-in. center spreads, so place each pipe (hot and cold water) 4 in. off center. The drain should exit the wall at least 16 in. above the kitchen floor and should be 12 in. in from one or the other side of the cabinet wall.

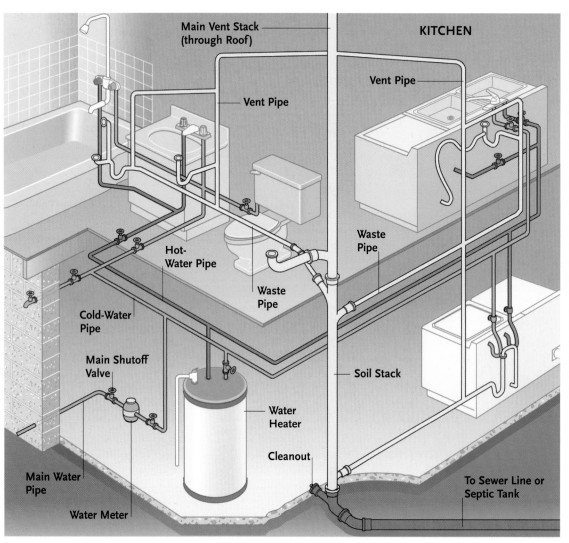

LEFT In a typical household plumbing system, water arrives from the municipal system or a private well. The cold-water supply lines branch from this main line; hot-water lines are first routed through the water heater. All fixtures receiving water are also connected to drainpipes and vent pipes. All drain and vent lines converge on soil and vent stacks, which extend through the roof.

scope of this book. However, an understanding of kitchen plumbing basics can help you deal knowledgeably with a plumbing contractor.

Kitchen Plumbing Anatomy

Hot and cold water come to a sink through a pair of supply lines, called risers, made of copper, brass, plastic, or galvanized steel. If your kitchen was originally plumbed with steel, the pipes should be replaced.

Because supply lines are small in diameter and the water flows under pressure, supply lines are easily rerouted. That's not so with drain lines, which depend on gravity. Water exits the sink through a curved trap, and a small amount retained in the trap forms an airtight seal that prevents sewer gases from leaking into the house.

The trap in turn connects to a drainpipe. Wastewater

from the trap typically drops down the drain to a larger pipe called a stack, which probably also serves one or more of your home's bathrooms. An upper extension of the drain, known as a vent, also typically connects to the stack, which rises as a main vent through the roof to expel gases and prevent suction that could siphon water from the trap.

Plumbing codes restrict the distance a sink's trap can be located from its drain/vent line. The distance varies somewhat from one community to another, but don't plan on moving the sink more than about 36 inches without having to break into the wall and extend branch lines or add a new stack.

Bringing Gas to a Range

Gas travels through black iron pipes threaded together with couplers, elbows, and T-fittings. You can hook up a range or cooktop with flexible gas piping, but moving or adding permanent gas pipes is a job for a professional plumber. Even if you routinely handle plumbing chores, working with gas is far more dangerous.

When you make any type of connection in a gas line, remember to always test your work after turning the gas back on by brushing all connections with soapy water; if the solution bubbles, tighten that connection.

Complying with Codes

If you plan extensive plumbing changes, you'll probably need a building permit. In some places, a licensed plumber must sign off on any work. In others, an inspector checks a job once while the walls are open, and again after all fixtures are hooked up.

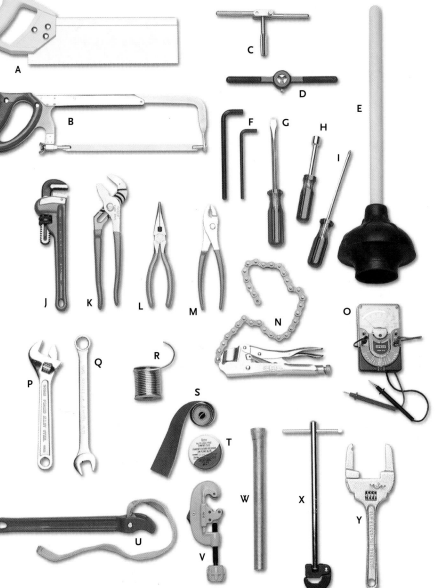

LEFT Basic tools for plumbing include: (A) backsaw, (B) hacksaw, (C) tap, (D) diestock, (E) plunger, (F) Allen wrenches, (G) flat-blade screwdriver, (H) nut driver, (I) Phillips screwdriver, (J) pipe wrench, (K) groove-joint pliers, (L) needle-nose pliers, (M) pliers, (N) chain wrench, (O) multitester, (P) adjustable wrench, (Q) open-end wrench, (R) solder, (S) emery cloth, (T) flux, (U) strap wrench, (V) tubing cutter, (W) tubing bender, (X) basin wrench, (Y) spud wrench.

CUTTING AND JOINING PLASTIC PIPE

project

Plastic pipe is easy to install: just measure the length you need and cut the pipe in a miter box. Then test fit the pipe and fitting to see if it works where it's supposed to work. Join the pieces with primer/cleaner, followed by solvent cement. Working quickly, push the pieces together, give them a slight turn, hold for 10 seconds, and you're done.

TOOLS & MATERIALS
- Plastic pipe ▌ Backsaw or hacksaw
- Miter box ▌ Pipe primer
- Work gloves and goggles
- Pipe ▌ Solvent cement
- Compression clamp fittings (when working with cast iron)
- Utility knife ▌ Emery cloth

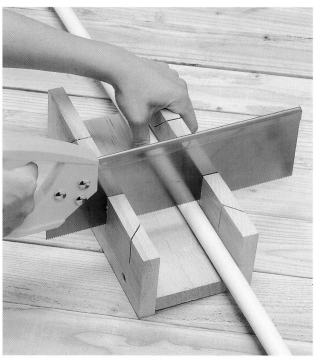

1 A simple wooden miter box is a great tool for making square cuts on plastic pipe. Just place the pipe in the box and hold it tightly against the side. Then make the cut using a backsaw, and remove the burrs from the cut end with emery cloth.

● BASIC PLUMBING SUPPLIES

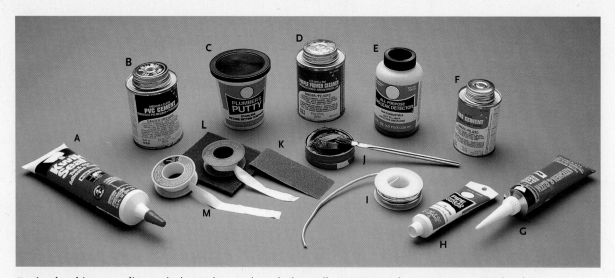

Basic plumbing supplies include (A) latex tub-and-tile caulk, (B) PVC solvent cement, (C) plumber's putty, (D) PVC primer, (E) leak-detection fluid, (F) ABS solvent cement, (G) silicone caulk, (H) pipe joint compound, (I) solder, (J) flux, (K) grit cloth, (L) abrasive pad, (M) pipe-thread sealing tape (yellow spool: gas, blue spool: water).

2 Once the pipe is cut, install the appropriate fitting and check if the assembly fits where it needs to go. If things look good, join the two.

BASIC PLASTIC DRAINAGE PIPING

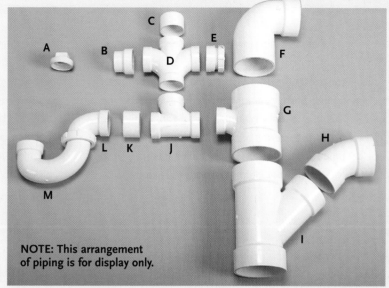

NOTE: This arrangement of piping is for display only.

Plastic drainage piping includes (A) cleanout plug, (B) threaded adapter, (C) coupling, (D) cross, (E) ground-joint adapter, (F) street 90-deg. elbow, (G) 3 x 1½-in. T-fitting, (H) 45-deg. elbow, (I) 3 x 2-in. Y-fitting, (J) sanitary T-fitting, (K) coupling, (L) trap arm, (M) trap.

3 The first step in joining pipe is to clean the end of the pipe and the inside of the fitting with pipe primer (inset). For PVC pipe, this cleaner is usually colored purple.

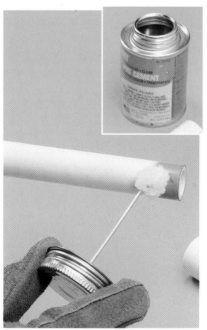

4 Once the primer is dry, apply a liberal coat of solvent cement (inset) to the end of the pipe and the inside of the fitting. Open the windows and use an exhaust fan to remove the cement fumes from the room.

5 Immediately after applying the cement, push the two parts together; turn them about one-quarter turn; and hold them for 10 seconds. This fuses the assembly so the pieces can't be taken apart.

SOLDERING COPPER PIPE

project

Before soldering copper pipe, make sure to don leather gloves and safety goggles to protect yourself against molten solder burns. Start by applying flux to the parts and pushing them together. Heat the joint, and press the solder onto the pipe. Protect combustible items with a piece of flashing, and wipe the joints clean when they are done.

TOOLS & MATERIALS
- Copper pipe
- Bristle brush
- Flux (soldering paste)
- Solder ▌ Propane torch
- Sparker ▌ Sheet metal
- Work gloves ▌ Clean rag
- Pipe fittings

INSULATING PIPES

For pipes that will carry hot water, it's smart to save a little on your energy costs with pipe insulation. Fit preformed polystyrene insulation tubes around hot-water pipes, and tape them in place. You can also wrap the pipes in strips cut from fiberglass batts. Either system will not only reduce heat loss but also prevent pipe sweating in the summertime.

If you have pipes running through an unheated crawl space, insulate (or protect with a heating cable) both hot- and cold-water pipes to keep them from freezing.

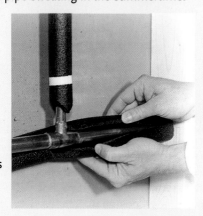

1 The first step in soldering copper pipe is to coat the pipe end and fitting with flux. Use a small brush and make sure everything is coated liberally.

2 Slide the fitting over the end of the pipe and twist it so the flux is spread around the entire joint.

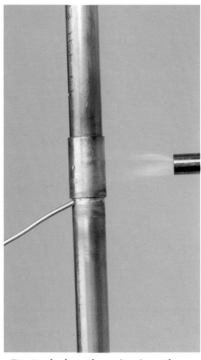

3 Push the other pipe into the coupling, and heat the fitting with a torch. Press the solder against the joint until the joint is filled.

• USING A PROPANE TORCH

If you're going to be working with metal pipe—whether copper, steel, or cast iron—you'll need to become familiar with the propane torch. Although it has the potential to be a dangerous tool, a few precautions and the proper safety gear will keep you safe from harm. Use a sparking tool to safely ignite the gas. Turn on a gentle supply of gas, and squeeze the sparker handle. Once you ignite the gas, increase the flow to enlarge the flame. It's wise to wear gloves when you handle heated pipes.

Before you try to heat up a pipe with a torch—to thaw a frozen section or to resolder a joint—first drain the line. You can't get copper hot enough to make solder flow when it is filled with water. Also, open a faucet just beyond the repair so that any steam that develops can escape. Be careful when using propane torches in tight spots where the flame may lick past the pipe and heat up building materials nearby. Use extra care working in framing cavities, particularly in older homes where the wood is very dry.

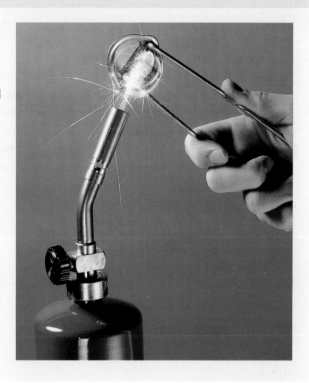

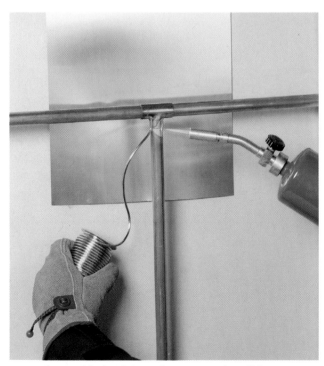

4 When soldering joints close to combustible materials, use a piece of flashing to protect these areas. Usually you can just tape the flashing in place with a piece of duct tape.

5 Once both sides of a joint are filled with solder, remove the torch and wipe the joint clean with a rag. Wear sturdy leather gloves to protect your hands from burns.

INSTALLING FAUCETS

If you are installing a new sink, add the faucet before the sink is attached to the countertop. It's much harder to make the connections from below once the sink is in place. The first step is to install the base plate gasket and base plate. Then slide the faucet into the middle sink hole, and tighten its mounting hardware. Finish up by connecting the faucet risers to the supply line shutoff valves.

TOOLS & MATERIALS

- Screwdriver
- Basin wrench
- Adjustable wrench
- Plumber's putty
- Pipe joint compound
- Faucet

1 Most single-handle kitchen faucets come with a base plate and gasket that are installed before the faucet head. Slide the base plate over the gasket and into the sink openings. Then hand tighten the jamb nuts.

2 Push the faucet assembly through the middle sink hole, and install the mounting hardware from below. Slide the retaining washer in place first; then thread the bracket against the washer and tighten its screws.

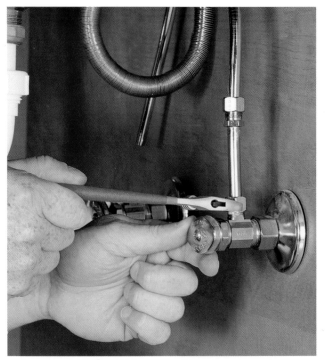

3 Connect the faucet's supply line risers to the shutoff valves with short lengths of tubing and compression fittings. Tighten the nuts securely; then install the drain piping before turning on the water and testing the connections.

INSTALLING DRAIN LINES

These days, many kitchen sinks are single-bowl models that require just a tailpiece between the strainer and the trap assembly. Double-bowl sinks, however, also need a T-fitting to join the two bowls together before connecting to the trap. While each bowl requires a drain, only one trap is needed. Start by installing a tailpiece below the strainer. Then add the T-fitting below this tailpiece and join it to the drain trap.

TOOLS & MATERIALS
- Hacksaw
- Sink-trap kit
- Groove-joint pliers
- PVC primer and cement

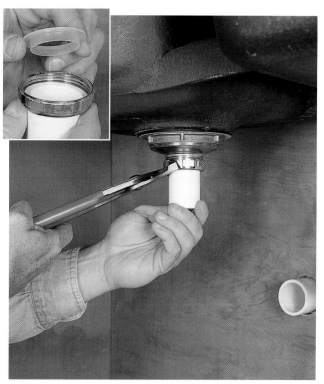

1 Once the sink strainer is installed, add a plastic tailpiece to the bottom of the strainer. Press a nylon washer into the top of the tailpiece (inset) and tighten the metal coupling nut onto the strainer spud.

2 Double-bowl sinks need a T-fitting to join the bowls together. To install one, slide a compression nut and a beveled nylon washer onto the tailpiece, followed by the T-fitting. Tighten the compression nut against the fitting.

3 Once the T-fitting is in place, install the drain trap to the bottom of the T-fitting tailpiece. Push on the compression nut followed by the nylon washer; then tighten the nut to the trap.

FIXING COMMON WATER-HEATER PROBLEMS

Water heaters are pretty simple devices that have only three common problems: a faulty temperature-and-pressure (T&P) relief valve, a sediment-clogged drain valve, and a corroded anode rod.

The T&P valve on every water heater is the unit's primary safety device. If a heater thermostat sticks and allows the temperature and pressure to increase dangerously inside the tank, the T&P valve automatically opens and relieves the high pressure and temperature inside.

These valves are great devices but it can be hard to tell if they are in good working order. So, make a small test every six months. Just lift up the test lever (inset right) and let it snap back. If hot water comes out in a short blast and then stops, the valve is OK. If no water comes out or the test lever won't operate, then replace the valve right away.

Sediment buildup is a fact of every water heater's life. To remove it, just turn off the gas or electricity to the unit. Then shut off the water supply to tank, and connect a garden hose to the bib on the bottom of the tank. Open the valve and drain the water and sediment together. Take off the hose, replace the valve, and fill the tank with water.

If the valve starts to drip after the tank is full, it is fouled with sediment. Turn off the power; drain the water; and replace the valve as shown below.

REPLACING A T&P RELIEF VALVE

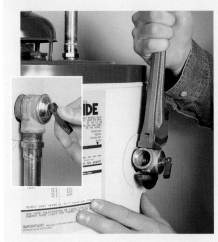

1. Test the T&P valve periodically (inset), and remove it if it seizes up or doesn't seem to work properly.

2. Wrap pipe-thread sealing tape around the threads of the new valve, and tighten it into the opening in the water heater.

REPLACING A SEDIMENT-CLOGGED DRAIN VALVE

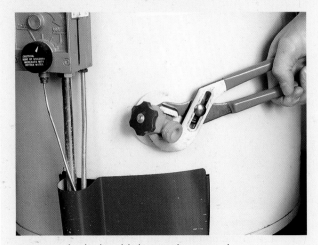

Remove the leaky old drain valve using large groove-joint pliers.

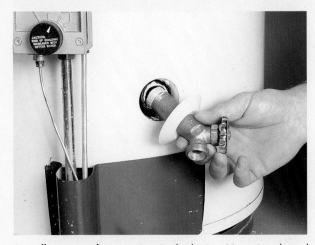

Install a new valve, turning it clockwise. Use pipe-thread sealing tape or pipe joint compound on the threads.

REPLACING AN ANODE ROD

project

Anode rods are sacrificial items. They are supposed to corrode over time, attracting the corrosive elements in the water rather than allowing those elements to react with the steel used to form the tank. Rod life is around 5 years; then replacement is a good idea. All that's required is to remove the old one with a socket wrench and thread in a new one. If the rod is not accessible from the top of the tank, as shown here, then check your tank owner's manual for its location.

TOOLS & MATERIALS
- New anode rod
- Breaker bar with 1¹⁄₁₆-in. socket
- Torch (as necessary)
- Pipe joint compound

1 The anode rod hangs on the inside of the tank and usually is held in place with a threaded fitting at the top. To remove the rod, put a 1¹⁄₁₆-in. socket on the anode nut and turn counterclockwise. If the nut won't budge, put a long breaker bar on the socket.

2 Pull the rod out carefully to avoid dropping corrosion in the tank. The anode shown here is about 5 years old and has exceeded any useful service life.

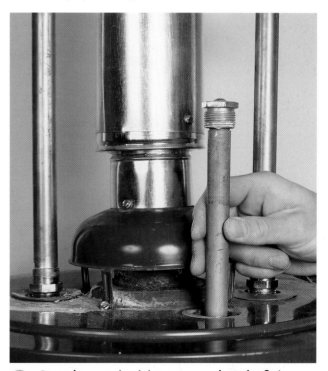

3 Spread some pipe joint compound on the fitting threads, and carefully lower the new anode rod into the tank. Tighten the nut using a socket wrench installed on a long breaker bar. Turn on the water, and check for leaks around the nut.

REPLACING A GAS WATER HEATER

Replacing a worn out gas water heater isn't very hard, if you get a new one that's close to the size of the old one. First, turn down the unit's thermostat; shut off the water supply; and drain the tank. Then turn off the gas; remove the flue; cut the water lines; and remove the heater. Slide the new tank into place and solder new supply lines. Install a new T&P valve and a new flue, and hook up the gas line. Fill the tank with water, and light the pilot.

TOOLS & MATERIALS
- New heater, T&P valve ▮ Garden hose
- Self-tapping screws ▮ Pipe wrenches
- Power drill-driver ▮ Nut driver
- Pipe joint compound ▮ Tubing and cutter
- Multipurpose tool ▮ Solder, flux, torch

1 The first step in replacing a water heater is to remove the old one. And the first step in removing the old one is to empty out the water. To do this, turn down the thermostat; shut off the water supply; and drain the tank using a garden hose.

4 Grip the cut supply lines and tip the heater toward you. Then carefully pivot it out into the room. Once everything is clear, get some help and carry the heater outside for trash pickup.

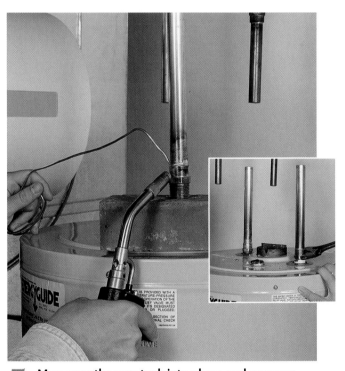

5 Maneuver the new tank into place, and measure from the tank to the existing water lines. Fill this space with a piece of pipe and a male adapter. Solder the two together; then thread the assembly into the tank (inset).

2 Shut off the gas supply by turning the gas valve handle 90 deg. (inset). Then separate the gas line by taking apart the union fitting just below the shutoff valve.

3 Gas heaters are vented to the outside through a flue hat at the top of the heater. Use a nut driver or socket wrench to take off the flue hat. Then cut the water lines above their unions with a tubing cutter (inset).

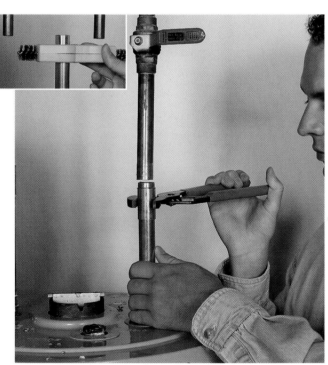

6 Clean all the pipes ends and the couplings using a multipurpose tool (inset) or emery cloth. Then add flux to both components of each joint, and solder the joints together using a propane torch.

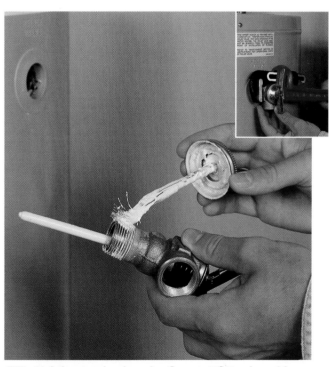

7 Lightly coat the threads of a new T&P valve with pipe joint compound. Then carefully slide the valve into the hole on the side of the tank and tighten with a pipe wrench (inset). Stop when the test handle is pointing toward the floor. *(continued on page 84)*

(continued from page 83)

8 To create a discharge tube for the T&P valve, measure the distance from the bottom of the valve to the floor, and subtract 6 in. Cut a section of pipe to this length, and solder a male adapter onto the end. Thread this into the bottom of the valve.

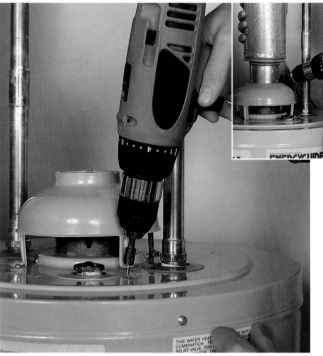

9 Install the new flue hat to the top of the tank using self-tapping sheet-metal screws and a drill-driver. Then screw the flue pipe to this flue hat using self-tapping screws (inset).

10 Join the gas line to the new heater with a black pipe union. Tighten the union using two pipe wrenches. Be sure to install a drip-leg pipe below the T-fitting that feeds the tank.

11 Make sure the tank is filled with water, and light the pilot light. A gas grill lighter works well for this job. Then attach the access panel and cover and turn up the thermostat.

INSTALLING AN ELECTRIC WATER HEATER

An electric water heater is easier to install than a gas-fired one because there are no flue and gas hookups to make. You do, however, have to make some electrical connections. The heater comes with a built-in electrical box for making the wiring splices. But you'll have to supply rigid conduit to protect the electrical cable between the top of the heater and a wall-mounted disconnect switch box. If your old electric water heater was properly installed, then you should be able to use the old connections. But local codes do change over time and some vary when it comes to mounting these disconnect boxes. So check with your building department before proceeding.

Usually the approved approach is to install a conduit connector and a piece of conduit in the tank (below left). Then run the cable through it and make the connections to the tank wires using wire connectors (below right). The other end of the cable goes to the disconnect switch and runs through conduit the whole way. The rationale for having a disconnect switch close to the heater is to make it easier and safer to shut off the power prior to working on the tank. Keep in mind, most electric water heaters require a 10-gauge cable and a 240-volt 30-amp breaker in your service panel.

smart tip

SAVING FUEL COSTS

TODAY'S WATER HEATERS ARE BETTER INSULATED THAN WERE THOSE OF EVEN A FEW YEARS AGO. STILL, YOU CAN BOOST EFFICIENCY BY INSTALLING AN AFTERMARKET INSULATION BLANKET. THE MORE HOURS YOU SPEND AWAY FROM THE HOUSE, THE MORE BENEFIT YOU'LL GET FROM THIS ADD-ON. CAUTION: BE CAREFUL NOT TO COVER THE ACCESS COVER, T&P RELIEF VALVE, OR CONTROL VALVE. YOU'LL ALSO NEED TO HOLD THE INSULATION AWAY FROM THE FLUE HAT BY SEVERAL INCHES ON GAS-FIRED HEATERS.

AN EVEN BETTER INVESTMENT IS TO INSULATE ALL HOT-WATER PIPES. THESE PIPES SHED A GOOD DEAL OF HEAT, AND THE MORE YOU CAN DO TO SLOW HEAT LOSS, THE LOWER YOUR ENERGY BILLS. YOU'LL FIND SEVERAL KINDS OF PIPE INSULATION ON THE MARKET. THE BEST IS PRE-SLIT FOAM RUBBER.

● INSTALLING A CONDUIT AND CABLE

1. Thread a conduit connector into the water heater, and run the wires in ½-in. EMT conduit.

2. Bind the grounding wire under the grounding screw, and join the like-colored wires in connectors.

WIRING BASICS

All of the intricacies of a home wiring system are beyond the scope of this book. But some basic information will allow you to complete simple electrical projects. To begin with, if your electrical system is up to current standards, the main service cable that enters your house will contain three wires—two hot wires and one neutral wire. The panel subdivides incoming current into individual circuits that are joined to lights, switches, receptacles, and appliances by means of electric cables.

The path the electricity takes is a closed loop. It leaves the panel in the hot wires and returns by the neutral wires. If you try to draw too much power through a circuit, the circuit breaker or fuse will shut off the power to this circuit, and thus reduce the possibility of shock or fire.

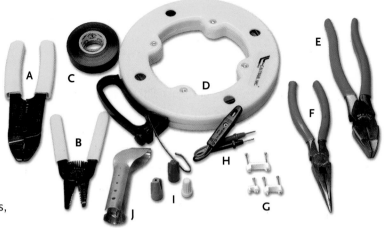

ABOVE Basic tools for wiring include (A) multipurpose tool, (B) wire stripper, (C) electrical tape, (D) fish tape, (E) lineman's pliers, (F) needle-nose pliers, (G) cable staples, (H) circuit tester, (I) wire connectors, and (J) cable ripper.

Grounding

Electricity always seeks to return to a point of zero voltage (the ground), along the easiest path open to it. Touch an electric fence, and the current goes right through you to the ground. If a short occurs in your electrical system, the normal circuit is broken. Touch the box, and you become part of the circuit unless the circuit is grounded.

Getting Power to the Kitchen

Your kitchen lights and receptacles are wired to circuits that are protected by 15-amp breakers (for most lights) and 20-amp breakers (for most receptacles). If you only want to replace old light fixtures, you may already have adequate power. It is possible to replace all of the outlets and switches without running new wiring. But if you plan on adding new appliances or additional lights or receptacles, discuss your power requirements with an electrician.

● SPLICING AND CONNECTING WIRES

Bare Wire

Insulated Solid Wire

Insulated Stranded Wire

Nonmetallic Cable (NM)

Armored Cable (AC)

To connect wires from different cables, strip ½ inch of insulation from the individual wires. Hold the wires parallel with one another, and twist them together by tightening down on a wire connector (turning clockwise) so that the exposed wires are covered. Tighten the connector by hand; don't use pliers.

STRIPPING CABLES AND WIRES

project

Electric cables carry current from your service panel to individual outlets and appliances. But the cables can't do anything unless the wires inside are hooked to the appropriate terminals. The cable sheathing and insulation must be stripped from the end of the wires to make them ready for the job. Do this with a cable ripper and multipurpose tool. Slice the sheathing with the ripper, and cut it off with a multipurpose tool; then strip the insulation from the wires.

TOOLS & MATERIALS
▌ Cable
▌ Cable ripper
▌ Multipurpose tool or utility knife

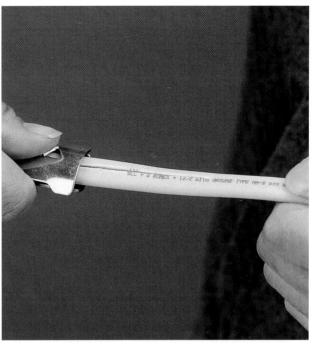

1 To remove the outside sheathing on electric cable, you can use a utility knife. But a cable ripping tool does a better and more professional-looking job, and takes less time. To use one, slide it over the cable and squeeze it at the point where you want to start stripping. Then pull to the end of the cable.

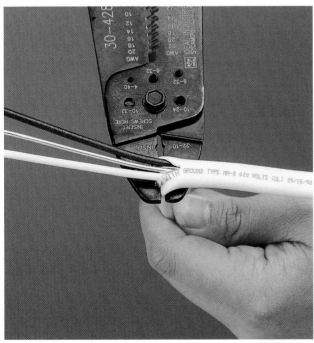

2 Pull the sheathing back to expose the individual wires inside the cable. Cut away the sheathing using a multipurpose tool or a utility knife. Be careful to avoid nicking the insulation on the wires.

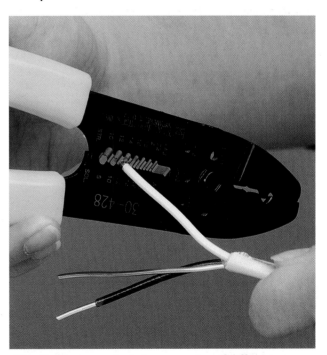

3 Multipurpose tools have a series of different diameter slots for stripping the insulation off a wide range of wire sizes. Find the slot that matches your wire; push the wire into the slot; squeeze the tool handles together; and pull. This will cleanly remove the insulation.

RUNNING NEW CABLE

project

Gutting your kitchen down to the framing gives you the chance to replace outdated wiring and to locate electrical fixtures just where you want them. The easiest kind of wiring to install is plastic-sheathed, nonmetallic cable called NM cable, or sometimes by the brand name Romex. NM cable contains a black-sheathed (hot) wire, a white (neutral) wire and a bare (ground) wire. Check with your electrical inspector to see what type and gauge of cable is acceptable for your project. As a rule of thumb, you can usually get by with 12-gauge cable for kitchen lights and receptacles. However, special equipment like waste-disposal units, dishwashers, and microwave ovens usually require heavier cable.

TOOLS & MATERIALS
- Power drill-driver with ¾-inch bit
- Basic electrical tools ▌ Cable staples
- 5d (1¾ in.) nails ▌ Cable
- Junction boxes, switch boxes
- Metal stud plates (if needed)
- Hammer

Outlet Boxes

Every receptacle, light, and switch must be installed in a metal or plastic box that is attached to house framing. Check with your building department to see what type of box is approved in your area. Round or octagonal boxes are usually used for ceiling fixtures and junction boxes. Rectangular boxes usually contain switches and receptacles. All these boxes are available with different fasteners to suit different situations. In most cases, the boxes are simply nailed to the wall studs or ceiling joists.

Begin running cable by laying out where you want all your boxes to go. Once you've formed a plan, attach the boxes to the framing. Then drill cable holes between the boxes or cut notches in the edge of wall studs. Insert the cable ends in the boxes, and staple loose cable to the sides of studs and joists. Cover notches with protective metal plates.

1 Lay out the kitchen for all the light, switch, and receptacle boxes. Then nail the boxes in place. These days, plastic boxes are popular. But galvanized-steel models are a good alternative.

2 Once the boxes are in place, determine the most efficient path for the cables that connect them. Drill ¾-in.-dia. clearance holes for the cables through the framing members. Keep the holes 1¼ in. from the side of the stud or joist.

SAFETY PRECAUTIONS

ELECTRICITY CAN BE DANGEROUS, BUT IF YOU USE COMMON SENSE, YOU CAN WORK WITH IT QUITE SAFELY. IT'S MOST IMPORTANT TO REMEMBER ALWAYS, WITHOUT FAIL, TO TURN OFF THE POWER AT THE MAIN SERVICE PANEL BEFORE WORKING ON A CIRCUIT. USE ONE HAND TO DISCONNECT OR REACTIVATE A FUSE OR CIRCUIT BREAKER, AND KEEP THE OTHER HAND IN YOUR POCKET OR BEHIND YOUR BACK. BEFORE STARTING WORK, CHECK THE CIRCUIT WITH A NEON CIRCUIT TESTER TO BE SURE THAT IT IS SHUT OFF. IF YOU ARE WORKING ON A SWITCH, TEST IT FOR CURRENT IN BOTH THE ON AND OFF POSITIONS. IF YOU ALWAYS FOLLOW THIS RULE, YOU SHOULD NEVER SUFFER AN ELECTRICAL SHOCK.

BOX CAPACITIES

Maximum number of wires permitted per box

Type of Box (Size in Inches)	Wire Gauge 14	12	10
Round or Octagonal			
4 x 1½	7	6	6
4 x 2⅛	10	9	8
Square			
4 x 1½	10	9	8
4 x 2⅛	15	13	12
Rectangular Boxes			
3 x 2 x 2¼	5	4	4
3 x 2 x 2½	6	5	5
3 x 2 x 2¾	7	6	5
3 x 2 x 3½	9	8	7

3 If you can't drill through the center of a stud, notch the edge of the studs for the cable. Install metal wire shields to protect the cable.

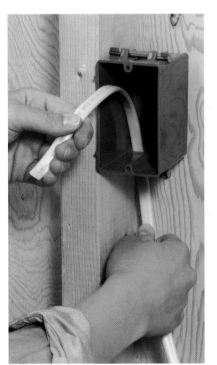

4 Run the cable from box to box as needed. Leave about 8 in. of cable extending from each box to make your connections.

5 Attach loose cable using cable staples. Be careful when driving the staples. They should hold the cable securely without cutting into the sheathing.

RUNNING CABLE BETWEEN FLOORS

project

Snaking new wire between floors can be a difficult job. But careful work and using a fish tape can make the job much easier. Start by cutting a box opening in the wall and marking its location by driving a nail into the floor. Then go into the basement and drill a cable hole up through the subfloor and the bottom plate of the wall above. Push a fish tape through the wall opening and down into the basement. Hook the cable to the fish tape, and pull both up through the box opening.

TOOLS & MATERIALS
▮ Power drill-driver with ¾-inch bit
▮ Fish tape ▮ Basic electrical tools
▮ Keyhole saw ▮ Electrical boxes
▮ Electrical tape ▮ Electrical cable

1 Cut an opening in the wall for a new box; then drive a nail through the floor just below the opening to mark the box location. Go into the basement and drill a cable hole up through the floor and the bottom wall plate.

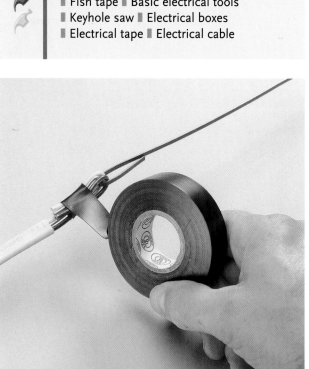

2 Carefully feed a fish tape through the box opening in the wall and down through the access hole into the basement. Make a hook at the end of the cable, and attach it to the end of the fish tape using electrical tape.

3 Slowly pull the fish tape and cable up through the box hole. The job will be easier if you have a helper down in the basement to guide the cable through the hole and prevent it from getting caught on something.

RUNNING CABLE THROUGH WALLS

project

One good way to run cable through finished walls is to install the cable behind the wall baseboards. Begin by marking a reference line along the top of the baseboard. Then remove the boards; cut the drywall behind; and take it out in pieces. Cut notches in the studs; install the cable; and cover it with protective steel plates. Replace the pieces of drywall that you removed. Then add the baseboards; touch up the paint; and you're done.

TOOLS & MATERIALS
▌ Basic carpentry tools
▌ Cable
▌ Wire shields

RETROFIT WALL WIRING

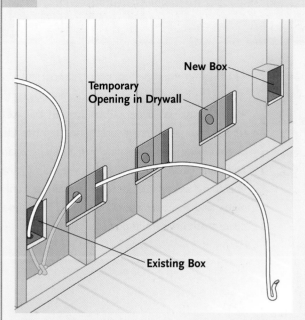

To run cable horizontally behind a finished wall, cut an opening for each stud and drill holes in the studs. Use fish tape to pull the new cable through the wall.

1 Draw a line along the top of your baseboards. Then carefully remove the baseboards, and draw a line ½ in. below the first line. Cut the drywall along this second line, and remove the panels.

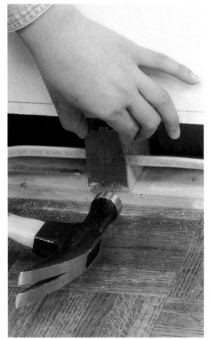

2 Notch the bottom of the studs for the cable, then cover up each notch with a metal plate. If you have room, you can also drill cable holes through the middle of the studs.

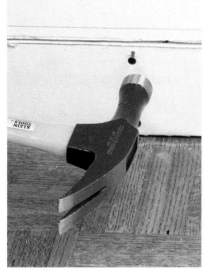

3 Once the cable is installed, replace the drywall panels. Nail them above and below the metal plates. Then reinstall the baseboards, and touch up the paint.

ADDING A NEW CIRCUIT

project

Kitchen remodeling plans almost always call for adding new electrical circuits to meet the increased demands. To start this job, turn off the main panel switch, and remove the cover. Check for the best location for the new circuit, and install the circuit cable. Strip the sheathing and insulation; then install the cable wires and the circuit breaker. Install the panel cover, and turn on the power.

TOOLS & MATERIALS
- Basic electrical tools
- Flashlight
- Cable (the type required by code)
- Cable clamps
- Circuit breakers of the required amperage and of the same make as your panel

1 To add a new electrical circuit to your service panel, start by opening the door and turning off the main circuit breaker. Then take off the panel cover by removing the four screws located near the corners of the box.

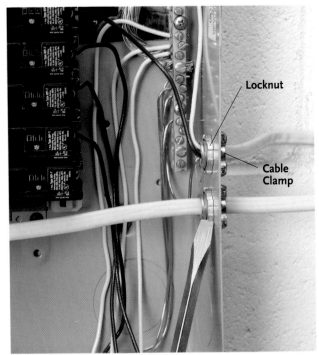

5 Finger-tighten the cable connector against the side of the panel. Then drive the locknut in a clockwise direction using a flat bladed screwdriver and a hammer. The locknut will dig into the panel and hold the connector securely in place.

6 Strip the sheathing from the end of the cable; then remove about ½ in. of insulation from the individual wires. Install the white wire in the neutral buss bar along with the other white wires. Install the ground wire in the grounding bus bar.

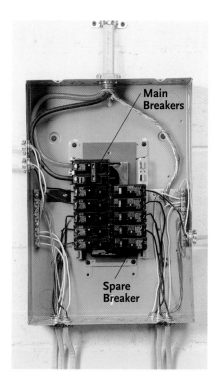

Main
Breakers

Spare
Breaker

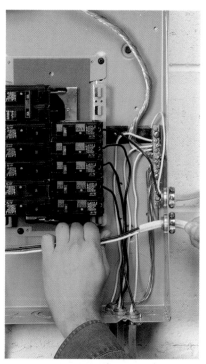

2 The locations of all the current circuits are labeled on the cover door. Each circuit breaker is connected to a cable of various types and gauges.

3 Once the cover is removed, check the panel for open slots or breakers that are not being used. Non-used breakers will have no cable attached.

4 To install a new cable, pry out one of the knockout plates and install a cable connector. Then push the cable through the connector, and tighten the clamp.

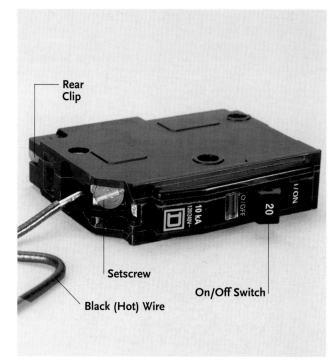

Rear
Clip

Setscrew

On/Off Switch

Black (Hot) Wire

7 A typical 120-volt, 20-amp breaker has a clip at the back that plugs into the hot bus bar in the panel. To install it, just engage the clip and push the breaker in. The hot (black) wire from the circuit cable is installed under the setscrew on the side of the breaker.

8 Remove the plate on the cover that falls where the new breaker is located. Then slide the panel cover in place and install the corner screws. Label the circuit on the inside of the door, and turn on the main breaker.

WIRING SWITCHES

Switches control the flow of current through a circuit. If a switch has two terminals (plus a grounding terminal), it is a single-pole switch. It alone controls a particular circuit. The incoming hot wire is hooked to one terminal and the outgoing hot wire is attached to the other. A switch with three terminal screws (plus ground) is called a three-way switch. Two such switches control one fixture from two different locations, such as switches located at different doorways to the kitchen that control the same light. There are also four-way switches that control lights from three or more locations, and double switches that serve more than one circuit.

When wiring switches, remember that the circuit can run from the switch to the fixture or through the fixture to the switch; see the samples below.

SWITCH STAMPS

Amp/Volt Rating

UL Label

Wire Types

Switches are stamped with code letters and numbers detailing operating specifications and safety information. Learn how to read these so that you buy the right switch. The switch at right is rated for 15-amp, 120-volt circuits on alternating current (AC) only; CU/ALR (or CU/AL) shows that it can be used with copper or aluminum wiring; CU WIRE ONLY switches can be used only with copper wire. UL or UND. LAB. means that the switch has been tested by Underwriters Laboratories. (CSA is the equivalent Canadian organization.)

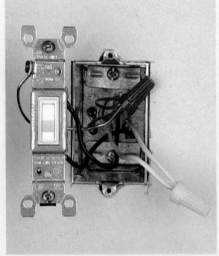

In a middle-of-the-run single-pole switch, connect black wires from both incoming and outgoing cables to the switch terminals. Splice together the white wires, and separately splice the green grounding wires, including a short grounding wire attached to the metal box.

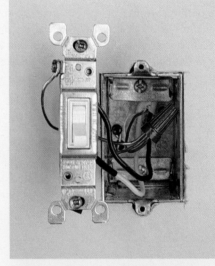

This switch is at the end of a circuit, which means the circuit actually passes through the light fixture before it gets to the switch. Both the black and white wires are hot, so be sure to code the white wire with black tape.

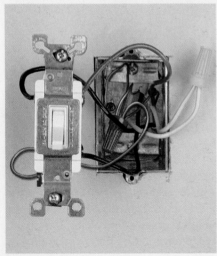
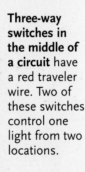

Three-way switches in the middle of a circuit have a red traveler wire. Two of these switches control one light from two locations.

Three-way switches at the end of a circuit run still have a red traveler wire to connect switches—for example, at each end of stairs.

ADDING NEW RECEPTACLES

Grounded receptacles accepted by the National Electrical Code contain three slots: two vertical slots of different sizes for the hot and neutral wires and a U-shaped slot for the ground wire. Don't install a three-prong plug on an ungrounded circuit. The circuit must be grounded back to the main panel through a grounding wire or a system of armored cable and metal boxes. Have a licensed electrician evaluate the circuit's wiring before substituting three-slot receptacles for old two-slot models.

High-Voltage Receptacles

Some appliances, such as electric ranges, require more power than the standard 120-volt circuit can deliver. These appliances need 240-volt receptacles to operate at full power, and most codes stipulate that they be the only receptacle on the circuit. In some cases, the circuit is wired directly to the appliance, but in many cases a high-voltage receptacle is mounted near the appliance.

A 240-volt receptacle uses a two-wire cable with ground. Both the black and white wires are hot (there is no neutral wire in this system). When wiring this type of receptacle, code the white wire as hot by applying some black electrical tape to it.

However, a high-voltage circuit that also requires 120-volt current to operate clocks, timers, and lights on the appliances does need a white neutral wire so that the appliance can split the entering current between 120 volts and 240 volts. These circuits use three-wire cable—black, red (also hot), and white—and a ground.

As a safety measure, all receptacles of high-voltage appliances have specific slot configurations that can only mate with the corresponding type of plug.

To wire a middle-of-the-run receptacle, connect the two black wires to the two brass-colored screws and attach the two white wires to the silver-colored terminals. Connect the bare grounding wire as shown.

For an end-of-run receptacle, bring the incoming cable into the box. Connect the black wire to the brass screw and the white wire to the silver-colored screw. Connect the grounding wire to the green screw and pigtail as shown.

A 240-volt receptacle uses a two-wire cable with ground. Both the black and white wires are "hot," so be sure to code the white wire with black electrical tape to alert anyone working on the receptacle later.

A 120/240 receptacle uses a three-wire cable with ground. The black and red wires are connected to the brass screws; the white wire goes to the neutral screw; and the grounding wire goes to the ground terminal.

HOW GFCIs WORK

Ground-fault circuit interrupters (GFCIs) are on the front line of keeping electricity safe to use in your home. They are relatively sophisticated electronic devices that sense and prevent current leakage in wiring circuits. Current leakage is normally defined as a discrepancy between the current being carried by the black hot wire and the neutral white wire. When there is a difference between the two, leakage is assumed.

Although a powerful current surging through your system will blow a fuse or trip a breaker, a less powerful current may not be sufficient to do this. Yet, a small current like this can be very dangerous, especially in wet or damp areas, like kitchens, bathrooms, basements, garages, and outdoor areas. A GFCI is designed to detect minute current leaks and to immediately break the circuit before you suffer a hazardous shock.

GFCI protection is available in three basics ways (below) and is required by The National Electrical Code in every situation where electrical fixtures and devices are likely to be exposed to wet or damp conditions. Check with your local building department for all the details.

project

INSTALLING A GFCI RECEPTACLE

To install a portable GFCI, you just plug it into a receptacle. To install a GFCI breaker, just replace a standard breaker with a GFCI model in the service panel. (Turn off the power first.) But a GFCI receptacle takes a little (but not a lot) more work. Begin by shutting off the power to the circuit and checking for current using a circuit tester. Then remove the existing receptacle from the box. Install the GFCI model in the same box, and test the installation.

TOOLS & MATERIALS
▌ Screwdriver
▌ Voltage tester
▌ Plastic wire connector
▌ GFCI receptacle(s)

● THREE WAYS TO PROTECT WITH GFCIs

The cheapest and easiest is a portable device that you simply plug into the outlet of the receptacle you want to protect. It protects only that outlet. At slightly more expense and effort, you can replace the receptacle with a GFCI receptacle, which offers the opportunity to protect receptacles downstream from the one you are replacing. Another way to protect all receptacles and devices connected to the kitchen is to wire them to circuits with GFCI breakers installed in the panel box. (See "Adding a New Circuit," page 92.) This is also the most expensive way to achieve protection, as GFCI breakers cost about four times as much as an ordinary 120-volt breaker.

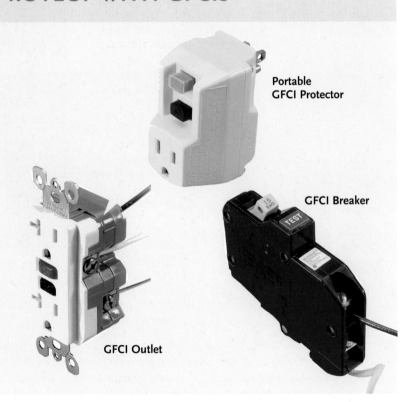

Portable GFCI Protector

GFCI Breaker

GFCI Outlet

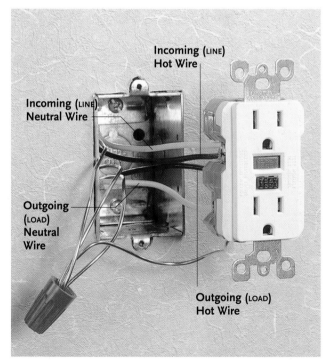

1 Turn off the power to the circuit at the service panel. Insert a neon circuit tester in a pair of plug slots to make sure there's no power present. If the indicator light comes on, then the wrong circuit was turned off.

2 Disconnect the existing receptacle by unscrewing the side terminal screws and freeing the wires. Remove the grounding wire, too. Check all the wire insulation to make sure it's still sound. If you see any nicks, cover them with electrical tape.

Incoming (LINE) Hot Wire

Incoming (LINE) Neutral Wire

Outgoing (LOAD) Neutral Wire

Outgoing (LOAD) Hot Wire

3 Attaching the existing wires to the GFCI receptacle is easy. First tighten the ground wire to its screw. Then join the incoming hot (black) and neutral (white) wires to the terminals marked LINE. If outgoing wires are present, connect these to the LOAD terminals.

Reset

Test

4 Carefully push the GFCI into the box, and screw it in place. Then install the cover (inset). Turn the power back on; press the RESET button; then the TEST button. If the GFCI is working properly, the RESET button should pop out.

Range Receptacle

In the past, cable for kitchen ranges included two hot wires and a stranded ground/neutral. This type of cable is called service-entrance conductor (SEU) cable. The range receptacle for this kind of cable accommodated a three-prong plug configuration. The problem with this arrangement was that the current-carrying neutral was also used as the grounding conductor for the appliance frame. Today, cables for kitchen ranges are still required to carry two hot conductors, but the neutral wire must also be insulated, and the grounding conductor can be either bare or insulated. It is a four-conductor cable containing three insulated wires and one grounding conductor. Usually, there are two hot wires, a neutral, and a ground wire that is green or bare. This category of cable is called service entrance round (SER) cable. Type NM cable with three conductors and a ground is also allowed. The size used for a kitchen range is usually 6-gauge cable. A range receptacle must accept a 4-prong plug configuration for this type of cable.

Of the four wires in SER cable, the two hot wires carry the 240 volts required to power the heating elements. The 120-volt power is carried across the neutral to either of the two hot wires—it doesn't matter which one. The 120-volt power is used to run the timer, clock, buzzer, etc. Drawing the neutral current away from the grounding conductor causes the return current to flow safely through an insulated conductor rather than through a bare copper grounding wire. The 4-slotted female receptacle into which the SER cable is wired can be surface- or

smart tip
INSTALLING APPLIANCES

IT'S A GOOD IDEA TO HAVE YOUR APPLIANCES ON SITE BEFORE YOU START RUNNING THE ELECTRICAL CABLES INSIDE THE WALLS AND CEILINGS. BY READING THE INSTALLATION INSTRUCTIONS THAT COME WITH EACH UNIT, YOU CAN MAKE SURE TO LOCATE THE WIRING AND RECEPTACLES (IF NECESSARY) IN THE BEST LOCATION. THIS IS ESPECIALLY TRUE FOR ELECTRIC RANGES THAT OFTEN COME WITH A PIGTAIL EXTENSION CORD ALREADY INSTALLED IN THE UNIT. CHECK THE LENGTH OF THIS CORD AND MAKE SURE THAT YOU LOCATE YOUR RANGE RECEPTACLE SO THAT THE CORD CAN REACH IT.

flush-mounted. For the average homeowner, a surface-mounted receptacle is often preferred because it is easier to wire. When a range is not hardwired but has a cord and plug, the plug must have four prongs to match the receptacle, as mentioned earlier, so that the neutral and grounding conductor will remain separate. If your kitchen has one of the older receptacles (shown below) and you plan on keeping your current range, no change is required. But new range models will have extension cord plugs that will only fit the new receptacles, so you'll have to plan on making the changeover.

● RANGE RECEPTACLES

Older range receptacles had only three slots, combining the current-carrying neutral with the appliance's frame grounding.

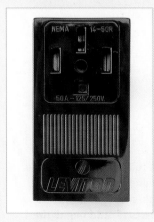

Modern range receptacles have four slots, for three insulated wires and a grounding conductor or wire, either bare or insulated.

INSTALLING A RANGE RECEPTACLE

First determine the location of the range receptacle so it can be reached by the built-in range pigtail. Then cut a hole in the wall for the circuit cable. Go into the basement and drill a cable access hole up through the floor. Attach a fish tape to the cable and pull it up through the hole in the wall. Then join the cable wires to the receptacle, and attach the receptacle to the wall. Join the other end of the cable to the appropriate breaker.

▮ Keyhole or saber saw ▮ Cable staples
▮ 50A or 60A 125/250v range receptacle
▮ Insulated screwdrivers ▮ Cable ripper
▮ Multipurpose tool ▮ Fish tape
▮ 6/3G SER copper cable ▮ Cable clamp
▮ 50A or 60A double-pole circuit breaker
▮ Knockout punch ▮ Long-nose pliers

1 Cut a hole in the drywall for the receptacle cable. Then go into the basement and drill a hole up through the floor. Feed the cable from the service panel into the wall hole. Use a fish tape to pull the cable.

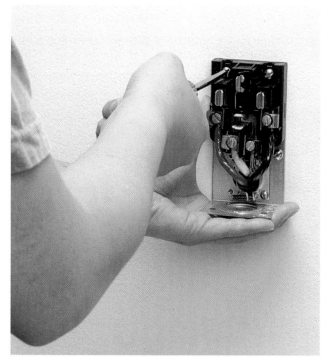

2 Strip the sheathing off the cable and the insulation off the individual wires. Then slide the wire ends under their corresponding clamps and tighten them in place. Attach the receptacle to the wall, and install the receptacle cover.

3 Shut off the power at the main-panel breaker switch. Then attach the black and red hot wires to the range breaker, and push the breaker into the bus bar. Install the white neutral wire and the bare ground wire to the neutral and grounding bus bars.

4 cabinets

Whether you typically prepare gourmet meals or prefer more simple fare, you'll want your new kitchen to allow you to do your best work. Nothing contributes more to this end than the cabinets you chose. And nothing makes cabinets work better than a good layout. Long trips from the refrigerator to the sink, or the sink to the stove, can turn something enjoyable, such as cooking, into something that feels much more like a chore.

Whether you work up your own layout, or pass this job onto a kitchen designer, don't lose sight of your primary goal: the kitchen has to work well for you. That means the cabinets should be well made and contain the extras that will make your time in the kitchen enjoyable.

CABINET STYLES AND OPTIONS

While it's true that cabinets help define the style and create the environment of a kitchen, their main job is to store the many items involved in preparing, serving, and cleaning up after meals. They must be durable enough to withstand thousands of openings and closings over years of use.

Regardless of the type and style of cabinets you choose, insist on quality construction. Good cabinets feature dove-tail and mortise-and-tenon joinery and solidly mortised hinges. The interiors are well finished, with adjustable

RIGHT and BELOW Choose from a variety of possible cabinet finishes. Choices range from natural looks, right, to glazed and painted finishes, below.

ABOVE Framed cabinets—those with a full frame across the cabinet box—are often used in traditional kitchens.

shelves that are a minimum of $\frac{5}{8}$ inch thick to prevent bowing under heavy loads. The drawers in good cabinets roll on ball-bearing glides, and they support at least 75 pounds when open.

Construction Styles and Options

There are basically two construction styles for kitchen cabinetry: framed and frameless. You can buy inexpensive ready-made cabinets directly from a retailer's stock in finished form, in unfinished form, or as knockdowns. These will usually be framed cabinets. If you prefer, choose more expensive semi-custom and custom-made cabinets. You can get custom cabinets from a large manufacturer, or have them built to your room's specifications by a carpenter or cabinetmaker.

Framed. Framed cabinets—or traditional-style cabinets—have a full frame across the face of the cabinet box. This provides a means of securing adjacent cabinets together and strengthens wider cabinet boxes with a center rail. Hinges may be either visible or hidden, and the front frame may or may not be visible around doors and drawers when they are closed.

Frameless. Frameless cabinets—also known as European-style cabinets—are built without a face frame. Close-fitting doors cover the entire front of the box, or they may be set into the box opening. Hinges are typically hidden. Both domestic and European manufacturers offer frameless cabinets. Prices can be high and delivery times lengthy if you want features that an import dealer does not have in stock.

Manufacturing Styles

Unless you have the time and skill to build the cabinets yourself or you can hire someone else to do it, you'll have to purchase them in one of three ways: stock, semi-custom, or custom. Prices vary from category to category, and even within each category.

Stock. Stock cabinets are literally in stock where they are sold or are quickly available by order. They are made in limited styles and colors, but in a wide variety of standard sizes that you can assemble to suit your kitchen space. The quality of stock cabinets may be fair, good, or excellent, depending on the manufacturer and price. Materials may be solid wood (hard or soft) and plywood, wood and particleboard, wood and hardboard, or all particleboard. They may be carefully jointed and doweled or merely nailed and glued together. Stock cabinets also come in steel and in several types of plastic, either in part or entirely. The quality of cabinets made from these materials also varies from barely adequate to exquisite. Stock cabinets range in price from inexpensive to moderately costly.

You can save some money by buying unfinished stock cabinets and staining or painting them yourself. You can save even more by purchasing knockdown cabinets, which are shipped flat to lower the costs of packing and delivery. Knockdowns are sometimes unfinished as well.

Semi-Custom. Like stock cabinets, semi-custom cabinets are available only in specific sizes, but there are many more finishes, colors, styles, options, and special features to chose from than you will find with stock cabinets. The extras aren't added to the cabinets until you place the order, so there will be a wait for delivery. Times vary, but expect to wait three to six weeks for delivery.

ABOVE Semi-custom cabinets are available with a variety of options, including refrigerator panels that match the cabinets.

Custom. Custom cabinets are built to the measurements of a particular project. Because custom cabinets are made from scratch, delivery may take from 4 to 16 weeks. The delivery delay rarely causes a problem because the preparation work for a new kitchen also takes time. But place your order well in advance of the date you will need your cabinets. Custom cabinets are almost always delivered completely finished, like fine furniture, whereas some stock cabinets may be bought unfinished. Prices for custom cabinets run from moderate to very expensive.

Carpenter-Built. If you have the time, some carpentry skills, and a work area, you can save money by constructing cabinets to your own specifications. Keep in mind that this work can be very time-consuming. Or, you can hire a carpenter to build them. This won't be a money saver, of course, but will give you great leeway in your design.

ABOVE AND LEFT
Custom touches improve any design. The carved corbel, above, is an option offered by a cabinet manufacturer. The spice drawers and open shelves, left, are a popular design element.

STORAGE OPTIONS

The type of storage in a kitchen is almost as important as the amount. Some people like at least a few open shelves for displaying attractive china or glassware; others want absolutely everything tucked away behind doors.

What are your storage needs? The answer depends partly on your food shopping habits and partly on how many pots, pans, and other pieces of kitchen equipment you have or would like to have. A family that goes food shopping several times a week and prepares mostly fresh foods needs more refrigerator space, less freezer capacity, and fewer cabinets than a family that prefers packaged or prepared foods and makes only infrequent forays to the local supermarket.

Planning

To help clarify your needs, mentally walk yourself through a typical meal and list the utensils used to prepare food, where you got them, and your progress throughout the work area. And don't limit yourself to full-scale meals. Much kitchen work is devoted to preparing snacks, reheating leftovers, and making lunches for the kids to take to school.

Food Preparation. During food preparation, the sink and stove come into use. Some families rely heavily on the microwave for reheating. Using water means repeated trips to the sink, so that area might be the best place to keep a steamer, salad spinner, and coffee and tea canisters, as well as glassware and cups. Near the stove you may want storage for odd-shaped items such as a fish poacher or wok. You can hang frequently used pans and utensils from a convenient rack; stow other items in cabinets so that they do not collect grease.

During the Meal. When the food is ready, you must take it to the table. If the eating space is nearby, a work

ABOVE Order cabinets that suit your storage needs. Mentally walk through a typical day in the kitchen to find what works best.

counter might turn into a serving counter. If the dining space is in another room, a pass-through facilitates serving.

After the Meal. When the meal ends, dishes must go from the table to the sink or dishwasher, and leftovers to storage containers and the refrigerator. Now the stove and counters need to be wiped down and the sink scoured. When the dishwasher finishes its cycle, everything must be put away.

storage checklist

■ *Do you like kitchen gadgets?* Plan drawer space, countertop sorters, wall magnets, or hooks to keep these items handy near where you often use them.

■ *Do you own a food processor, blender, mixer, toaster oven, electric can opener, knife sharpener, juicer, coffee maker, or coffee mill?* If you're particularly tidy, you may want small appliances like these tucked away in an appliance garage or cupboard to be taken out only when needed. If you prefer to have frequently used machines sitting on the counter, ready to go, plan enough space, along with conveniently located electrical outlets.

■ *Do you plan to store large quantities of food?* Be sure to allow plenty of freezer, bin, and shelf space for the kind of food shopping you do.

■ *Do you intend to do a lot of freezing or canning?* Allow a work space and place to stow equipment. Also plan adequate freezer storage.

■ *Do you bake often?* Consider a baking center that can house your equipment and serve as a separate baking pantry.

■ *Do you collect pottery, tinware, or anything else that might be displayed in the kitchen?* Eliminating soffits provides a shelf on top of the wall cabinets for collectibles.

■ *Do you collect cookbooks?* If so, you'll need expandable shelf space and perhaps a bookstand.

Personal Profile of You and Your Family

■ *How tall are you and everyone else who will use your kitchen?* Adjust your counter and wall-cabinet heights to suit.

■ *Do you or any of your family members use a walker, leg braces, or a wheelchair?* Plan a good work height, knee space, grab bars, secure seating, slide-out work boards, and other convenience features.

■ *Are you left- or right-handed?* Think about your natural motion when you choose whether to open cupboards or refrigerator doors from the left or right.

■ *How high can you comfortably reach?* If you're tall, hang your wall cabinets high. If you're petite, you may want to hang the cabinets lower and plan a spot to keep a step stool handy.

■ *Can you comfortably bend and reach for something in a base cabinet?* Can you lift heavy objects easily and without strain or pain? If your range is limited in these areas, be sure to plan roll-out shelving on both upper and lower tiers of your base cabinets. Also, look into spring-up shelves designed to lift mixer bases or other heavy appliances to counter height.

■ *Do you frequently share cooking tasks with another family member?* If so, you may each prefer to have your own work area.

Types of Storage

Storage facilities can make or break a kitchen, so choose the places you'll put things with care. Here's a look at a few alternatives:

Open versus Closed Storage. Shelves, pegboards, pot racks, cup hooks, magnetic knife racks, and the like put your utensils on view, which is a good way to personalize your kitchen. Here's an area where you can save some money, too. Open storage generally costs less than cabinets, and you don't have to construct and hang doors.

But open storage has drawbacks. For one thing, items left out in the open can look messy unless they are kept neatly arranged. Also, objects collect dust and grease, especially near the range. This means that unless you reach for an item almost daily, you'll find yourself washing it before, as well as after you use it.

ABOVE AND BELOW Closed storage like under-counter pantries, above, keep items close to their point of use. Glass-fronted cabinets, below, put items on display.

LEFT AND RIGHT Speciality storage is key to a well-designed kitchen. A full-height pantry, left, can hold supplies for the long term. A revolving shelf, right, placed near the cooking center is a good place to store spices.

If extra washing and dusting discourages you from the idea of open storage but you'd like to put at least some objects on view, limit your displays to a few items. Another option is to install glass doors on wall cabinets. This handily solves the dust problem but often costs more than solid doors.

Pantries. How often you shop and how many groceries you typically bring home determine the amount of food storage space your family needs. If you like to stock up or take advantage of sales, add a pantry to your kitchen. To maximize a pantry's convenience, plan shallow, 6-inch-deep shelves so that cans and packages will never be stored more than two deep. This way, you'll easily be able to see what you've got on hand. Pantries range in size from floor-to-ceiling models to narrow units designed to fit between two standard-size cabinets.

Appliance Garages. Appliance garages make use of dead space in a corner, but they can be installed anywhere in the vertical space between wall-mounted cabinets and the countertop. A tambour (rolltop) door hides small appliances like a food processor or anything else you want within reach but hidden from view. This form of mini-cabinet can be equipped with an electrical outlet and even can be divided into separate sections to store more than one item. Customize an appliance garage any way you like. Reserve part of the appliance garage for cookbook storage, for example, or outfit it with small drawers for little items or spices.

LEFT Appliance garages keep countertop appliances in easy reach but out of sight when not in use.

Lazy Susans and Carousel Shelves. Rotating shelves, such as lazy Susans and carousels, maximize dead corner storage and put items such as dishes or pots and pans within easy reach. A lazy Susan rotates 360 degrees, so just spin it to find what you're looking for. Carousel shelves, which attach to two right-angled doors, rotate 270 degrees; open the doors, and the shelves swing out allowing you to reach items easily. Pivoting shelves are a variation on the carousel design and may or may not be door-mounted. In addition, units may be built into taller cabinets, creating a pantry that can store a lot in a small amount of space.

Fold-Down Mixer Shelf. A spring-loaded mixer shelf swings up and out of a base cabinet for use, then folds down and back into the cabinet when the mixer is no longer needed.

Slide-Outs and Tilt-Outs. Installed in base cabinets, slide-out trays and racks store small appliances, linens, cans, or boxed items, while slide-out bins are good for holding onions, potatoes, grains, pet food, or potting soil—even garbage or recycling containers. A tilt-out tray is located in the often-wasted area just below the lip of the countertop in front of the sink and above base cabinet doors. Use it to hold sponges and cloths.

Pivoting Shelves. Door-mounted shelves and in-cabinet swiveling-shelf units offer easy access to kitchen supplies. Taller units serve as pantries that hold a great deal in minimal space.

Pullout Tables and Trays. In tight kitchens, pullout tables and trays are excellent ways to gain eating space or an extra work surface. Pullout cutting boards come in handy near cooktops and microwaves. Pullout tea carts are also available.

Drawer Inserts. A drawer insert is a good way to keep packaged spices organized and easily accessible. Inserts are made for flatware and other items, too.

Tray Storage. A narrow base cabinet with horizontal slots is perfect for storing cookie sheets and trays on edge. Locate this in a baking center.

Customized Organizers. If you decide to make do with your existing cabinets, consider refitting their interiors with cabinet organizers. These plastic, plastic-coated wire, or enameled-steel racks and hangers are widely available at department stores, hardware stores, and home centers. And they cover just about every type of specialized storage you can imagine.

ABOVE Pivoting shelves save you from stooping to retrieve items from the back of base cabinets.

RIGHT Pullout trays provide extra work surfaces near cooking and baking centers.

RIGHT Turn wasted space to valuable storage with pullout tray holders.

Some of these units slide in and out of base cabinets, similar to the racks in a dishwasher. Others let you mount shallow drawers to the undersides of wall cabinets. Still others consist of stackable plastic bins with plenty of room to hold kitchen sundries.

Beware of the temptation to overspecialize your kitchen storage facilities. Sizes and needs for certain items change, so be sure to allot at least 50 percent of your kitchen's storage to standard cabinets with one or more movable shelves.

Recycling Storage. Slide-out shelves can hold two or three large containers for sorting recyclable materials. Some products also include bins for holding newspapers.

Herb and Spice Racks. Be aware that herbs and spices lose their flavor more rapidly when exposed to heat or sunlight, so don't locate a spice rack or shelving intended for storing herbs too close to the cooktop or a sunny window. Choose opaque containers, or keep seasonings in a cool, closed cupboard or in a drawer outfitted with a rack so you can quickly reach what you need.

Wine Storage. Some contemporary kitchens show off bottles of wine in open racks and bins that hold as much as a couple of cases. If you regularly serve wine with

ABOVE Glass-fronted drawers put pasta, beans, or rice on display, making them part of the kitchen's design.

meals, by all means keep a few bottles on hand—but bear in mind that the kitchen is far from the ideal place to store wine for any length of time.

The problem is that heat and sunlight are two of wine's worst enemies, which is why fine wines are stored in cellars. The temperature in a wine cellar should be about 55 to 60 degrees F, so if you'd like to age new vintages for a year or two, keep them in a cool, dark location, such as the basement or an attached climate-controlled garage, where the bottles won't be disturbed.

Cabinet Hardware

Door and drawer pulls and knobs not only serve a functional purpose, they also contribute to the overall look of your kitchen. When selecting hardware, make sure you can grip it easily and comfortably. If your fingers or hands get stiff easily or if you have arthritis, select C- or U-shaped pulls because they are easier to grab and hold on to. If you like a knob, try it out in the showroom to make sure it isn't slippery or awkward when you grab it. Knobs and pulls can be inexpensive if you stick to unfinished ones that you can paint in an accent color picked up from the tile or wallpaper. If you don't plan to buy new cabinets, changing the hardware on old ones can redefine their style. The right knob or pull can suggest any one of a number of vintage looks or decorative styles.

ABOVE Create a recycling center with units that hold tall containers for bottle and can storage.

ABOVE AND LEFT Open storage puts items on display. The cabinet above stores dishes and bowls near the prep and cleanup areas. Shelving under the cooktop, left, holds pots and pans.

BELOW AND BOTTOM Dealing with necessities is central to a storage plan. Pullout pantries, below, allow you to stock up on packaged goods. Recycling cabinets help organize a room, bottom.

TOP AND ABOVE Unusual configurations can help meet storage needs. The cabinet, top, combines drawers with shelves. The baskets, above, hold cooking ingredients.

113

project

INSTALLING WALL CABINETS

The best time to install wall cabinets is before the base cabinets are in place. Without the base cabinets taking up room, you can work close to the wall.

Your first step is to draw a level line across all of the walls that need cabinets. Then, install a ledger board beneath this line by driving screws into the wall studs. With a helper, lift the first cabinet into place and rest it on the ledger. Level and plumb the cabinet; then screw it to the wall.

Lift the second cabinet onto the ledger, and clamp it to the first cabinet. Screw the cabinets together through the stiles, and attach the second cabinet to the wall using screws driven through the back. Continue until all the wall cabinets are in place. Remove the ledger, and install the door hardware.

TOOLS & MATERIALS

- Stud finder
- Cabinets and hardware
- 48-inch level
- Measuring tape
- Pencil
- Wood shims
- Utility knife
- 3- and 3½-inch wood screws
- Handsaw
- Power drill-driver with assorted bits
- C-clamps or adjustable bar clamps
- Screwdrivers (flat-bladed and Phillips)
- Lumber for ledger

smart tip

HARDWARE HOLE JIG

IF YOU HAVE A LOT OF IDENTICAL HARDWARE HOLES TO DRILL IN CABINET DOORS, MAKE A SIMPLE CARDBOARD TEMPLATE WITH A HOLE DRILLED AT THE PROPER PLACE. THEN HOLD THE TEMPLATE AGAINST EACH DOOR, AND BORE THE HOLE THROUGH THE DOOR.

1 Establish the proper height of the bottom of your wall cabinets, and draw a level line on the wall. Then, screw a ledger board beneath this line. Make sure the board is level and that the screws reach into the wall studs.

4 Attach the cabinets to the wall using 3-in. screws driven through the cabinet back and into the wall studs behind. Two screws at the bottom and top of each cabinet back are all that is required.

2 Start hanging the wall cabinets with a corner unit. Get some help to lift it onto the ledger board and to push it tight against the wall. One person will have to hold the cabinet until it's screwed to the wall.

3 Position the cabinet so that it is level and plumb. If necessary, use shims between the cabinet and the wall. If the first cabinet is installed plumb, the other cabinets in the row will also be plumb.

5 Lift the next cabinet onto the ledger board, and have one person hold it in place. Clamp the cabinets together at the top and bottom, and fasten them together using screws driven through the cabinet stiles.

6 Once the cabinets are screwed together, attach the second cabinet to the wall by driving screws through the back into the wall studs. Finish up by installing the door hardware (inset).

INSTALLING BASE CABINETS

project

Base cabinets are difficult to install because both the floor and the wall surface can be out of level or plumb. To correct any problems, make liberal use of cedar shimming shingles.

Start by installing the corner cabinet. Add the next cabinet in line, and shim it in place using wood shims. Be sure to check for level as you work. Screw the cabinet to the wall, and continue installing the rest of the cabinets along the wall. Finish up by installing the toe-kick boards next to the floor.

TOOLS & MATERIALS

- Stud finder (or nail)
- Cabinets and hardware
- 48-inch level
- Measuring tape
- Pencil
- Wood shims
- Utility knife
- 2½-, 3-, and 3½-inch wood screws
- Handsaw
- Power drill-driver with assorted bits
- C-clamps
- Screwdrivers
- Vinyl or wood kickplates
- 1x3 ledger board
- Quarter-round molding

smart tip

DRILLING HOLES FOR PLUMBING LINES

DRILL HOLES FOR PLUMBING AND WASTE LINES BEFORE INSTALLING THE CABINETS. IT IS EASIER TO WORK WHEN THE CABINETS ARE OUT IN THE MIDDLE OF THE FLOOR. JUST TAKE CAREFUL MEASUREMENTS OF WHERE THE SUPPLY AND DRAIN LINES ARE, AND TRANSFER THESE TO THE CABINET BACK.

1 Measure the height of base cabinets, and transfer this dimension to the walls. Mark a level line on the wall where the cabinets fall. Then screw ledger strips behind any corner cabinets to support the back of the countertop.

4 The next step is to screw the back of the cabinet to the wall. Just locate the wall studs, and drive screws through the back cleat and into the studs. Make sure to check level between cabinets.

2 After installing the corner cabinets, start adding the adjacent units. Make sure these are aligned square to the wall and are level and plumb. To raise the cabinet, slide wood shims underneath the sides.

3 Also use shims between cabinets to maintain proper alignment. First, clamp the cabinet stiles together. Then install the shims, and when the fit is right, drive screws to join the stiles. Remove the clamps.

5 Once all the cabinets are installed, attach the toe-kick boards at the bottom of the cabinets. These boards will hide any gaps between the bottom of the cabinets and the floor.

TOE-KICK HEATERS

Toe-kick heaters have a short profile designed to slide into the normally empty space under kitchen cabinets. They are a good solution for providing auxiliary heat when needed or to provide spot heat on particularly cold days. To install one, you will need to bring power from an existing junction box to a new switch and pull cable from the switch to the heater—similar to the method used for installing under-cabinet lighting. Cut out the opening in the toe-kick space; then pull the cable into the room. Make the necessary electrical connections, and slide the heater into position.

INSTALLING AN ISLAND

Building a kitchen island may look complicated, but most are nothing more than a couple of base cabinets crowned with a countertop. To install one, start by drawing the outline of the island on the floor; then draw another line on the inside that represents the inside edge of the cabinet cases. Screw cleats along the inside line; lower the cabinet over the cleats; and screw the cabinets to the cleats. Cover any unfinished sides with plywood veneer set in contact cement and nailed with finishing nails. Attach the countertop base using wood screws driven from below the cabinet corner blocks, and add your finish material—plastic laminate, tile, solid surfacing—to the top. Apply trim to the corners to cover the joints; then finish up by painting or staining and finishing the veneer.

TOOLS & MATERIALS
- Base cabinets or island cabinets
- Straightedge ▐ Pencil or marker
- 2x4 cleats ▐ Power drill-driver
- Wood/utility screws
- Plywood veneer
- Hammer ▐ Contact cement
- Finishing nails
- Wood molding
- Corner molding
- Countertop materials

MOST BUILDING CODES REQUIRE THAT ISLANDS BE EQUIPPED WITH ELECTRICAL OUTLETS. HERE'S THE REASON: IF YOU HAVE AN OUTLET ON THE ISLAND, YOU WILL NOT BE TEMPTED TO PLACE A COUNTERTOP APPLIANCE ON THE ISLAND AND THEN DRAPE THE CORD ACROSS THE AISLE TO A WALL OUTLET, CREATING A POTENTIAL HAZARD.

1 Locate the position of the island on the kitchen floor. Then, using a straightedge guide, draw an outline of the island on the floor. Draw another line, inside the first, that indicates the inside surface of the cabinet.

5 Cut the countertop base to size, and place it on the cabinets. Drive a screw up through the corner mounting blocks and into the top. Make sure that the screw doesn't break through the top of the counter.

2 Measure and cut 2x4 cleats to fit along the inside line that's drawn on the floor. Screw these down securely with 3-in. screws.

3 Lower the island cabinets over the floor cleats, and screw the bottom cabinet sides to the cleats to secure the island to the floor.

4 Cover the back of the cabinets and any unfinished sides of the island with plywood veneer. Cut to size, and install it using contact cement and finishing nails.

6 Install cement board over the countertop base if you plan to install tile. For solid-surfacing countertops, spread a bead of caulk around the perimeter of the base and lower the top in place.

7 You have many trim options for hiding the corner joints between the sides. One good one is to install wood corner molding using 4d finishing nails.

REVIVING OLD CABINETS

Sometimes it is not necessary or practical to replace existing cabinetry. Cabinets that are in reasonably good condition can be painted or refaced.

Painting Cabinets

A fresh coat of paint is often a good short-term solution. Begin by removing all the cabinet hardware and setting the doors and drawers aside. Fill any dents or gouges with wood filler, and when it's dry, sand it flush with the surrounding surfaces. Clean the cabinets with a strong detergent and water, and wipe them dry with an old towel. Repair and clean the doors and drawer fronts in the same way. Then sand all the exposed surfaces with 150-grit

sandpaper, and wipe off all the dust with a damp rag or a tack cloth.

You'll get the smoothest finish if you spray paint all the components. But this is usually difficult for most homeowners to do because it's hard to control the overspray. You can spray the doors and drawers in the garage or basement, but the cabinets are generally brushed. Just use the best quality brush and paint you can find. Apply one coat of primer and two top coats on all the parts, sanding between coats with 220-grit sandpaper. Be sure to remove all the sanding dust before applying the next coat of paint.

Refacing Cabinets (See page 124.)

Refacing cabinets is a big step up from painting them. This job involves replacing the doors and drawer fronts and covering the cabinet frames and sides with wood veneer or plastic laminate that matches the doors and drawer fronts. Refacing is a good option if your existing kitchen is well designed and the cabinets are structurally sound. It costs less than half of what new cabinets cost and when combined with buying all new appliances can dramatically change the look of your kitchen. You can do the work yourself as shown on page 124, or you can hire a contractor that specializes in refacing to handle the job.

Before

ABOVE AND RIGHT
Refacing cabinets consists of removing old doors and drawer fronts and replacing them with new ones, and covering the cabinet frames with a matching material.

Refacing is a good solution for updating a kitchen that has an efficient layout.

After

REPAIRING DOORS AND DRAWERS

Cabinets are not the only components in a kitchen that create a big impression. The flooring, wall coverings, paint, appliances, and furniture all make a big statement. If you upgrade some or all of these things, you can often get by with simply cleaning and making minor repairs to cabinet doors and drawers. Fixing warped doors, replacing old drawer slides, and refinishing or replacing drawer fronts, can give old cabinets a new life.

TOOLS & MATERIALS
- Powdered chalk
- Block plane
- Screwdrivers
- Wood/utility screws
- Metal drawer guides

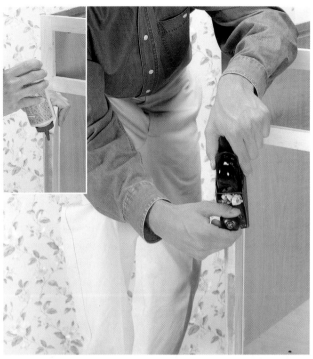

1 Sticking doors can often be fixed by tightening all the hinge screws. But when a door warps, it may need to be planed. Spread chalk on the door edge, then close it. Places where the chalk rubs off need stock removed with a block plane.

2 Replace worn-out drawer slides with new ones. You may have to add a new rail to the inside of the cabinet to support this hardware. Once it's in place, attach one side of the slide to the cabinet and the other to the drawer side.

3 You can either refinish or replace drawer fronts. In both cases, remove the old ones by backing out the screws from the inside of the drawer. Attach the new ones using the same screws.

121

INSTALLING ROLLOUT SHELVES

project

Cabinet manufacturers offer dozens of storage options to make their products more efficient and useful. Many of these kits can be purchased separately for updating older cabinets. Installation directions vary, but in general, you first assemble the storage unit; then install support rollers in the bottom of the cabinet; and slide the kit onto the rollers.

TOOLS & MATERIALS
- Shelving kit ▪ Tape measure
- Screwdrivers ▪ Masking tape
- Power drill-driver with screwdriver attachment
- Wood screws (if not provided)
- Metal screws (if not provided)

1 There are many different storage systems available for updating cabinets. Each is installed somewhat differently, so follow the instructions that come with your product. Generally, you start by attaching the basket or shelf to the upright brackets.

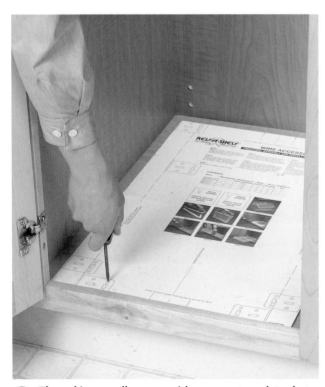

2 These kits usually come with a paper template that clearly shows where to drill for the mounting hardware. Tape the template to the bottom of the cabinet, and mark the screw holes with an awl.

3 Install the roller guides on the cabinet bottom using the screws that came with the kit. Install half the screws, and test the performance. If satisfied, drive the rest of the screws.

INSTALLING PULLOUT PLATFORMS

Pullout platforms are a great way to store countertop appliances out of the way. Most simply move in and out, but more-elaborate models can swivel from side to side and are often used for small TVs. Before buying one of these platforms, make sure it's rated to carry the weight you want it to support. Installation isn't difficult; just lay out the cabinet so the platform is in the middle; attach the platform with screws; and screw the shelf to the platform from underneath.

TOOLS & MATERIALS
- Shelf kit ▮ Clamps
- Wood screws (if not provided)
- Power drill-driver with screwdriver attachment
- Screwdriver ▮ Tape measure

1 A pullout platform is a hardware fixture that slides in and out of a cabinet and supports a wide shelf for holding countertop appliances. Begin installation by marking the middle of the cabinet. The middle of the platform should line up with this cabinet mark.

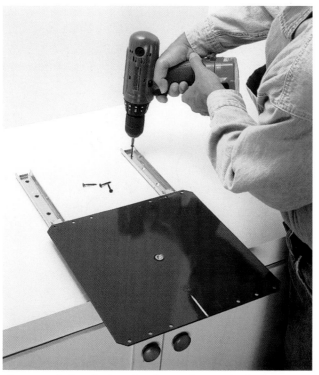

2 Install the platform hardware first in the bottom of the cabinet. To do this, extend the platform to expose the slides; then drive the screws, making sure the slides are square to the front of the cabinet.

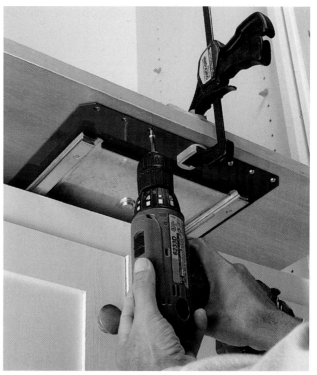

3 Cut the shelf to a size that fits inside the cabinet, and lay it on the platform. Hold it in place with a clamp, and attach it to the platform by driving screws up from below the platform.

REFACING CABINETS

project

Refacing cabinets is usually a job done by contractors. But experienced do-it-yourselfers can tackle it. First prepare the cabinets as shown in this sequence; then install veneer on the side of a cabinet. Cover the stiles, the vertical sections, and rails, the horizontal, with flexible veneer that has pressure-sensitive adhesive on the back. Finish up by installing the doors and drawers.

TOOLS & MATERIALS
▌ Screwdriver ▌ Scraper and sandpaper
▌ Paint and brushes (if necessary)
▌ Wood putty ▌ Putty knife ▌ Utility knife
▌ Veneer ▌ Contact cement ▌ Laminate roller
▌ Power drill-driver and assorted bits
▌ Spring and/or C-clamps ▌ Router
▌ Hinges ▌ Handsaw

1 Begin by cleaning the cabinets with detergent and water; sand all surfaces with 150-grit sandpaper; and remove the dust. Mask off adjacent surfaces to the ends of the cabinets, and spray contact cement on the surface of the cabinet.

4 Make sure the veneer is positioned plumb on the stile; then press it down and roll it with a laminate roller. Using a utility knife, cut the veneer so that it can be wrapped around the edges.

5 Fold the veneer around the stile so that the edges are completely covered, and roll the veneer smooth with a laminate roller. Trim off any excess veneer using a utility knife and metal straightedge.

2 Cut a piece of veneer slightly larger than the cabinet side, and carefully press it into the contact cement so there's just a slight overhang on all sides. Smooth the panel in place using a laminate roller. Trim the panel flush with a router.

3 Use flexible veneer with adhesive on the back for covering the stiles. Cut the piece to a width that covers the stile front and two side edges. Expose some of the adhesive at the top of the veneer; press it onto the stile; then pull off the rest of the protective paper.

6 Install flexible veneer on the rail the same way as it was done on the stiles. First cut it to length; then press it against the rail. Wrap the top edge, and roll the whole thing smooth. Trim the bottom edge using a utility knife.

7 Once all the veneer is installed, fill any voids between veneer pieces with wood putty that matches the color of the veneer. Apply a finish to everything; then install the doors and drawer fronts to complete the job.

5 countertops, sinks, and faucets

The hardest part about installing most new countertops is choosing the countertop material because so many options are available, from inexpensive plastic laminate to solid stone treatments that can dwarf the cost of new appliances. No matter what material you choose, keep one simple rule in mind: include as much uncluttered open space as possible in your kitchen design. If you can't add more countertop space, then improve the storage above the counter so you can put away most of your small appliances. You will also need to decide on the type of sink and faucet you want. It makes sense to pick a sink and faucet style at the same time you choose a countertop.

COUNTERTOP MATERIALS

The surfaces of your kitchen help define how it looks and determine how well it cleans up and withstands wear and tear. Choose countertops, wallcoverings, and flooring to suit your style and lifestyle. Make sure all of these materials are easy to clean, especially the countertops. You'll spend more time cleaning these areas than you'll ever spend washing the walls or mopping the floor. The market offers lots of countertop materials, all of which are worth consideration for your kitchen. Pick the materials and designs that best suit your needs and the look of the room. You can also enhance a basic design by combining it with an eye-catching edge treatment. Another option is to combine different materials on the same surface.

Plastic Laminate. This thin, durable surface comes in hundreds of colors, textures, and patterns. The material is relatively easy to install; its smooth surface washes easily; and it is heat-resistant, although very hot pots can discolor or even burn it. Laminate stands up well to everyday wear and tear, but it can be easily scorched by hot pots and pans or scratched with knives and other

sharp utensils, and surface damage is difficult to repair.

Laminate countertops are available in three ways. You can buy sheets of laminate and adhere them to a plywood base yourself. Home centers and kitchen supply dealers sell post-formed counters. These are the types that come in 8- or 10-foot lengths that you trim yourself. Both the laminate sheets and the post-form counters are available in a limited number of colors and patterns. Another option is to order a laminate counter from a counter fabricator—some home centers and kitchen dealers offer this service as well. The counter will be built to your measurements, and you will get a wide variety of colors and patterns to choose from. Most fabricators also offer a variety of edge treatments.

Ceramic Tile. Glazed tile can be magnificently decorative for counters, backsplashes, and walls, or as a display inset in another material. Tile is smooth and easy to wipe off, and it can't be burned by hot pots. In addition to the standard square tiles, ceramic tiles are available in a number of specialty shapes and sizes, allowing you to create a truly custom look. Ceramic tile costs more than laminate, but you can save money by doing the installation yourself.

When shopping, you should also consider the finish. There are two kinds: unglazed and glazed. Unglazed tiles are not sealed and always come in a matte look. They are not practical for use near water unless you apply a sealant. On the other hand, glazed tiles are coated with a material that makes them impervious to water—or spills and stains from other liquids, too. This glaze on the tile can be matte or highly polished, depending on your taste.

The upkeep of tile is fairly easy, but you must regrout and reseal periodically. White grout shows dirt easily, but a dark-color mix can camouflage stains. Still, unless it is sealed, grout will harbor bacteria. So clean the countertop regularly with a nonabrasive antibacterial cleanser. Tile that is well-maintained will last a lifetime, but beware: your glassware and china may not. If you drop them on this hard surface, they'll break.

Solid-Surfacing Material. Made of acrylics and composite materials, solid surfacing comes in $1/2$ inch and $3/4$ inch thicknesses. This is a premium material that resists moisture, heat, stains, and cracks.

There is almost no limit to the colors and patterns of

OPPOSITE Granite, marble, and other natural stones make truly elegant and functional countertops.

ABOVE AND BELOW Laminate counter materials, above, are available in hundreds of colors and designs. Customize the job with a colorful backsplash. Ceramic-tile countertops, below, should be sealed.

solid surfacing. It can be fabricated to resemble marble and granite, or it can be a block of solid color. Either way, the material can be carved or beveled for decorative effects just like wood. Manufacturers recommend professional installation.

The surface becomes scratched fairly easily, but the scratches are not readily apparent. Because the material is a solid color, serious blemishes can be removed by sanding or buffing.

Natural Stone. Marble, slate, and granite can be formed into beautiful but expensive counters. Of the three, granite is probably the most popular because it cannot be hurt by moisture or heat, nor does it stain if finished properly. Installers polish granite to produce a high-gloss finish.

Marble scratches, cracks, and stains easily, even if waxed. Slate can be easily scratched and cracked and cannot take a high polish.

These are heavy materials that should be installed by a professional. However, you can get the look of granite and marble by installing granite or marble tiles. Cut from the natural stones, these products are available in 12 x 12-inch tiles and are installed and cut in much the same way as ceramic tiles.

Wood. Butcher block consists of hardwood laminated under pressure and sealed with oil or a polymer finish. Because it's thicker than other materials, butcher block will raise the counter level about ¾ inch above standard

ABOVE AND BELOW Wood may be unusual for counters, above, but when done properly it makes a striking addition to the kitchen. Granite tiles, below, are a good way to get the look of natural stone at a fraction of the cost.

ABOVE Different countertop materials like solid surfacing and granite can work well together.

MAKE USE OF COUNTER INSERTS TO HELP WITH THE COOKING CHORES. FOR EXAMPLE, CERAMIC TILES INLAID IN A LAMINATE COUNTER CREATE A HEAT-PROOF LANDING ZONE NEAR THE RANGE. A MARBLE OR GRANITE INSERT IS TAILOR-MADE FOR PASTRY CHEFS. AND A BUTCHER-BLOCK INLAY IS A GREAT ADDITION TO THE FOOD PREP AREA.

height. Also, wood is subject to damage by standing water or hot pans. Butcher-block tops are moderately expensive, but can be installed by amateurs.

Other kinds of wood counters may be used, especially in serving areas. Any wood used near water must be resistant to moisture or well sealed to prevent water from penetrating below the surface.

Concrete. There aren't a great number of concrete counters, but the material is catching on with some in the kitchen design community. If your goal is to install a cutting-edge material in your kitchen, concrete is it. Thanks to new staining techniques, concrete can be saturated with color all the way through, and it can be preformed to any shape and finished to any texture. That gives kitchen designers a lot of latitude when developing custom looks. Set stone or ceramic tile chips into the surface for a decorative effect. Form it to drain off water at the sink. Be cautious, however, as a concrete countertop must be sealed, and it may crack. Installation is best left to a professional counter fabricator.

Stainless Steel. Stainless steel used for a countertop, whether it is for the entire counter or just a section of it, can look quite sophisticated, especially with a wood trim. What's practical about it is its capacity to take high heat without scorching, which makes it suitable as a landing strip for pots and pans straight from the cooktop. It is also impervious to water, so it's practical at the sink. On the negative side, stainless steel can be noisy to work on, it will show smudges, and even fingerprints can be seen easily, which never happens with other countertop materials. Depending on the grade of the material, it may also be vulnerable to scrapes, stains, and corrosion. The higher the chromium and nickel content (and therefore the grade), the better. Also, look for a thick-gauge stainless steel that won't dent easily.

ABOVE AND BELOW Stainless-steel counters, above, provide a sleek, contemporary look to any kitchen. Concrete counters, below, are usually fabricated on site. They work well with other materials, as shown here.

SINKS AND FAUCETS

The kitchen sink is the focal point in the cleanup center. This includes the sink, 18 to 24 inches of counter space on either side for dishes and food that you need to wash, a dishwasher, a waste-disposal unit (where local codes permit), and storage for glassware, frequently used utensils, detergents, colanders, and other sink accessories. The trash receptacle and recycling bins are also in the cleanup center; a trash compactor may be included here as well.

Because it's often located under a window and always tied to the plumbing system, the sink is one of the most fixed of kitchen fixtures. If you're thinking about moving your sink and dishwasher more than 60 inches from the current location, you'll probably have to rework vent and drain lines, and you might have to move a window as

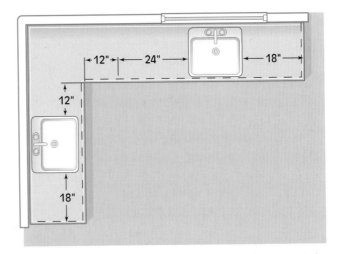

ABOVE Plan adequate counter space near the main sink. For smaller second sinks, plan on 3- to 18-in. landing spaces. As with all kitchen fixtures, be sure there is enough counter space on both sides of the sink. Experts recommend 18 and 24 in. of counter space.

well. If cost containment is important to you, it's wise to begin your kitchen plan by trying to locate the sink at or near the place the old one occupies.

Where there's no window behind the sink, decide what you'll do with the wall space there. One choice is to integrate the space into a run of cabinets with units that are shorter than those on either side so that you'll have headroom. Another possibility is to install full-height cabinets only 6 inches deep. Whatever treatment you select, be sure your cleanup center includes adequate daytime and nighttime light falling directly onto the sink and adjacent counters.

Sinks

Sinks come in a great variety of sizes and shapes. Materials include stainless steel, pressed steel, cast iron, and the same solid-surfacing material used for countertops. Sinks of each material come in single-, double-, and triple-bowl models.

A single-bowl sink is large enough for soaking big pots and pans. Two-bowl sinks may have identical-size basins, or one may be smaller or shallower than the other. Three-bowl sinks include a small disposal basin at one side or between the larger bowls. These sinks usually require about 12 inches more counter space than a double-bowl unit.

LEFT Cleanup centers revolve around the main sink. To save money, locate the new sink where the old one stood.

TYPES OF SINKS

Stainless-Steel Sinks. Stainless steel, made with nickel and chrome to prevent staining, continues to be a popular choice for sinks, although some homeowners complain about spotting. This kind of sink offers the greatest selection of bowl sizes and configurations. Choose 18-gauge stainless for a large sink or one with a disposer, lighter 20-gauge material for smaller sinks. Stainless steel also differs in grade, depending on the amount of nickel and chrome it contains. High levels of both are included in good-quality sinks.

Pressed-Steel and Cast-Iron Sinks. Both of these sinks have porcelain-enamel finishes. Cast iron is heavier and less likely to chip than pressed steel. Cast iron is also quieter than both stainless and pressed steel when water is running. These sinks are available in a wide range of colors.

Solid-Surface Sinks. Solid-surface, or acrylic sinks, can be molded directly into a solid-surface countertop, creating a seamless unit that is especially easy to keep clean. Separate drop-in models are also available. Sinks of this material are even quieter than cast iron, but costly.

Besides the common kitchen varieties, there are sinks for virtually every practical and aesthetic need—perfect circles, sinks that turn corners, deep farm-style kitchen sinks, and so on.

Under-mount sinks are attached to the underside of the counter. They work with stone or solid-surface counters.

Two- and three-bowl configurations are gaining popularity. This arrangement allows you to separate clean dishes from dirty ones as well as from waste materials. Some sinks come with a colander and cutting board that fits over one of the bowls. Typically, a waste-disposal unit is installed with one of the bowls, usually the larger one.

Like every other kitchen product, there are numerous options open to you. In terms of durability, any one of the materials mentioned above will hold up for years, if not decades, with the right care. Enameled cast-iron sinks tend to discolor but can be cleaned easily with a nonabrasive cleanser recommended by the manufacturer. Stainless steel and stone should be cleaned the same way. However, solid-surface sinks can take a lot of abuse. Minor scratches can be sanded out without harming the finish. You can use an abrasive agent on them. Expect a quality sink to last as long as 30 years.

Stainless-steel sinks come in several sizes and configurations. Quality sinks are made of 18-gauge steel.

Second Sinks

Many homeowners find that adding a second, small sink to their kitchen greatly improves the kitchen's efficiency. The primary sink is usually a full-size model that anchors the main food-preparation and cleanup areas, while the secondary sink serves outside of the major work zone. A second sink is a must when two or more people cook together routinely, but it is also handy if you practice crafts in the kitchen or entertain often and would use it as a wet bar. You can also use a secondary sink as an extra place for washing hands and the like when someone is using the main sink for preparing a meal.

Many manufacturers offer second sinks and faucets that match their full-size models. You have the same options regarding finishes, colors, styles, and the like. If you do install a second sink, you must route water, drain, and vent lines to it. Allow at least 3 inches of counter space on one side and 18 inches on the other.

Faucets

State-of-the-art technology in faucets gives you not only much more control over water use, but better performance and a wider selection of faucet finishes as well. Fea-

tures to look for include pullout faucet heads, retractable sprayers, hot- and cold-water dispensing, single-lever control, anti-scald and flow-control devices, a lowered lead content in brass components, and built-in water purifiers to enhance taste.

For a quality faucet, inquire about its parts when you shop. The best are those made of solid brass or a brass-base material. Both are corrosion-resistant. Avoid plastic components—they won't hold up. Ask about the faucet's valving, too. Buy a model that has a washerless cartridge;

● SINK INSTALLATIONS

In terms of installation, there are five types of kitchen sinks to consider:

▌ **Under-Mounted.** If you want a smooth look, an under-mounted sink may be for you. The bowl is attached underneath the countertop.

▌ **Integral.** As the word "integral" implies, the sink and countertop are fabricated from the same material—stone, faux stone, or solid-surfacing. There are no visible seams or joints in which food or debris can accumulate.

▌ **Self-Rimming or Flush-Mounted.** A self-rimmed sink has a rolled edge that is mounted over the countertop.

▌ **Rimmed.** Unlike a self-rimming sink, a rimmed sink requires a flat metal strip to seal the sink to the countertop.

▌ **Tile-In.** Used with a tiled countertop, the sink rim is flush with the tiled surface. Grout seals the sink to the surrounding countertop area.

TOP AND BOTTOM Apron-front or farmhouse sinks, top, have exposed fronts and are gaining popularity. Two-sink kitchens, bottom, can make cooking more efficient.

it will cost more, but it will last longer and be less prone to leaks. This will save you money in the long run.

Besides selecting a spout type (standard, arched, gooseneck, or pullout), you may choose between single or double levers. Pullout faucets come with a built-in sprayer. Others require installing a separate sprayer. Until recently, a pressure-balanced faucet (one equipped with a device that equalizes the hot and cold water coming out of a faucet to prevent scalding), came only with single-lever models. Now this safety feature is available with faucets that have separate hot- and cold-water valves. You may mix your spout with one of many types of handle styles: wrist blades, levers, scrolls, numerous geometric shapes, and cross handles. If your fingers or hands get stiff, choose wrist blades, which are the easiest to manipulate.

Chrome, brass, enamel-coated or baked-on colors, pewter, and nickel are typical faucet finishes. Some finishes, such as chrome, are easier to care for than others; brass, for example, may require polishing. Technologically advanced coatings can make even delicate finishes, such as the enameled colors, more durable unless you use abrasive cleaners on them, which will scratch the finish. You may expect a good-quality faucet to last approximately 15 years; top-of-the-line products will hold up even longer.

ABOVE Pot fillers save you steps to the sink while cooking. Choose one that can reach most of the burners on your cooktop.

● TYPES OF FAUCETS

▌**High Gooseneck.** Gooseneck spouts facilitate filling tall pitchers and vases and make pot cleaning easier when the sink bowl is shallow. This faucet type is great at a bar sink or auxiliary food preparation sink for cleaning vegetables.

▌**Single Lever.** One lever turns on and mixes hot and cold water. Styles range from functional to sleek.

▌**Double-Handle Faucet.** Temperature may be easier to adjust with separate hot and cold controls. Most contain washers and seals that must occasionally be replaced.

▌**Single-Handle Faucet with Pullout Sprayer.** A pullout faucet allows single-handed on, off, temperature control, and spraying.

▌**Pot Fillers.** Pot fillers are mounted to the wall over the cooktop. Some versions have a pullout spout.

Others feature a double- or triple-jointed arm that can be bent to reach up and down or swiveled back and forth, allowing the cook to pull the faucet all the way over to a pot on the farthest burner of a wide commercial range.

Don't be sidetracked by how good today's sinks and faucets look, the products you pick must function well in your new kitchen. As a practical matter, compare the size of your biggest pots and racks to see whether the sink and faucet you are considering will accommodate them. You may be able to compensate for a shallow sink by pairing it with a pullout or gooseneck faucet. But a faucet that is too tall for a sink will splash water; one that is too short won't allow water to reach to the sink's corners. If you plan a double- or triple-bowl sink, the faucet you select should be able to reach all of the bowls.

Compression Faucets

The most familiar faucet is probably the washer-equipped compression-type faucet, sold under many brand names. These are the least expensive faucets and they have been around the longest. They control water by means of a threaded, washer-fitted stem that moves up and down over a flat brass seat. Every compression faucet consists of a handle, a packing nut and/or a bonnet nut, a threaded stem with a washer, a washer screw, and a brass seat. When the handle is turned off, the washer bears against the flat seat and shuts off the water. When the faucet is opened, the stem and washer move away from the seat and water passes between the two.

Compression faucets are not designed so that a single stem can mix water from hot and cold supply lines. Therefore, there are no single-handle compression faucets for kitchen sinks. Your only option is a two-handle, single-spout unit. Of course some single-handle compression faucets do exist. In fact there are lots of them sold every year, including sillcocks and boiler drain valves.

Ball-Type Faucets

Ball-type faucets are always single-handle units. The ball contains inlet ports that align with faucet body ports to allow water flow. Movement of the ports alters the flow rate and the hot-cold mixture. Delta and Peerless are two of the major ball-type faucet brands. Most people consider these faucets preferable in the kitchen because you can turn on and adjust the temperature of the water with just one hand.

Cartridge Faucets

A cartridge faucet may have two handles, such as compression faucets, or a single handle like ball-type unit. If your faucet is an Aqualine, Moen, Price Pfister, or Valley brand single-handle model, it is probably a cartridge type. If it is a dual-handle model, the only way to tell if it has a cartridge is to take it apart. This faucet mixes and diverts water in a way that's similar to ball-type faucets. It just features a cartridge and diverter fitting instead of a ball.

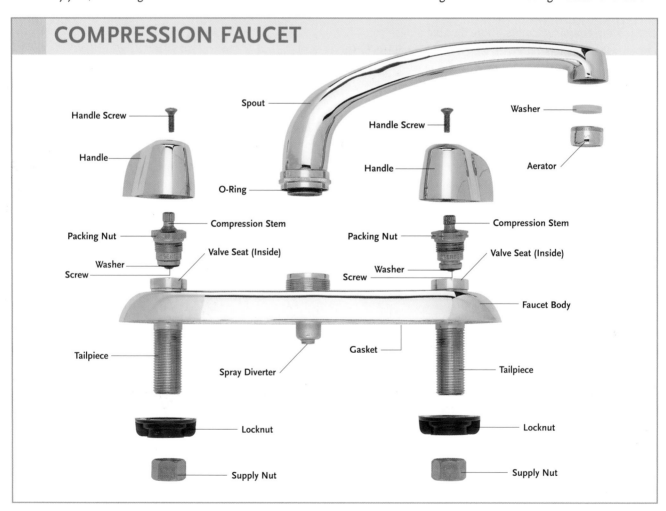

COMPRESSION FAUCET

ABOVE Two-handle faucets are often compression-type units.

ABOVE The ball mechanism in this faucet arches and rotates.

ABOVE The stem in this cartridge faucet travels vertically.

BALL-TYPE FAUCET

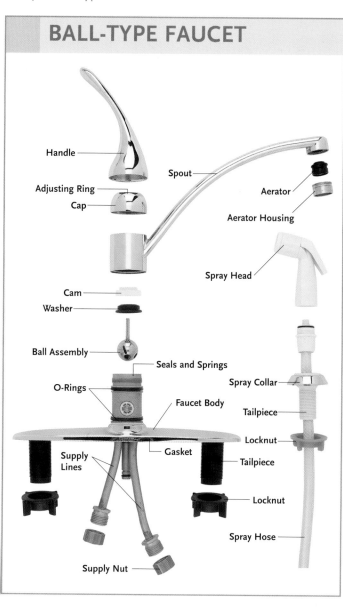

Handle

Spout

Adjusting Ring

Cap

Aerator

Aerator Housing

Spray Head

Cam

Washer

Ball Assembly

Seals and Springs

O-Rings

Spray Collar

Faucet Body

Tailpiece

Supply Lines

Locknut

Gasket

Tailpiece

Locknut

Spray Hose

Supply Nut

CARTRIDGE-TYPE FAUCET

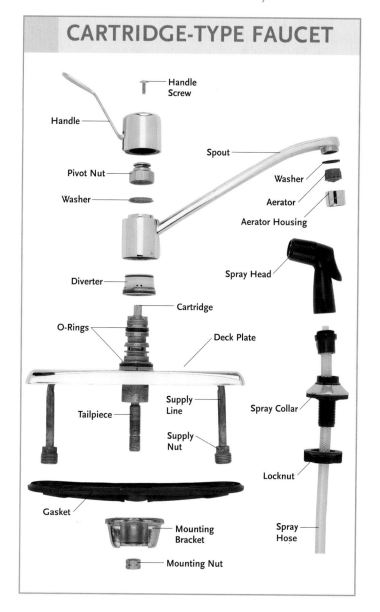

Handle Screw

Handle

Spout

Pivot Nut

Washer

Washer

Aerator

Aerator Housing

Diverter

Spray Head

Cartridge

O-Rings

Deck Plate

Tailpiece

Supply Line

Supply Nut

Spray Collar

Tailpiece

Gasket

Locknut

Mounting Bracket

Spray Hose

Mounting Nut

MAKING A LAMINATE COUNTERTOP

Plastic laminate is a durable, affordable, and attractive countertop finish material. It's available in solid colors, patterns, and metallic-coated sheets, to name just a few design options. Working with it requires some special skills. But compared to other counter materials, such as natural stone or solid surfacing, building a laminate countertop is a breeze.

Start by building the countertop substrate using either ¾-inch-thick exterior-grade plywood or particleboard. A double layer is best, but a single layer with the edges built up with 4-inch-wide strips is acceptable. Join the layers using carpenter's glue and drywall screws.

Begin applying the plastic laminate to the edges of the substrate. Use contact cement and make sure to roll all the pieces flat with a laminate roller. Install the top sheet as shown below in step 4; then trim the edges flush with a router and a bevel bit with a ball-bearing guide.

TOOLS & MATERIALS
- ¾-inch plywood and cement backer board (optional)
- 1½-inch screws
- Basic carpentry tools ▌ Laminate
- Contact cement and brush
- Laminate roller
- Brown wrapping paper or lattice strips
- Router with carbide flush-trimming bit and roller-guided bevel bit

USE CONTACT CEMENT ONLY IN WELL-VENTILATED AREAS. EXPOSURE TO ITS FUMES CAN IRRITATE YOUR NOSE, THROAT, AND LUNGS. BE SURE TO WEAR EYE PROTECTION AND RUBBER GLOVES AS WELL.

1 Start by cutting the laminate for the countertop edges. You can rough cut these pieces using a sharp utility knife. Just use it, with a metal straightedge, to score the back of the sheet. Then snap the sheet along the score line. You can also use a laminate scoring tool for this job.

2 Laminate is glued to the countertop substrate with contact cement. This adhesive is spread on both mating surfaces, allowed to dry a bit, and then the parts are pressed together. Use a disposable brush and wear gloves, eye protection, and a respirator to avoid breathing the fumes.

● COUNTERTOP OPTIONS

There are a number of countertop options available to you, including laminate, ceramic tile, solid surfacing, natural stone, stainless steel, and concrete. Of this list, laminate and ceramic tile counters are best suited for the do-it-yourselfer because the tools and materials are widely available. Setting a solid-surface countertop in place is relatively easy, but fabricating the actual countertop requires skill and expertise. Besides, most manufacturers deal with professional countertop fabricators only.

If you have decided on a laminate countertop, you can fabricate one yourself by attaching the laminate to a substrate or by purchasing a prefabricated countertop that you install. There have always been ready-made countertops available in standard lengths that you cut to fit your needs. Called post-formed countertops, they come with integral rounded backsplashes and are available in a limited range of colors. (See "Installing a Prefab Countertop," page 140.) But an increasing number of home centers and dealers are serving as the middle men

Solid-surface counters are installed by professional counter fabricators. Each countertop is custom made.

between countertop fabricators and homeowners. You can order a countertop cut to your specifications in any one of a wide range of laminate colors and textures. You can also specify edge treatments. If you go this route, have the retailer or fabricator take the measurements for the countertop. That way, if the countertop doesn't fit, the fabricator is responsible for fixing the problem.

3 Once the cement has set properly, carefully align the edge laminate and push it in place. Roll it smooth with a laminate roller, and trim all the edges with a router and a flush-trimming bit.

4 Place lattice strips on the counter, and lower the laminate onto them. Make sure the sheet overhangs on all sides. Pull out the strips one at a time, and press down on the sheet.

5 Roll the laminate across the top of the counter to make a complete bond. Then cut off the overhanging edges using a router and a roller-guided bevel bit.

INSTALLING A PREFAB COUNTERTOP

project

Prefabricated countertops, also called post-formed countertops, are stock units at the large chain home centers. You just buy one that looks good to you and is the right size. Installing these tops is usually easy. First make sure the base cabinets are level; then lower the top in place; scribe its backsplash to the wall; attach it to the cabinets; and caulk around its perimeter. These tops can be cut to any length and mitered to form right angles.

TOOLS & MATERIALS
- Countertop ▌ 48-inch level ▌ Belt sander
- Caulking gun and adhesive caulk
- Shims (if necessary) ▌ Sandpaper or file
- Power drill-driver and assorted bits
- Wood screws as needed ▌ Tub-and-tile caulk
- Iron (optional)

1 Before installing the countertop, check the cabinets for level from side-to-side and front-to-back. Use a 4-ft. level for the most accurate results. If necessary, shim the cabinets until all are aligned.

4 To place the countertop, get a couple of helpers to lift it and lower it onto the cabinets. Make sure that one person supports any joint in the top to reduce the bending stress.

5 Push the top against the wall, and carefully scribe the backsplash to the wall using a wide, flat carpenter's pencil. Remove the top and sand the back of the backsplash so it conforms to the scribe line. A belt sander works well for this job, but it does create a lot of dust. Be sure to wear a dust mask when using one.

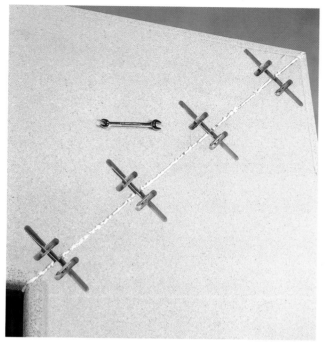

2 Corner joints, like the mitered joint above, are joined with adhesive and I-bolts. You order the counter sections with the miter and the T-slots (for the I-bolts) already cut. Spread the adhesive; then insert the bolts and slowly tighten them. Keep the sections aligned as they are drawn together.

3 Before putting the top in place, check the height of the cabinets. If they aren't at least 34 1/2 in. high (which is the rough-in clearance for most under-counter appliances), then cut and screw small riser blocks to the back and front edges of the top to yield more clearance.

6 The countertop is held to the cabinets by screws driven up through the cabinet corner blocks and into the underside of the top. Don't use screws that are long enough to break through the surface of the top.

7 Once the top is screwed to the cabinets, use silicone caulk to fill the seam where the backsplash meets the wall. This caulk will prevent moisture from getting behind the top.

8 On exposed countertop ends, install preformed end strips that match the top laminate. These strips usually are coated with a heat-activated adhesive. Use a hot clothes iron to press the strip in place.

INSTALLING BACKER BOARD FOR TILE

project

The key to a good tile job is to create a stable base that won't move. If the base does move, it can easily cause cracked grout and even broken tiles. The best approach is to start with a ¾-inch-thick plywood substrate and then cover this with a layer of ½-inch-thick cement-based backer board. Maintain ⅛-inch-wide gaps between panels, and fill these with thinset mortar and fiberglass mesh tape.

TOOLS & MATERIALS
▌Power drill-driver and bits
▌Utility knife ▌Square ▌Template
▌Screwdriver ▌Notched trowel
▌Construction adhesive ▌Caulking gun
▌Thinset adhesive ▌4-mil polyethylene
▌Stapler ▌Backer board ▌Screws
▌Fiberglass mesh tape

1 Install backer board over an exterior-grade plywood substrate using 4-in.-wide perimeter reinforcing strips. Once the substrate is fabricated, run a bead of construction adhesive along the top edges of all the cabinets, and lower the plywood top in place.

4 Cut out the sink opening and test the sink for fit. Then apply a moisture barrier to top. Use a sheet of 4-mil polyethylene or 15-lb. roofing felt. Keep the barrier smooth and staple it in place with ¼-in.-long staples. Make sure all the staples are driven completely into the top, not sticking up.

5 Using a notched trowel, spread thinset adhesive over the entire plywood top. Then cut ½-in.-thick backer-board panels to size and lower them into the thinset. Leave a space of about ½ in. between any abutting panels.

2 Hold the countertop in place with screws driven up through cabinet corner blocks into the underside of the top. Make sure to use screws that aren't long enough to extend through the top surface of the plywood.

3 Before installing any cement backer board, you have to make a cutout in the plywood for the sink. Put the template that comes with the sink onto the top, and trace it according to the manufacturer's instructions. Make sure to keep the template square to the front edge of the counter.

6 Install backer-board panels up to the sides of the sink cutout, using corrosion-resistant screws. Add narrow strips along the front and back of the sink cutout to fill those voids. Make sure to maintain a ⅛-in.-wide space between all the pieces of backer board.

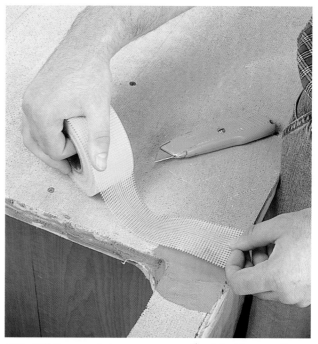

7 Fill the gap between any panels with thinset adhesive, and trowel the surface smooth. Then embed fiberglass mesh tape over all the joints and carefully trowel it smooth. Once the backer-board adhesive dries, lightly sand the entire top with 100-grit sandpaper and a sanding block to make sure it is smooth.

143

TILING A COUNTERTOP

Once your countertop substrate is prepared, take the time to dry fit the tile. Lay out all the field tile, and check for satisfactory appearance. Usually, starting with a full tile at the front of the counter and cutting the tiles along the wall will look best because these partial tiles will almost always be covered with small appliances and other things. It's also a good idea to use full tiles alongside the sink or other countertop cutouts.

TOOLS & MATERIALS
- Chalk-line ▌Framing square
- Rented tile cutter and nippers
- Sponge ▌Tape measure
- Hammer ▌Rubber float
- Ceramic tiles ▌Masking tape
- Plastic spacers ▌Putty knife
- Tile adhesive
- Notched trowel

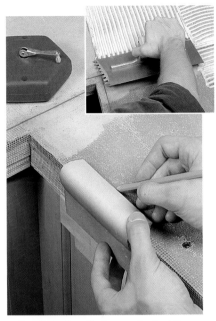

1 Start the tile layout by holding an edge tile to the edge of the substrate, and mark the back of the tile on the top. Snap chalk lines at these marks; then spread adhesive on the top using a notched trowel (inset). The chalk lines will show through the adhesive.

2 Starting at the chalk lines, lay the field tiles using small plastic spacers between the tiles. Periodically check the surface of the tiles to make sure each is lying flat. High spots can be pushed down with gentle hand pressure.

3 After all the full tiles have been set, begin marking the partial tiles for cutting. Hold the partial tile over a full tile, and mark the length. Allow for the grout gap between the tiles; then cut the full tile using a tile cutter, and place it on the top so the cut edge faces the wall.

4 Apply adhesive to the edge of the countertop using a notched trowel. Then cover the back of the trim tile with adhesive, using a putty knife. Make sure both surfaces of the tile are completely covered with adhesive, but don't apply so much that it squeezes out around the tile when it's installed.

● BACKSPLASH OPTIONS

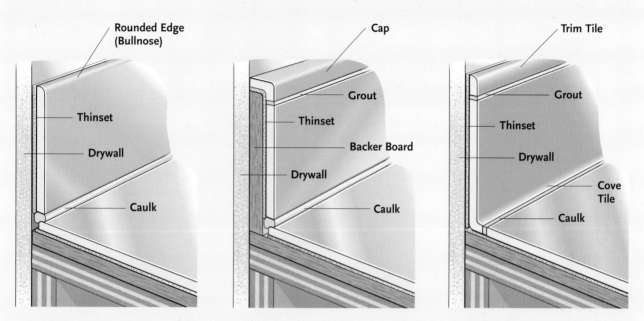

One of these three designs can be used to create a simple tile backsplash. Only the center option requires a backer board or plywood substrate. Be sure to caulk the joint between the field tiles and the vertical backsplash.

5 Install plastic spacers on the field tiles; then press the edge tiles against the countertop. Make sure to align the grout joints, and slightly wiggle the edge tile from side-to-side to embed the tile completely. The inside corner edge tiles must be mitered before they're installed.

GREAT-LOOKING GRANITE

Granite countertops are usually installed by professionals, but you can get the same look by installing granite tiles. The installation procedure is similar to the one shown at left. Use special granite and marble mortar rather than tile thinset. Seal the stone before grouting to prevent staining.

INSTALLING A SELF-RIMMING SINK

Self-rimming sinks are installed so they sit on top of the counter. Cast-iron models, like the one we show here, are heavy enough so that once installed they won't move. But lighter models will have clips that must be added after the sink is lowered into the hole. The hardest part of the job is cutting the hole in the countertop. Just take your time while cutting and be sure to use a new, sharp blade in your saber saw.

TOOLS & MATERIALS
▪ Template ▪ Saber saw
▪ Power drill-driver with bit ▪ Utility knife
▪ Spud wrench or groove-joint pliers
▪ Caulking gun ▪ Silicone caulk ▪ Sink
▪ Drain kit ▪ Plumber's putty ▪ Gloves

1 Many sinks come with a template that makes locating the sink opening easy. Just tape it to the counter and trace around its perimeter. If your sink doesn't have a template, invert your sink on the top; trace around its edge; and mark the cut line inside this traced line, following the manufacturer's instructions.

3 Place the sink upside down on the counter and run a fat bead of silicone caulk around the underside of the sink rim. When the caulking is done, install the faucet and spray hose, which is much easier to do when the sink is inverted.

4 Carefully lower the sink into the opening by holding it in the drain hole. Check the sink for proper alignment and adjust as necessary. For heavy sinks, like this cast-iron model, the weight of the sink combined with the silicone caulk will keep the sink from moving.

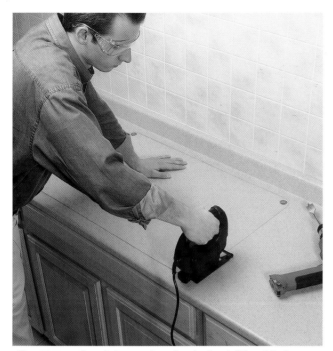

2 To cut the sink opening, begin by drilling blade-entry holes at all four corners. Then make the side cuts with a saber saw. Work slowly and hold the saw firmly to keep it from bouncing up and down, which can scratch the countertop.

5 It's usually best to install the drain hardware after the sink is in place. First, spread an ample roll of plumber's putty on the underside of the drain flange; then push the flange into place from above. Hold the gaskets in place, and thread the spud nut onto the drain piece. Tighten the nut.

SINK OPTIONS

The installation method you choose not only depends on the type of sink you purchase but also on the countertop. Laminate and ceramic tile countertops consist of substrates that cannot be exposed, so the sink should rest on the countertop. For these countertops choose either a self-rimming or metal rim sink. Solid surfacing and natural stone are not necessarily installed on substrates, and their edges may be exposed. This gives you the opportunity to install an undermount sink.

INSTALLING A RIMMED SINK

1. Set the rim over the sink, and use a screwdriver to bend the tabs inward on the sink rim. With a cast-iron sink, install supporting corner brackets.

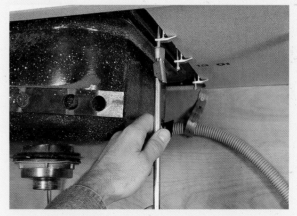

2. Use a sink-clip wrench (or a long nut driver or screwdriver) to drive the clip bolts against the underside of the countertop. Space clips about 8 inches apart. If the corners do not draw down, use an extra clip at each corner.

HOOKING UP A NEW FAUCET

project

Each manufacturer has slightly different requirements for installations, but the basics connections remain the same. In most cases, it is best to mount the faucet in the sink before you install it in the countertop because it is easier to secure the faucet to the sink before the fixture is in place. Shown here is a faucet with a pullout spray that requires a supply adapter that connects to the hose.

TOOLS & MATERIALS
▊ New faucet
▊ Screwdriver
▊ Groove-joint pliers
▊ Latex tub-and-tile caulk
▊ Pipe joint compound
▊ PVC trap and drain line
▊ Supply risers, compression fittings

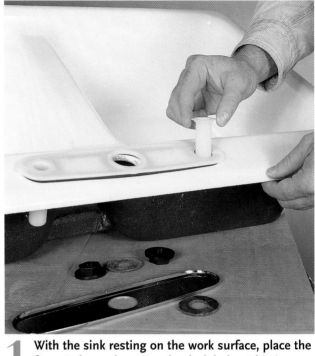

1 With the sink resting on the work surface, place the faucet's base plate over the deck holes. This is a single-column faucet, but it can be installed in a sink with three holes as shown here. The base plate will cover the holes. Install the plastic jamb nuts on the shanks that protrude below the sink. Make the nuts finger-tight.

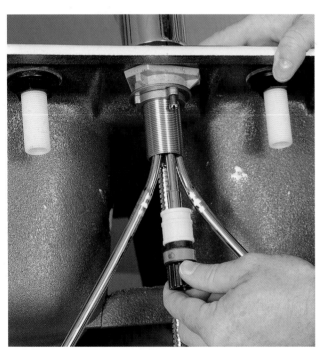

4 This faucet has a pullout spray in the spout and requires a supply adapter that is attached under the sink. Install the adapter on the faucet nipple. Most faucets use a slip fitting with an O-ring seal. With the adapter on the nipple, thread the spray hose onto the adapter. Tighten until the attachment feels snug.

5 From above, thread the outlet end of the spray onto the hose. Pull the hose out several feet to test. Make sure the drain assembly is in place as shown on page 147.

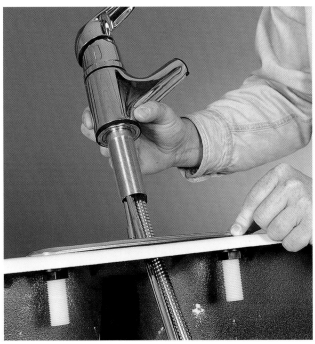

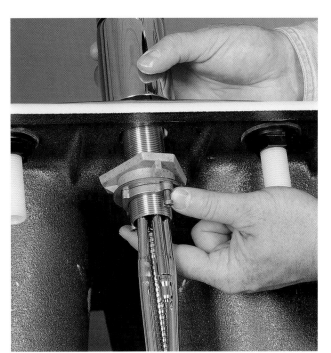

2 Snap the decorative base plate over the plastic support. The base plate should be parallel with the back edge of the sink. Straighten the plumbing lines on the faucet, and insert the faucet body into the middle hole in the sink deck.

3 Slide the mounting hardware onto the column, and thread the hardware up the shank of the faucet. This model has a plastic spacer, a steel washer, and set screws. When the assembly is snug against the bottom of the sink, tighten the set screws using a screwdriver.

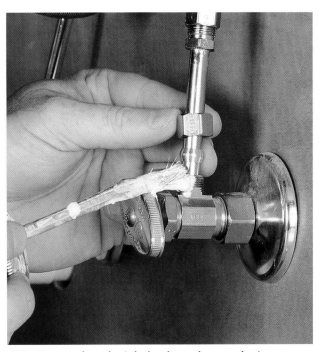

6 A short tailpiece attached to the drain by a chrome nut connects the drain to the trap assembly. This photo shows a T-fitting that connects the trap to a second sink. Measure and cut the pipe to fit your requirements. Follow the attachment steps in "Cutting and Joining Plastic Pipe," pages 74-75.

7 To complete the job, hook up the supply risers to the shutoff valves. Cut the risers to size if necessary. Connect the riser to the faucet and to the shutoff valves. Here compression fittings are used to make the connection. Coat the threads and ferrule with pipe joint compound. Tighten the compression nuts.

6 appliances

Appliances are the real workhorses of any domestic kitchen. They are usually very reliable and long-lived, and they don't gobble up huge piles of energy compared with the human effort they save. They can also be pretty inexpensive because they are sold in so many different retail outlets. Some of the best of these outlets are the big-box stores because the prices are low and, on many items, the inventory is high. Buying countertop appliances in these stores makes good sense because they are plug-and-play devices. Larger appliances, such as those discussed in this chapter, are a little more difficult to install but well within the capabilities of a typical homeowner. Just follow our step-by-step photos and the manufacturer's instructions that come with the appliance, and you should be all set.

FOOD PREPARATION

Preparing food requires fire and ice. Luckily for us in the modern world, these are provided by a wide choice of functional and beautiful appliances: the ice by refrigerator/ freezers, of course, and the fire by cooktops and ovens.

ABOVE AND BELOW Food-preparation centers require a range or cooktop, above, and a refrigerator, below. Note how the range, refrigerator, and sink are within easy reach of one another.

Refrigerators and Freezers

To estimate the refrigerator/freezer capacity your family needs, allow 12 cubic feet of total refrigerator and freezer space for the first two adults in your household, then add 2 more cubic feet for each additional member. Typically, a family of four would need a refrigerator/freezer with a capacity of 16 cubic feet. You must increase this capacity, however, if you prepare meals for the week in advance and keep them in the refrigerator or freezer. If your teenagers down a half-gallon of milk in a swallow, increase milk storage capacity. If you freeze produce from your garden for use out of season, increase your freezer space or consider buying an additional standalone freezer.

As you make a selection, be aware that the fuller a refrigerator or freezer is kept, the less it costs to run. This fact is a compelling reason not to buy a refrigerator or freezer too large for your household or for the amount of food you normally keep on hand, especially where electricity costs are high.

Refrigerator sizes vary by more than capacity. Many require a space that extends out beyond the full depth of a base cabinet and upward into the overhead cabinet space. In recent years, however, manufacturers have been offering 25-inch-deep freestanding models, which do not protrude too far beyond the front edges of counters. Built-in 24-inch-deep designs further minimize the

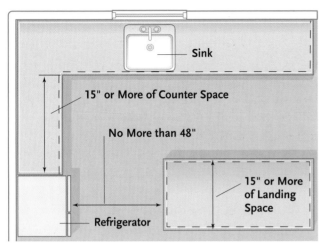

ABOVE Plan adequate counter space near refrigerators. Island landing space should be no more than 48 inches away.

bulk of this massive piece of kitchen equipment. Shallower refrigerators and freezers are wider than standard models, however, and often taller as well, so allocate kitchen space accordingly. Most conventional refrigerators come in one of these styles:

Top Freezer. The freezer and refrigerator sections are separate, usually with automatic defrosting. The freezer will maintain food for long periods of time.

Bottom Freezer. Similar in look to top-mounted freezer units, bottom mounts have a large freezer section under the main refrigerator area. The benefit: no need to bend down to look into the refrigerator.

Side-by-Side. A side-by-side offers the greatest access to both compartments and requires the least door-swing clearance in front. Side-by-side models are wider than up-and-down versions, and their narrow shelves may not handle bulky items, such as a large frozen turkey.

Modular. Modular refrigerators offer a departure from the vertical box we're used to. This concept allows refrigerator or freezer drawer units and cabinets to be located strategically throughout the kitchen—or house. The units are only 27 inches wide and are standard cabinet depth. They accept all types of paneling and handles, so they can blend in with cabinetry. Drawer units and cabinets may be individually temperature-controlled for optimal food storage—32 to 34 degrees F for vegetables, 38 degrees for milk, and 30 to 32 degrees for meats.

Under-counter-style refrigerators, freezers, and combination units may solve some design difficulties where tall units pose a problem and provide for some specialized needs—such as keeping wine at the right temperature.

COOL OPTIONS FOR REFRIGERATORS

Today refrigerators can be loaded with options unheard of even a few years ago. As with any purchase, extras tend to drive up the price of the appliance, but many options can make your life easier or the appliance more efficient. Here are some to consider:

▌ Adjustable shelving
▌ Automatic ice maker
▌ Automatic defroster
▌ Wine rack
▌ Through-the-door water and ice dispenser
▌ Extra-deep door shelves for gallon jugs
▌ Zoned temperature controls
▌ Separate controls for crisper drawers
▌ Slide-out shelves
▌ Leak-proof shelves
▌ The ability to accept panels that match cabinets

LEFT Wine coolers keep your favorite vintages at optimal temperature.

LEFT Modular drawer units can be placed throughout the kitchen.

Cooking Center

The term "cooking center" may sound a bit grand, but with all of the options available, including restaurant-style ranges, modular cooktops, microwaves, and convection ovens, many home chefs want more than just a set of burners with an oven underneath.

As you begin to plan your cooking center, take yourself through the process of meal preparation in your household. Make a mental inventory of the range-top utensils you now have or plan to acquire.

Ranges

Until the late 1950s, the heart of every American kitchen was a "stove" that stood off by itself so heat would not damage nearby cabinets and countertops. Today the successors to the stove are drop-in or slide-in ranges that are insulated at the sides and rear so that they can fit flush against cabinets and other combustible surfaces. Like stoves, ranges include gas or electric burners on top and an oven/broiler below. The most common range styles are:

- *Freestanding.* Typical freestanding models are 30, 36, or 40 inches wide. Both sides are finished.
- *High-Low.* A second oven, regular or microwave, on top provides extra capacity.
- *Drop-In.* Drop-ins look the most built-in but leave dead space beneath. They are usually 30 inches wide.
- *Slide-In.* The sides are not finished. Most are 30 inches wide; compact units are 20 or 21 inches wide.

Gas or Electric? Whether you choose gas or electric with which to cook depends in part on what's available locally. If natural gas is not available, appliance dealers can convert ranges to run on bottled liquid propane—but you'll need to arrange for regular delivery.

Many accomplished chefs prefer to cook with gas because gas burners heat up fast, cool quickly, and can be infinitely adjusted to keep food simmering almost indefinitely. Electric cooktops, on the other hand, are easier to clean. Also, new developments in cooktops, such as magnetic-induction cooking and smooth-top surfaces, are designed for electricity, not gas. Although many people prefer gas for surface cooking, ovens are a different story. Electric ovens maintain more even temperatures than gas units. So, many people choose a dual-fuel unit that combines a gas cooktop with an electric oven.

ABOVE Restaurant-style ranges look similar to commercial appliances but without the ventilation and clearance drawbacks.

RESTAURANT-STYLE RANGES

True restaurant, or commercial-quality, ranges with heavy-duty burners deliver more heat more quickly than the usual kitchen range, and their ovens have superior insulation. Commercial-type cooking surfaces are made of cast iron, making them ideal for prolonged, low-intensity cooking. The sturdy appearance of a restaurant range appeals to serious cooks.

However, restaurant ranges are for restaurants. The tremendous heat that they generate will increase the risk of fire and injury in your home. Codes for installing this type of range are strict—some areas even prohibit the installation of commercial equipment for residential use. A commercial range also requires special venting and minimum clearances between it and adjacent cabinets or other combustible materials or surfaces.

As an option, you may want to consider a commercial-style range. They look like those used in restaurants, but more importantly they produce less heat—though more than standard ranges. They allow you to set flames as high as 15,000 Btu—30 to 50 percent higher than regular residential ranges—and to bring them down to 360 Btu (on some models) for low simmering. Some units come with the option of one high-flame burner (12,000 to 15,000 Btu).

● COOKTOPS

A surface cooking unit has top burners only and fits into the countertop. Most of the space underneath can be used for conventional storage.

Gas. Usually 30 or 36 inches wide, gas cooktops have brushed-chrome or porcelain-enamel finishes. If you think gas cooktops are difficult to keep clean, new sealed gas burners may be the answer, because the cooking surface is extended around the heating element. No more drip plates or escaping flames.

Electric. Conventional electric cooktops have coil or cast-iron disk burners. Disks heat more evenly than coils and are easier to clean.

Ceramic Glass. Also called a radiant-heat cooking surface, a ceramic top features electric coils directly under translucent glass, which transfers heat more efficiently to the cookware than do older, opaque, white ceramic surfaces. It also uses higher-wattage heating elements. The smooth, sleek appearance of ceramic glass cooktops appeals to contemporary tastes. The finish is scratch- and stain-resistant, but can be damaged by abrasive cleansers. You'll need flat-bottomed, heavy-gauge metal pans to heat food quickly and effectively with ceramic glass.

Halogen. Similar to ceramic glass cooktops, especially with regard to cookware and cleaning, halogen units combine resistant heating wires and halogen

Gas cooktops, top, provide the precise temperature control many cooks desire. Ceramic glass cooktops, bottom, have smooth, easy-to-clean surfaces.

lamps that are located beneath a ceramic-glass cover to create heat.

Induction. This ceramic-glass cooking surface uses electromagnetic energy to heat the cookware, not the cooktop, making it safe because no heat is generated by a flame or coil. An induction cooktop is also easy to keep clean; because the surface remains relatively cool, and spills don't burn and turn into a crusty mess that requires scrubbing.

Below the surface, the coils produce a high-frequency alternating magnetic field that flows through the cookware. Most of the heat from the cooktop is absorbed by the pan. Without a pan or utensil, the heating coil is de-energized and turns itself off. Induction cooktops require magnetic-responsive cookware, which means pots and pans for use with this appliance must be steel, porcelain-on-steel, stainless steel, or cast iron. Manufacturers of induction cooktops boast of its quick response—it can go from high heat to low heat instantly—and the precise temperature control.

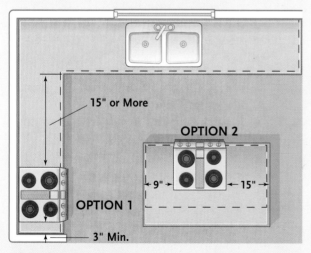

15" or More

OPTION 2

OPTION 1

9"   15"

3" Min.

Plan adequate counter space near cooktops and ranges. Provide heat-proof surfaces in these areas.

Ovens

Ovens that are separate from cooktops can be located in a wall cabinet at a height that permits safe handling of heavy or awkward pans. The main features to consider, after making a choice between gas and electric, are the size of the oven's interior, whether you need one or two ovens, and what attachments are practical for your family. Most standard ovens, for instance, will hold a 20-pound turkey. But if your requirements are greater, shop for an oven that's more spacious.

Convection Ovens. You also may want to consider a convection oven. You'll pay more for a full-size convection oven, and because the heat source is outside the cooking cavity of a true convection oven, it won't broil. But here's what a convection unit does: it circulates heated air around the food, pulls the air out of the cooking cavity, reheats the air over a hot element, and returns the reheated air to the cavity. Because the convection system is closed, moisture is retained in the unit and therefore in the food. Cooked meats tend to be juicier and baked goods moister. Convection ovens bake and roast faster than conventional models at temperatures that are 25 to 75 degrees F lower, which saves energy. Because superheating the air over hot elements burns off odors, it's possible to bake dissimilar items, such as an apple pie and an onion/garlic casserole, at the same time without corrupting the flavor of either.

Microwave Ovens. Microwave units cut down cooking time for some foods to mere minutes. However, food cooked in a microwave oven often demands a certain amount of coddling and doesn't turn out the same as with traditional methods.

Even if you're not hooked on microwave cooking, you may want the convenience of quick reheating and defrosting. A microwave unit needn't be located in your primary cooking center, although some brands feature built-in range hoods that make them naturals for hanging over a range. Position the oven at about eye level, with 15 to 18 inches of counter space adjacent to or under it.

Fast-Cooking Ovens. Hybrid products that combine cooking technologies such as microwaves and radiant heat, fast-cooking ovens cut in half baking and roasting times for most foods. They are available as standalone ovens or as part of a range.

RIGHT Wall ovens are available with traditional gas or electric heating elements or with convection elements.

WARMING DRAWERS

Another practical device is a warming drawer. They range in size from 24 to 30 inches wide and can keep food moist and warm for long periods of time. Most manufacturers make warming drawers to match other appliances in their lines, but you can outfit them with a trim finish that blends with the cabinetry, as well. Look for a model with adjustable temperature settings—from about 90 to 200 degrees F is a good range—flexible racks, automatic shutoff, and removable pans.

Warming drawers keep food warm and moist until you are ready to serve. They range in size from 24 to 30 in.

ABOVE Ventilation hoods and fans remove unwanted moisture and odors, and can be a design element.

Ventilation

No discussion of cooking equipment is complete without addressing ventilation. Unvented grease, smoke, heat, and steam generated when you cook will take its toll on your new cabinets, countertops, floors, walls, and other surfaces, which will collect the residue along with germs and general grime.

The only efficient way to combat this residue and the stale cooking odors that linger is with an exhaust system. A fan over the range or cooktop is not enough. The most effective way to ventilate a kitchen is with a hooded system. The hood, which is installed directly over the cooking surface, captures the bad air as it heats and naturally rises. A fan expels the contaminants to the outside through a duct. A damper inside the hood closes when the system is turned off so that cold air can't enter the house from the outside. Don't try to save money by installing a ductless fan: any system that isn't ducted to the outside is useless.

Although handsome hoods can create a focal point in the kitchen, most people don't regard ventilation as a glamorous feature. However, it is one of the most impor-

SIZING VENTILATION FANS

No matter how attractive the hood may be, it is the fan in the system that actually takes the air out of the kitchen. Fans are sized by the amount of air they can move in cubic feet per minute (CFM). Here are some guidelines to help you size the ventilation fan to suit your needs: multiply the recommended CFM below by the linear feet of cooking surface. Note: The length of the ductwork, the number of turns in the duct, and the location of the fan's motor also contribute to the size of the fan needed.

Ranges and Cooktops Installed Against a Wall
Light Cooking: 40 CFM
Medium to Heavy Cooking: 100 to 150 CFM

Ranges and Cooktops Installed in Islands and Peninsulas
Light Cooking: 50 CFM
Medium to Heavy Cooking: 150 to 300 CFM

tant—not only for preserving the good looks of your new room, but for your safety and health too. When installing a range hood, keep in mind that manufacturers recommend a maximum distance of 24 to 30 inches between the cooktop and the bottom of the hood in order to get the best ventilation. The actual distance depends on the depth of the range hood. A 16-inch-deep hood should be no more than 24 inches above the cooktop; a 24-inch-deep hood can be installed the full 30 inches above the cooking surface. The width of the hood should overlap the cooking surface by about 3 inches on each side to capture all the steam from boiling pots.

An alternative to a system that uses a hood is downdraft ventilation, which is often installed in conjunction with an island cooktop or grill. The vent is in the countertop and the fan is below it. Downdraft venting works by forcing the air above the burners through a filter and then moving it out of the house via ductwork. This method is not as effective as a hooded system, but it is more effective than a ductless fan. Both hooded and nonhooded systems require a powerful fan. The more cooking you do, the more power you need.

INSTALLING A WASTE-DISPOSAL UNIT

project

These days every well-appointed kitchen features a waste-disposal unit. These products are sold either as batch feed or continuous feed models. Batch feed units are safer because after they are filled, the motor is turned on only when the opening is closed by a plug. The continuous feed units, on the other hand, are more convenient because they are activated by a wall-mounted switch. So you can turn them on and feed waste into the opening while the unit is operating.

TOOLS & MATERIALS
- Waste-disposal unit ▮ Plumber's putty
- Screwdrivers (flat-bladed and Phillips)
- Plastic wire connectors ▮ Pliers
- Wire stripper ▮ Cable ▮ Switch

1 If you are installing the disposal unit in an existing sink, start by removing the drain hardware and cleaning the lip around the drain opening. If you are working on a new sink, start by applying a ½-in.-dia. rope of plumber's putty to the underside of the disposal unit's drain flange.

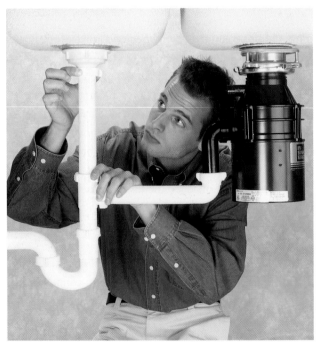

5 Connect the pipes and fittings that form the drain system. The second sink bowl has a standard tailpiece that goes from the drain fitting to a T-fitting. This fitting receives an extension tube from the disposal unit, then directs the waste from both bowls to a standard trap. Tighten all fitting nuts.

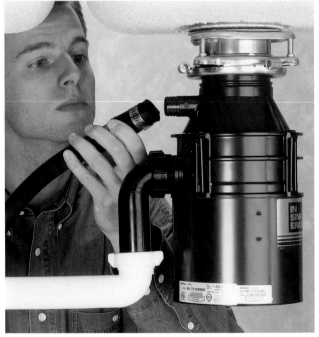

6 Once all the drainpipe connections are made, install the dishwasher drain hose, connecting it with a hose clamp. If pushing the hose on the fitting is too hard, spread some dishwashing liquid on the fitting and inside the end of the hose to make both slippery.

2 Turn the sink over, and hold the drain flange to keep it from falling out. Then install the disposal unit's mounting assembly following the manufacturer's instructions.

3 Disposal units come with a fitting for attaching the drain hose from a dishwasher. If you are installing a dishwasher, use a hammer and screwdriver to break through the seal of this port.

4 Lift the disposal unit against the mounting assembly, and engage the mounting ring. Rotate the unit clockwise until it is tight and the drain openings are pointing in the right direction.

7 Remove the electrical cover plate from the bottom of the disposal unit, and install a cable clamp in the knockout hole. Then slide the switch cable into the unit, and join the like-colored wires from the cable and unit using wire connectors. Replace the cover, and tighten the cable clamp.

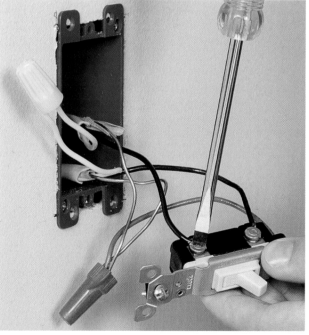

8 Install a switch box above your countertop, and run a power line to it from an existing circuit (if it has the room for a disposal unit) or from the service panel. Attach the black wires to the switch terminals and the ground wires to the switch grounding screw. Join the white wires together using a wire connector.

INSTALLING A DISHWASHER

The typical kitchen dishwasher is a great labor-saving device, especially because the labor that's being saved is washing dishes. Even inexpensive models do a good job of cleaning thousands of loads without having any serious trouble. And while their designs may be complicated from an engineering point of view, their operation could hardly be easier: load 'em up, and turn 'em on.

Although wrestling the dishwasher out if its box and into its opening without scratching the floor or adjacent cabinets can be difficult, attaching the appliance to the plumbing and electrical systems is relatively easy. Start by running a discharge hose from the dishwasher to the waste-disposal unit; then replace the existing hot-water shutoff valve with a dual-stop model. Hook the dishwasher's water line to this valve, and make the electrical connections at the front of the appliance.

TOOLS & MATERIALS
■ Dishwasher ■ Compression T-fitting
■ Compression shutoff valve
■ Copper tubing (⅜ inch or larger)
■ Adjustable wrench ■ Bucket
■ Rubber or plastic drain line ■ Hose clamps
■ Backflow preventer ■ Wire connectors
■ 12-gauge electrical cable
■ Basic electrical tools ■ 1-inch wood screws

MOST DISHWASHERS COME WITH A DISCHARGE HOSE. IF THE UNIT YOU BUY DOES NOT HAVE ONE, YOU'LL NEED TO SUPPLY THE HOSE. APPLIANCE SUPPLY STORES MAY HAVE WHAT YOU NEED, BUT IF THEY DON'T, AUTOMOTIVE HEATER HOSE IS A REASONABLE SUBSTITUTE. IT CAN HANDLE PROLONGED EXPOSURE TO HEAT AND DETERGENT.

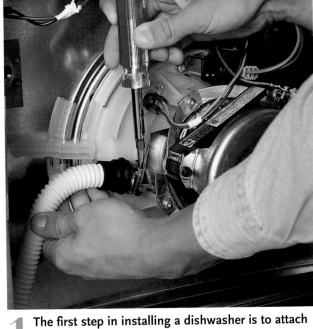

1 The first step in installing a dishwasher is to attach the discharge hose that takes the wastewater to the waste-disposal unit port. Tip the dishwasher on its back to gain easy access to the underside. Then attach the discharge hose to the unit's pump using a hose clamp.

5 Attach the existing hot-water supply tube to the top of the dual-stop shutoff valve. Then slide a compression nut and ferrule over the end of the dishwasher tubing, and connect this tubing to the side of the valve. If this joint leaks once the dishwasher is running, use pipe-sealing tape to seal the threads.

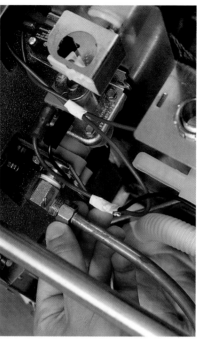

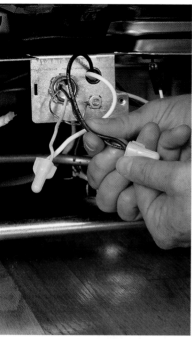

2 To supply hot water to the dishwasher, remove the existing hot-water shutoff valve and replace it with a dual-stop valve. This will send water to both the sink and the dishwasher.

3 Use ³/₈-in.-dia. flexible copper tubing to connect the shutoff valve under the sink to the bottom of the dishwasher. Connect the two with a compression nut and ferrule.

4 Run 12-gauge cable into the electrical box, and tighten the cable clamp. Connect like-colored wires with wire connectors; then attach the ground wire to the grounding screw.

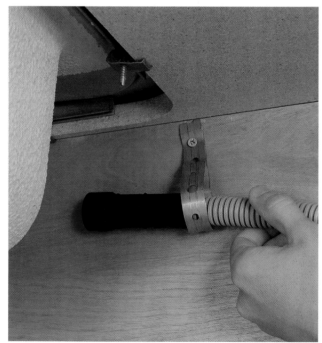

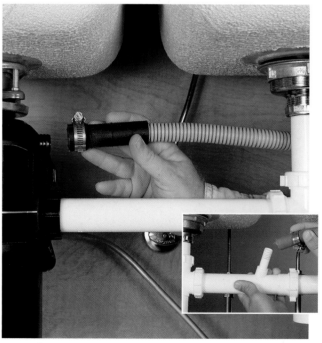

6 To prevent a clogged sink drain from backing up into the dishwasher, local codes may require installing a backflow preventer. But in most cases, it's okay to simply loop the dishwasher hose up near the countertop, hold it there with pipe strapping, and connect the end to the waste-disposal unit.

7 There are two ways to connect the dishwasher drain hose. If you have a waste-disposal unit, connect the hose to the dishwasher port on the side of the unit. If you don't have a disposal unit, attach the hose to a T-fitting installed in the connecting pipe between the sink drains (inset).

INSTALLING A GAS RANGE

Before you try to install a new gas range, check with your building department. Some local codes prevent the use of flexible gas line between the range and the gas valve, as shown here. Instead, these codes stipulate the use of rigid steel pipe. The flexible line is easy to work with for just about anybody. But rigid pipe is quite a bit harder to install, and you may want to hire a plumber for this work. No matter how you get the work done, your building department may require an inspection of the job.

TOOLS & MATERIALS
▌ Gas range ▌ Flexible gas connector
▌ Adjustable wrenches ▌ Pipe joint compound
▌ Groove-joint pliers ▌ Brush and soapy water

1 To replace a gas range, first pull the unit away from the wall so you have access to the gas valve. Turn off the valve; remove the old gas line; and take the range away. Bring in the new range, and attach its gas supply line to the gas valve. Tighten the nut securely with an adjustable wrench.

2 It's essential that you check all your gas connections to prevent small leaks from creating dangerous concentrations of gas inside your house. To do this, turn on the gas valve and spread soapy water around any joints. If bubbles appear, you have a leak. The nut has to be tightened or the fittings replaced.

3 Once the gas connection passes the soapy water test, plug in the electrical cord on the back of the range that provides power to any oven lights and clocks. Then carefully push the range against the wall, and level it in place by adjusting the feet with pliers.

INSTALLING AN ELECTRIC COOKTOP

Installing a cooktop is very much like installing a typical kitchen sink. You just trace a template on the countertop, cut an opening, and lower the appliance into the hole. Most cooktops are held in place by simple clips that are screwed to the underside of the countertop. It's usually a good idea to run some silicone caulk under the rim to provide the best seal.

TOOLS & MATERIALS
▌Cooktop ▌Junction box ▌Electrical cable
▌Wire connectors ▌Tape measure
▌Template ▌Saber saw
▌Power drill-driver ▌Drill bits

CHECK WITH YOUR LOCAL BUILDING INSPECTOR BEFORE ATTEMPTING THIS TYPE OF INSTALLATION. THE LATEST VERSION OF THE NATIONAL ELECTRIC CODE STATES THAT IF THE CIRCUIT IS NEW, THE APPLIANCE MUST BE WIRED HOT TO HOT, NEUTRAL TO NEUTRAL, AND GROUND TO GROUND. THE WIRING SHOWN HERE IS WIRING FOR AN EXISTING CIRCUIT.

1 Place the cooktop template on the countertop according to the manufacturer's instructions. Then trace the template, and cut the hole with a saber saw. Test fit the cooktop by lowering it into the opening. When satisfied, remove it, apply silicone caulk to the bottom of the rim, and put the cooktop back in the opening.

2 Once the cooktop is aligned properly in the countertop cutout, move inside the cabinet and attach the mounting clips from below. Use a drill-driver and short screws.

3 If you're replacing an old cooktop with a new one, the electrical connections are easy. Just bring the new cable from the appliance into the existing electrical box and tighten the cable clamp. Then join the red wires together and the black wires together using wire connectors. Finish up by joining the white and ground wires.

INSTALLING A RANGE HOOD

The hardest part of installing a range hood is installing the duct work between the hood and the outside of your house. If the range is located on an outside wall, the best choice is to run the duct from the back of the hood straight through the wall. If the range is on an interior wall, the preferred route is usually from the top of the hood through the roof or a roof soffit. No matter where it ends up, the exhaust duct has to be covered with a duct cap, soffit grille, or roof cap.

TOOLS & MATERIALS
■ Range hood ■ Electrical cable
■ Basic carpentry tools
■ Sheet-metal screws ■ Duct tape
■ Metal duct sized to fit unit

1 The cutout in the back wall of the cabinet connects to ducts that are installed inside the wall. Install the ducts before installing the new cabinets. To install the hood, cut a duct hole in the bottom of the cabinet using a saber saw. Also drill a hole for the electrical cable that supplies power to the unit.

2 With the circuit power turned off and the hood resting on the range, pull the power cable into the hood and tighten it with a cable clamp. Then join like-colored wires with wire connectors, and attach the ground wires to the green grounding screw.

3 Attach the hood to the underside of the wall cabinet using screws. It's a good idea to also drive a couple of screws through the two sides of the hood and into the adjacent cabinets. Have a helper hold the hood while you work.

● DUCTING OPTIONS

If the duct comes out through the side wall of the house, install a duct cap. Make sure to seal around the perimeter of the cap with exterior caulk. If the duct goes through a soffit, you'll need a transition fitting to connect the round duct to the square grille.

4 Connect the duct at the top of the hood to the duct inside the wall. Two 45-deg. adjustable elbows will usually do the job. Once the parts fit together properly, join the elbows to the ducts and each other using sheet-metal screws and duct tape.

5 If the duct passes through the roof, you need to install a weatherproof duct cap. To do this, cut an opening in the shingles that matches the size of the cap. Then slide the cap over the duct and under the shingles. Hold it in place by applying plastic roof cement over the cap flange and under the roof shingles.

appliance options

LEFT AND ABOVE Side-by-side refrigerators, offer a variety of options, such as through-the-door water and ice. Built-in appliances add sophistication to a kitchen. The refrigerator above is designed to fit narrow spaces.

LEFT AND RIGHT Sleek finishes and distinctive handles help the dishwasher at left and refrigerator at right to stand out.

CLOCKWISE FROM LEFT Cooking options include restaurant-style ranges, that provide higher than normal burner temperatures; unique AGA cookers, which are always on; and modular cooktops that combine gas and electric burners.

INSTALLING A WATER FILTER

There are many different water-treatment systems. The best one for you depends on what's in your water. So, your first step is to have your water tested. There are simple do-it-yourself test kits available. But you'll get a more thorough analysis if you send your sample to a testing laboratory. Once you get your results back, shop for a filter that will remove the impurities you have.

TOOLS & MATERIALS
- Filtration system
- Installation kit (saddle valve, water lines with compression fittings if not included with the system)
- Adjustable wrench or appropriate open-end wrenches
- Pliers ▪ Screwdriver

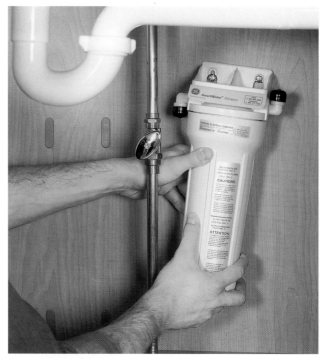

1 The carbon filter unit is designed to mount under the kitchen sink. Clear a space near the cold-water supply pipe, and mount the canister on the side of the cabinet. Some units simply hang on a couple of screws, like this one. Others are installed on a simple bracket.

2 If your sink has a knockout plug for a sprayer or hot-water dispenser, this is the perfect spot for the filter faucet. Just remove the knockout using a flat-blade screwdriver. If you don't have a hole, you can drill one through the sink or the countertop next to the sink to provide easy access.

3 Lower the filter faucet into the hole; then tighten it in place by installing a mounting nut from below the sink. Have someone above hold the faucet so that it points in the preferred direction while you tighten it from below.

TYPES OF WATER TREATMENT

Residential water filters can be either point-of-entry or point-of-use systems. The first treats all the water that comes into the house. The second is located near one sink and only filters the water that's used for drinking and cooking at that specific sink. A point-of-use system is relatively inexpensive and easy to install and is the type shown here. The most popular models are activated carbon filters, reverse osmosis (RO) filters, and distillation units.

Carbon Filters. These units are effective at eliminating a wide variety of odors, tastes, and contaminants. Usually available in separate canisters, as shown here, carbon filters have to be changed regularly.

RO Systems. In these units, the water is forced through a membrane that allows water molecules through but traps contaminants. Once filtered, the water is held in a storage unit until it's used.

Distillation. These units don't filter water; they boil it and capture the steam in a condensing coil. This water is impurity-free and is held in a tank until it's used.

POINT-OF-USE SYSTEMS

Problem	Possible Solutions
Bacteria	Activated carbon, distiller, RO
Low suds	RO
Rusty stains	Activated carbon
Rotten egg smell	Activated carbon
Yellow/brown tinge	Activated carbon, distiller, RO
Chlorine odor	Activated carbon, RO
Pesticides, volatile organic compounds, benzene	Activated carbon, distiller, RO
Lead, mercury	RO, distiller
Nitrates, sulfates	RO, distiller

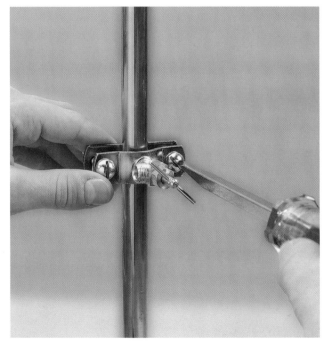

4 Make the water connection to the cold-water pipe using a simple saddle valve that comes with the filter kit. Back out the tapping pin on the valve; then hold the plates against the pipe and alternately tighten the bolts a little at a time until the assembly is tight. Turn the tapping pin clockwise until it pierces the pipe.

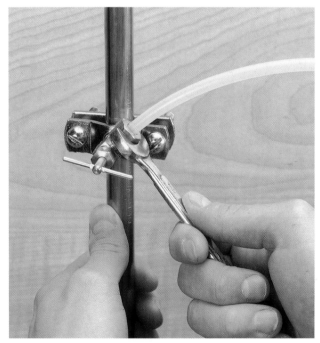

5 Join the filter unit to the saddle valve with a plastic hose and a compression fitting. Then run hose between the filter and the faucet, again using compression fittings. Turn on the water supply, and check the installation for any leaks. If you find any, try tightening the compression nuts.

INSTALLING A HOT-WATER DISPENSER

project

Hot-water dispensers can deliver 190-degree water for brewing tea, making instant soups, and blanching vegetables. The heating unit mounts below the sink and comes with a three-pronged plug. You'll need to install a receptacle in the cabinet for this plug. These heaters do not, however, require a dedicated plumbing line. You can simply tap into the sink's cold-water supply line with a saddle valve, as shown below.

TOOLS & MATERIALS
▌ Dispenser and fittings
▌ Flat-blade screwdrivers
▌ Groove-joint pliers
▌ Open-end wrenches
▌ Tubing cutter (optional)

1 The first job is to install the heater unit in the sink knockout opening. Push it up through the hole from below, and attach a mounting nut from above (inset). Complete the job by tightening the jamb nut from below.

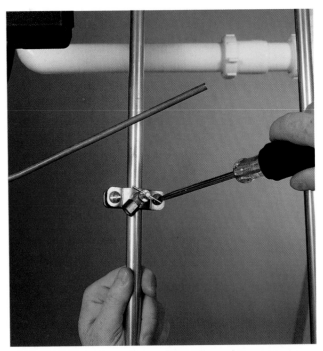

2 Install a self-piercing saddle valve on the cold-water supply pipe under the sink. Back out the tapping pin and mount the brackets on both sides of the pipe. Tighten the bolts a little at a time, alternating between sides. Join the tubing from the heater to the saddle valve using a compression fitting.

3 Turn the tapping pin on the saddle valve until it punctures the pipe. Then turn on the water; plug in the heater cord; and test for leaks. These units typically come with a temperature-adjusting feature. On this model, all that's required is to turn the screw on the front of the unit.

INSTALLING AN ICE MAKER

project

Refrigerator manufacturers now include automatic ice makers or chilled water dispensers as standard equipment on most of their new products. You can also retrofit most existing refrigerators with ice makers, as long as you get the kit from the same company that made your refrigerator. In both cases, you'll have to supply the appliance with water. Usually the best place to do this is under the kitchen sink.

TOOLS & MATERIALS
- Ice-maker installation kit
- 1/4-inch copper or plastic tubing
- Fixture shutoff valve (optional)
- Flat-blade screwdriver ▪ Groove-joint pliers
- Adjustable or open-end wrenches
- Tubing cutter (optional)

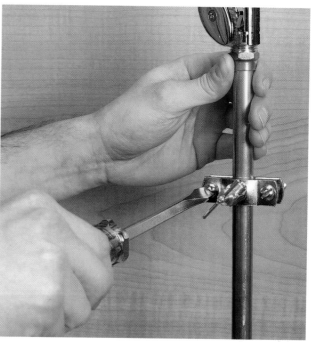

1 To supply water to the ice maker, install a saddle valve in a cold-water supply line. Under the kitchen sink is usually a good place to access a cold-water line. But if your refrigerator is a long way from the sink, it may be easier to drill a hole through the floor, below the refrigerator, to access the water pipes in the basement.

2 Carefully pull the refrigerator away from the wall to avoid scratching the floor, and remove the back access panel. The ice maker connection fitting is usually located in one corner, near the floor. It's easy to identify because tubing runs from it to the ice maker in the freezer compartment.

3 Run 1/4-in.-dia. tubing from the saddle valve to the connection fitting. Use compression fittings to join the tubing to both fixtures. Then turn on the water, and test the installation. If there are no leaks, replace the access panel and push the refrigerator back into place.

171

7 lighting

One of the hard facts of kitchen life is that there's never enough storage space. Two months after moving into a remodeled kitchen, most of us have it positively bursting with the essentials of our complicated lives.

Another hard fact is that there's never enough light. The room may have more bulbs than a Broadway marquee, but there's always a dark spot here and there that can drive you crazy. The best way to get enough light is to plan carefully for it beforehand, then add 20 percent more light. You don't have to use a fixture just because it's there. But you can't ever use it if it's not. There are all sorts of fixture and bulb choices that make the design job easier. But nothing is more important than considering exactly how you and your family will use the room.

LIGHTING OPTIONS

Good lighting plays a key role in efficient kitchen design—and goes a long way toward defining the personality of the room. With the proper fixtures and in the proper places, lighting can help you avoid working in shadows. Install several different lighting circuits, controlled by different switches, and you can change your kitchen's atmosphere easily. Lighting falls into three broad categories:

General, or ambient, lighting illuminates the room as a whole and helps to create a mood.

Task lighting focuses on work surfaces like sinks, countertops, ranges, eating areas, and other places where you need to get a clear look at what you're doing.

Accent lighting brings drama and architectural flavor to a kitchen. Accent lighting controlled with a dimmer switch can also serve as general lighting.

For an effective lighting scheme, plan a mix of these three types, in the amounts specified in "How Much Light Do You Need?" on page 177. Bear in mind, though, that several factors affect how much general and task lighting a given kitchen needs. Dark surfaces absorb more light than lighter ones. Glossy surfaces reflect more light (and glare) than matte finishes. And different fixture types do different lighting jobs.

ABOVE A good lighting plan includes general illumination, task lighting over work areas, and accent lighting.

FIXTURE TYPES

Suspended — Globes, chandeliers, and other suspended fixtures can light a room or a table. Hang them 12 to 20 inches below an 8-foot ceiling or 30 to 36 inches above table height.

Surface-Mount — Attached directly to the ceiling, it distributes very even, shadowless general lighting. To minimize glare, surface-mount fixtures should be shielded. Fixtures with sockets for several smaller bulbs distribute more even lighting than those with just one or two large bulbs.

Recessed — Recessed fixtures, which mount flush with the ceiling or soffit, include fixed and aimable downlights, shielded fluorescent tubes, and totally luminous ceilings. Recessed fixtures require more wattage—up to twice as much as surface-mount and suspended types.

Track — Use a track system for general, task, or accent lighting—or any combination of the three. You can select from a broad array of modular fixtures, clip them anywhere along a track, and revise your lighting scheme any time you like. Locate tracks 12 to 24 inches out from the edges of wall cabinets to minimize shadows on countertops.

Under-Cabinet — Fluorescent or incandescent fixtures (with showcase bulbs) mounted to the undersides of wall cabinets bathe counters with efficient, inexpensive task lighting. Shield under-cabinet lights with valances, and illuminate at least two-thirds of the counter's length.

Cove — Cove lights reflect upward to the ceiling, creating smooth, even general lighting or dramatic architectural effects. Consider locating custom cove lights on top of wall cabinets, in the space normally occupied by soffits.

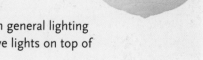

Types of Bulbs

Most homes include a combination of warm and cool tones, so selecting bulbs—called lamps by professionals—that provide balanced lighting close to what appears normal to the eye is usually the most attractive choice. Experiment with balancing various combinations of bulbs to create the desired effect. To help you achieve the balance you want, here is a brief description of the different bulbs.

Incandescent. Like sunlight, incandescent bulbs emit continuous-spectrum light, or light that contains every color. Illumination from these bulbs, in fact, is even warmer than sunlight, making its effect very appealing. It makes skin tones look good and enhances the feeling of well-being. Also, the bulbs come in a variety of shapes, sizes, and applications. One type even features a waterproof lens cover that makes it suitable for use near a sink or above the cooktop where steam can gather. Incandescent bulbs may be clear, frosted, tinted, or colored, and they may have a reflective coating inside. The drawback is that incandescents use a lot of electricity and produce a lot of heat. Therefore, they cost more to run than other types.

Fluorescent. These energy-efficient bulbs cast a diffused light that makes them great for general illumination. They are economical, but the old standard fluorescents produce an unflattering light, making everything and everyone appear bluish and bland. Newer fluorecent bulbs, called triphosphor fluorescent lamps, are warmer and render color more closely to the way sunlight does. Fluorescents are available both in the familiar tube versions and in newer, compact styles. Mixing these bulbs with incandescent lamps, plus adding as much natural light to the kitchen plan as possible, can make fluorescents more appealing. Be aware, though, that in some parts of the country local codes require fluorescent lights be the first type turned on when entering a room to conform to energy conservation mandates.

Halogen. This is actually a type of incandescent lamp that produces a brighter, whiter light at a lower wattage, with greater energy efficiency. The disadvantages are a higher price tag and higher heat output that requires special shielding. However, although halogens cost more up front, they last longer than conventional incandescents. A subcategory of halogen is the low-voltage version. It produces an intense bright light but is more energy efficient than standard halogen. Compact in size, low-voltage halogens are typically used for creative accent lighting.

Fiber Optics. One of countless innovations gradually finding their way into the home, a fiber-optic system consists of one extremely bright lamp to transport light to one or more destinations through fiber-optic conduits. Used to accent spaces, fiber-optic lighting has the advantage of not generating excessive heat. This makes it ideal as an alternative to decorative neon lights, which get very hot and consume a great deal of energy.

ABOVE AND BELOW Hanging fixtures, above, can provide either general or task lighting. The tops of the wall cabinets, below, glow from low-voltage accent lights.

ABOVE When used correctly, lighting becomes an important design element in the kitchen.

HOW MUCH LIGHT DO YOU NEED?

Type	Incandescent	Fluorescent	Location
General (ambient) lighting	2–4 watts per square foot of area. Double this if counters, cabinets, or flooring are dark.	1–1½ watts per square foot of floor area	90 inches above the floor
Task lighting			
Cleanup centers	150 watts	30–40 watts	42 inches above the sink
Countertops	75–100 watts for each 3 running feet of work surface	20 watts for each 3 running feet of work surface	14–22 inches above the work surface
Cooking centers	150 watts	30–40 watts	18–25 inches above burners. Most range hoods have lights.
Dining tables	100–120 watts	Not applicable, usually	25–30 inches above the table
Accent lighting	Plan flexibility into accent lighting so that you can vary the mood with a flick of a switch or the twist of a dimmer. Suspended, recessed, track, and cove fixtures all work well.		

INSTALLING A SURFACE-MOUNTED CEILING FIXTURE

project

The hardest part of this job is getting the box and cable installed. (For help on this job see "Running Cable Between Floors," on pages 90 and 91.) Once both are in place, strip the sheathing and wire insulation from the cable, and screw a light fixture hanging strap to the box. Join the wires from the fixture and the cable using wire connectors. Then tighten the fixture in place; install the proper light bulb (or bulbs); and screw on the fixture globe.

TOOLS & MATERIALS
▌ Insulated screwdriver
▌ Electrical box ▌ Cable ripper
▌ Needle-nose pliers ▌ Wire stripper
▌ Cable clamps ▌ Wire connectors
▌ Light fixture ▌ Threaded nipple
▌ Mounting strap

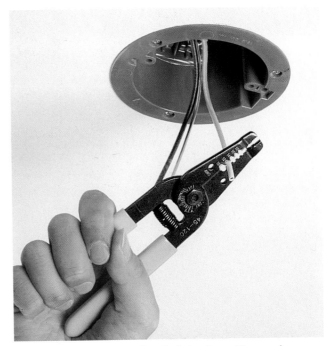

1 Begin by cutting a box hole in the ceiling and fishing new cable from the switch box into the ceiling opening. Install a retrofit ceiling box, and tighten the support wings against the drywall. Remove the cable sheathing, and strip the ends of the wires using wire strippers.

2 Screw a metal light-fixture hanging strap to the bottom of the box. This strap provides threaded holes for mounting different fixtures.

3 Screw a threaded pipe nipple into the collar of the hanging strap. After the fixture is installed you'll thread another nut onto the bottom of this nipple that will hold the fixture securely in place. Make sure the threads are clean so the fixture nut is easy to install.

RETROFITTING BOXES

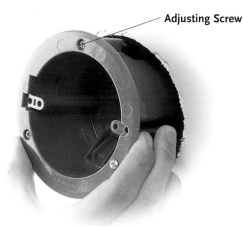

Adjusting Screw

Support Wing

Cut-in or old-work boxes are designed for installation in a finished wall or ceiling. Although you will still need to fish cable to the box, installing the box does not damage the finished surface. To install, cut an opening with a keyhole saw, pull the cable into the box, and then insert the box.

Tighten the adjusting screws to set the wings against the back of the finished wall. Usually these boxes will not support fixtures that weigh more than 15 pounds, but check the manufacturer's literature.

4 Join the fixture wires to the cable wires by combining like-colored wires with wire connectors. Add a short pigtail wire to the ground wires, and then tighten this pigtail wire under a green grounding screw. If possible, have someone hold the fixture while you make these connections.

5 Slide the fixture over the box, and turn the retaining nut onto the threaded nipple. Tighten the nut until the fixture is against the ceiling. Add the recommended bulbs, and install the globe that came with the fixture. Do not use bulbs, with more wattage than the manufacturer recommends.

INSTALLING A RECESSED CEILING FIXTURE

project

Recessed lights come in different styles. But generally, the unit has a housing mounted on sliding brackets and a separate electrical box for making the wiring connections. Start the job by installing the unit between ceiling joists. Then open up the electrical box, and install the cable that comes from the wall-mounted light switch. Join the cable wires to the fixture wires using wire connectors. Replace the box cover, and install a bulb, lens, gasket, and trim ring.

TOOLS & MATERIALS
- Insulated screwdrivers ▪ Nails or screws
- Hammer (if necessary) ▪ Power drill-driver
- Cable ripper ▪ Needle-nose pliers
- Multipurpose tool ▪ Cable clamps
- Recessed lamp housing ▪ Wire connectors

1 Begin by establishing the location of the light unit and cutting a hole in the ceiling drywall. Then take the fixture into the attic; pull back the insulation; and adjust the extension bars until the fixture is centered over the hole. Screw the brackets to the sides of the joists.

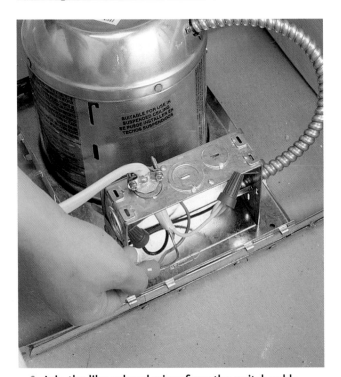

4 Join the like-colored wires from the switch cable and the fixture by hand tightening wire connectors. Make sure to install the proper size connector for the wire gauges you are joining. In this case, the connector must be rated for at least two 14-gauge wires.

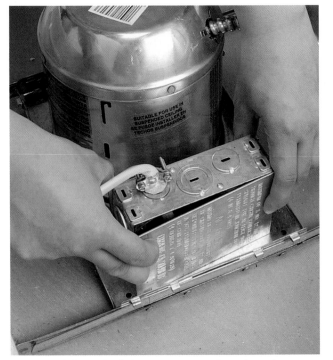

5 Carefully tuck all the wire connections into the box, and replace the side cover. Then go back to the kitchen and install the gasket, lens, and trim ring to the bottom of the fixture. Turn on the circuit, and test the performance of the fixture and switch.

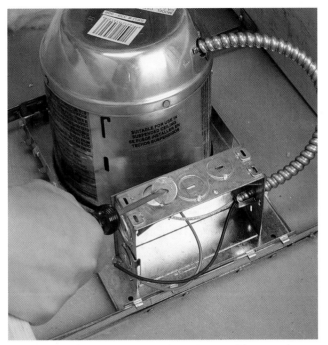

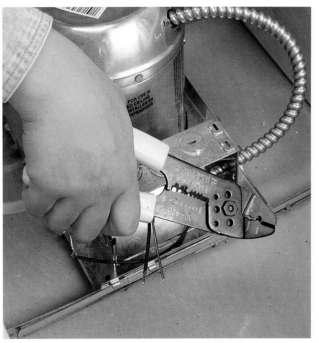

2 Take off the side cover to the electrical box, and using a flat-bladed screwdriver, remove one of the box knockouts. Install a cable connector in this hole; then slide the switch cable through the connector, and tighten it in place.

3 Strip the sheathing from the switch cable, and remove approximately ½ in. of insulation from the end of each wire. The fixture wires are usually stranded wire instead of solid wire. If you have to strip the insulation from them, be careful to avoid cutting the wires.

caution

WORKING IN AN ATTIC CAN BE VERY HOT IN THE SUMMER OR VERY COLD IN THE WINTER. BUT THE WORST PART ISN'T THE TEMPERATURE, ESPECIALLY IF YOU HAVE FIBERGLASS INSULATION BETWEEN THE JOISTS. YOU SHOULD LIMIT YOUR EXPOSURE TO THIS MATERIAL. WEAR LONG SLEEVES AND LONG PANTS, GLOVES, EYE PROTECTION, AND A GOOD DUST MASK. AND WHEN YOU ARE DONE, IMMEDIATELY WASH ALL YOUR CLOTHES AND TAKE A COOL SHOWER.

TYPES OF RECESSED LIGHTS

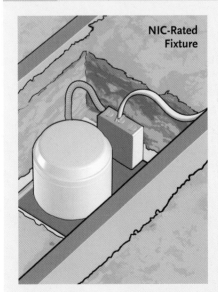

NIC-Rated Fixture

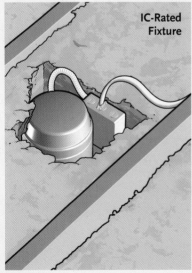

IC-Rated Fixture

Recessed-light housings are rated for either non-insulated ceilings (NIC), left, or insulated ceilings (IC), right. Keep insulation at least 3 inches away from any NIC housing. IC housings are permitted to be in direct contact with insulation.

ABOVE The soft glow near the ceiling helps to separate the eating area from the kitchen.

ABOVE AND RIGHT Fixtures should match the style of the room. Hanging fixtures, above, are a good choice for tables and breakfast nooks. Pendant lights, right, provide task lighting.

LEFT AND BELOW Task lighting makes kitchen work areas more efficient. The track lighting system at left illuminates all of the counter space. The decorative fixture below lights this snack counter.

INSTALLING TRACK LIGHTS

project

If you'd like to try some track lighting to change the look of your kitchen or to direct more task lighting where you need it, then you're in luck. Installing one of these systems is not difficult, especially if you already have a switch-operated ceiling fixture where you want the track to go. All you have to do is shut off the power to the fixture, remove it and start installing the tracks. Once they are attached to the ceiling, install the light heads and turn on the power.

TOOLS & MATERIALS
- Track lighting kit ▮ Insulated screwdrivers
- Basic electrical tools
- Drywall nails or screws
- Straightedge ▮ Power drill-driver

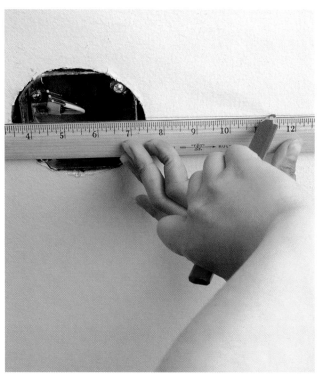

1 Turn off the power at the service panel, and remove the old ceiling fixture. Mark the ceiling for the location of the tracks according to the manufacturer's instructions in the track lighting kit.

2 Start installing the tracks by threading the wires from the power connector through its mounting plate holes. Then connect like-colored wires from the connector to those in the ceiling box. Make the wire splices usihng the right size wire connectors.

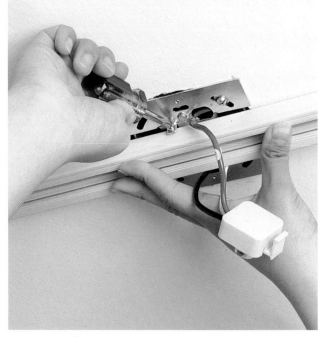

3 Screw the power connector mounting plate to the electrical box. Make sure the plate is tight and doesn't pinch any of the cable or fixture wires. Then lift up a section of track; slide it between the connector wires; and attach it temporarily to the mounting plate.

ABOVE Track fixtures can be used for general lighting or to provide task lighting to specific areas.

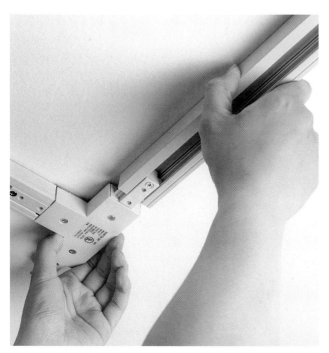

4 Temporarily install all the tracks and the connectors. When you are satisfied with the layout, mark all the track-mounting holes on the ceiling, and then take down the tracks. Where the track passes under a ceiling joist, you can use drywall screws to attach it. In the spaces between joists, use toggle bolts.

5 Permanently install the tracks and any T- or L-connectors, and make sure they are all tight against the ceiling. Slide the light fixtures onto the track, and lock them in place. Turn on the lights, and adjust the direction of the lamps if necessary. Then touch up the ceiling paint to cover any installation marks.

INSTALLING UNDER-CABINET LIGHTING

The best way to add task lighting to your kitchen is to install under-cabinet lighting. These fixtures usually use fluorescent bulbs, but some newer versions feature halogen bulbs. When either type of fixture is located near the front of the wall cabinet, it completely washes the counter with bright, even light. There's more good news. Installing these lights is straightforward, even if your walls are already finished. The hardest part is fishing a power cable into the wall-mounted switch box.

TOOLS & MATERIALS
- Drywall saw ▌ Needle-nose pliers
- Cable ripper ▌ Wire stripper
- Wire connectors ▌ Insulated screwdrivers
- Cable ▌ Fixture ▌ Single-pole switch

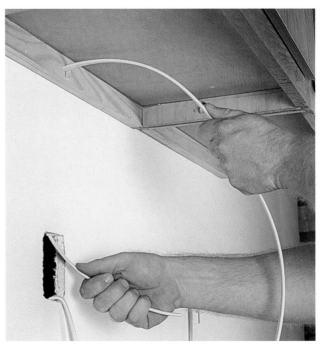

1 Start by cutting a switch box opening in the wall under the wall cabinets. Then fish a power cable from a close-by circuit—one that still has some capacity available—or a new circuit cable from the service panel. Also fish a cable from the back of a wall cabinet and into the wall opening.

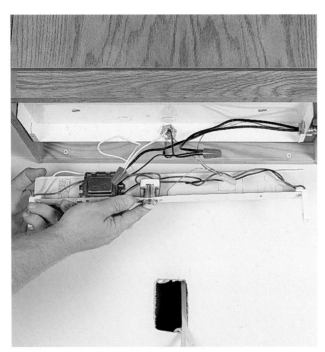

2 Attach the base of an under-cabinet fluorescent fixture to the bottom of the wall cabinet. Then pull the switch cable through a cable connector mounted in the back of the base. Tighten the connector, and join the switch wires to the fixture wires using wire connectors. Lift the light fixture onto the base, and attach it securely.

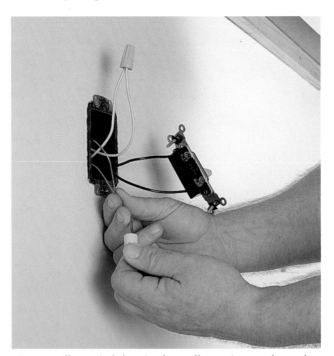

3 Install a switch box in the wall opening, and attach both black wires to the switch terminals. Join the white wires together and the ground wires together using wire connectors. Screw the switch securely to the box, and test the installation. When satisfied, install a cover plate on the switch box.

INSTALLING A CHANDELIER

A chandelier is a great way to provide a lot of light to a specific area, such as kitchen island or a dining table. Because these fixtures are usually heavy, they shouldn't be hung from a cut-in box. They have to be mounted on a box that is securely attached to the ceiling framing. If you are replacing an existing fixture, chances are the box will be nailed or screwed to the framing. So you can use it for a chandelier or other type of hanging light fixture.

TOOLS & MATERIALS
▌ Cable ripper ▌ Wire stripper ▌ Stud
▌ Hickey ▌ Threaded nipple
▌ Insulated screwdrivers ▌ Wire connectors
▌ Needle-nose pliers

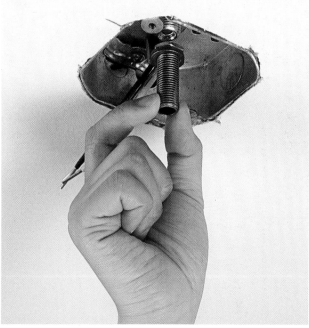

1 Turn off the circuit power, and remove the existing ceiling fixture. Make sure the electrical box is securely mounted to the ceiling framing. Then remove the center knockout plate in the top of the box, and install a stud in the knockout hole. Then screw a hickey into the stud and a threaded nipple into the hickey.

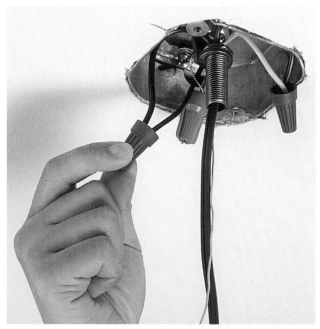

2 Have someone hold the chandelier for you or support it on a stepladder while you work. Thread the chandelier wires through the threaded nipple. Then connect the fixture wires to the box wires using wire connectors.

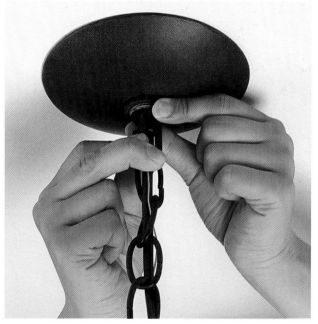

3 Once the wires are joined, slide the chandelier escutcheon plate up against the ceiling box. Hold it in place as you screw the collar nut onto the threaded nipple in the middle of the box. When the escutcheon is tight, turn on the power and test the installation.

8 flooring

Installing the finished floor is usually one of the last major construction components of a project. You will find it easier to protect the floor if you wait until most of the other messy work is completed before you install the finished flooring. If you already have a wood floor that you like, you may be able to repair and refinish it to look like new. If not, then you'll have to install a new finished floor. It is also a good idea to check insulation levels at this point. For instance, you may need to insulate the foundation walls of an unheated crawl space. At the very least, you'll have to prepare the subfloor and install underlayment to get the floor ready for a new surface. In addition to wood, common choices for kitchen floors include resilient vinyl tile, vinyl sheet flooring, laminate flooring, and ceramic tile.

FLOORING TYPES

Floor coverings fall into two broad categories: resilient flooring, which has some resiliency, or bounce, and hard flooring, with no flex whatsoever. Resilient floors are less tiring to stand on than hard-surface floors and less likely to produce instant disaster for dropped glasses or chinaware. But the flooring you select plays more than a practical role in your kitchen.

Before replacing an old surface, make sure the subfloor is in good condition. Subflooring that is in need of repair will eventually ruin any new flooring material that you install.

Resilient Vinyl Tile and Sheet Flooring. Vinyl flooring wears fairly well to very well, needs only occasional waxing or polishing (in some cases none at all), and is easy to clean. It comes in a wide variety of colors and patterns, and is an economical flooring choice.

These products are available in individual tiles or in large sheets. (The sheets can look like individual tiles as well as a wide range of designs.) Installing vinyl tile is a popular do-it-yourself project. Installing sheet goods is a bit more complex but well within the skills of an experienced do-it-yourselfer.

Vinyl does have disadvantages, however. It dents easily when subjected to pressures such as high-heel shoes or furniture legs. Vinyl surfaces may also scratch or tear easily, and high-traffic areas are likely to show wear. You can control some degree of wear by the type of vinyl flooring you choose. Look for a minimum 10-mil thick-

ABOVE An individual tile look, complete with grout lines, is only one of the designs possible with vinyl sheet flooring.

BELOW LEFT Vinyl sheet flooring comes in a variety of styles, designs, and colors. Some manufacturers offer textured surfaces.

BELOW RIGHT Real linoleum fell out of favor during the 1970s. New manufacturing techniques are making it popular again.

ness up to the most expensive 25-mil-thick flooring. Inlaid vinyl flooring is solid vinyl with color and pattern all the way through to the backing. This most expensive vinyl flooring is designed to last 20 to 30 years.

Hard-Surface Flooring. Ceramic tile, stone, and slate floors are hard, durable, and easy to clean, especially

when you use grout sealers. Because these floors are so inflexible, anything fragile dropped on them is likely to break. Also, they are tiring to stand on and noisy, and they conduct extremes of temperature. For those who love the look of this kind of flooring, however, the drawbacks can be mitigated with accent and area rugs that add a cushion.

Ceramic tile makes an excellent kitchen floor when installed with proper grout and sealants. The tiles range from the earth tones of unglazed, solid-color quarry tiles to the great array of colors, patterns, and finishes in surface-glazed tiles. Grout comes color-keyed, so it can be either inconspicuous or a design element. Ceramic and quarry tiles are best suited to a concrete subfloor, though you can lay them over any firm base. Cost ranges from moderate to expensive. Installation is hard work, but straightforward if the subfloor is sound. This is a great project for do-it-yourself remodelers who want to create special designs with the tiles.

Stone and slate are cut into small slabs and can be laid in a regular or random pattern. Materials are inexpensive or costly, depending on quality and local availability. Even if you find these materials more expensive than other floor coverings, don't dismiss them because of price. They will never need to be replaced, making your initial investment your final one. Because stone and slate are laid in mortar and are themselves weighty materials, a concrete slab makes the ideal subfloor. In other situations, the subfloor must be able to carry a significantly heavy load. Installation is a complex do-it-yourself job.

Laminate. This type of flooring consists of laminate material, a tougher version of the material used on counters, bonded to a fiberboard core. The decorative top layer of material can be made to look like just about anything. Currently, wood-grain patterns are the most popular, but laminates are available in many colors and patterns, including tile and natural stone designs.

Available in both plank and tile form, they are easy to install, hold up well to normal traffic, and are easy to clean. Most laminates can be installed directly over any other floor finish with the exception of carpeting.

Wood. Thanks largely to polyurethane coatings that are impervious to water, wood flooring has made a comeback in kitchens. You already may have a wood floor buried under another floor covering. If this is the case, consider exposing it, repairing any damaged boards, and

ABOVE Laminate flooring is available in both tiles and plank configurations. The finish is designed to last for years.

BELOW Wood-look designs are the most popular laminate floors. For kitchens, choose products that can stand up to moisture.

refinishing it. Or install an all-new wood floor. Wood can be finished any way you like, though much of the wood flooring available today comes prefinished in an assortment of shades.

Hardwoods such as oak and maple, are popular and stand up to a lot of abuse. Softwoods such as pine, give a more distressed, countrified look. Flooring comes in 2¼-inch strips as well as variable-width planks. Parquet flooring, another good option for the kitchen, consists of wood pieces glued together into a geometric pattern. These prefinished squares can be installed in a way similar to that used for vinyl tiles.

INSULATING CRAWL SPACES

Kitchens located over crawl spaces or uninsulated basements often feel uncomfortable because the floor may be cold. Solve the problem by adding fiberglass batts between the floor joists or insulating the foundation walls.

Insulating the Floor

Cut sections of unfaced insulation to fit snugly between the floor joists. Keep them in place by stapling sheets of house wrap or polyethylene plastic to keep the material from falling down.

Protect pipes from freezing and ductwork from losing energy by wrapping them in insulation. Buy insulation designed for these jobs, and seal all joints with duct tape. If the ducts also serve the air conditioning system, the insulation will help save energy during the summer as well.

Insulating the Foundation

The most important part of this project is to keep moisture vapor generated in the ground from migrating into the house and the house framing. Spread a 6-mil sheet of polyethylene plastic over the exposed ground in the crawl space. Staple sheets of polyethylene to the sill plate, and let the plastic drape down the wall and overlap the sheet on the ground by about 12 inches. (See the drawing below.) Each sheet of plastic attached to the rim joists should overlap the one next to it by 12 inches.

Measure the distance from the top of the rim joist to the ground, and add 36 inches. Cut insulation to this length. Push the cut batts against the rim joist and between the floor joists. Staple the batts in place with the kraft-paper covering facing into the crawl space. The batts should overlap the ground by about 36 inches. Hold them in place with 2x4s. Connect the batts together, creating a good seal, by stapling the seams together every 8 inches.

INSULATING CRAWL SPACES

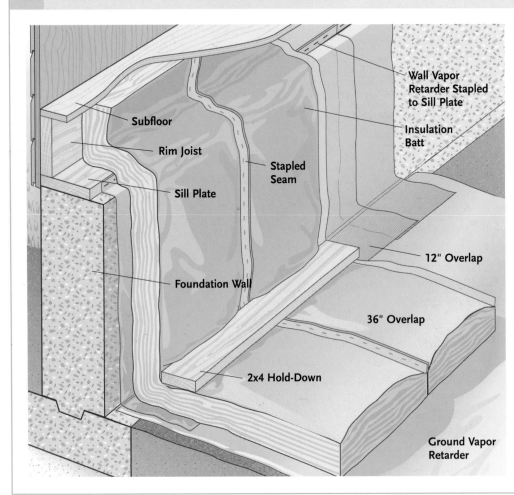

Subfloor

Rim Joist

Sill Plate

Foundation Wall

Stapled Seam

2x4 Hold-Down

Wall Vapor Retarder Stapled to Sill Plate

Insulation Batt

12" Overlap

36" Overlap

Ground Vapor Retarder

If your kitchen sits above a crawl space, prevent cold feet by making sure there is enough insulation in either the floor or on the surrounding foundation. If you insulate the floor by installing fiberglass batts between the joists, be sure to wrap water pipes and ductwork in the crawl space with insulation. An alternative is to insulate the foundation walls and install a continuous vapor retarder as shown at left.

REINFORCING OLD FLOORS

You should never install a new floor over an old subfloor that squeaks or sags. These conditions will shorten the life of your new floor, in some cases dramatically. It's a better idea to take a few hours to make the old floor sound, as shown here, before proceeding. Start by thoroughly screwing the old plywood to the floor joists. Then reinforce any problem joists by gluing and screwing new ones next to them. Finish up by installing new plywood or backer board underlayment over the subfloor.

TOOLS & MATERIALS
▌Power drill-driver and screwdriver bit
▌Galvanized screws ▌4-foot level
▌Lumber to match existing joists
▌Construction adhesive ▌Caulking gun

1 If a floor squeaks when it's walked on, the joists may be weak. But a more likely cause is loose subflooring. Begin by pulling any loose nails; then drive new screws through the subfloor and into the joists. Use galvanized screws every 10 in. in the middle of a panel and every 6 in. around the perimeter.

2 Check for weak joists by seeing if any are sagging down. Hold a 4-ft. level on the bottom of the joists, and see if it rocks over any of these framing members. If any joist sags more than $1/2$ in., it needs reinforcement.

3 Strengthen a weak joist using construction adhesive and screws to attach a new joist to one side of the old one. In severe cases (sagging more than 1 in.), the old joist should be jacked up and held while the new joist is being installed.

INSTALLING PLYWOOD UNDERLAYMENT

project

The correct underlayment will make your new flooring stay flat and resist water for many years. But it needs to be installed properly. First prepare the existing floor so that it provides a solid base. Then select an underlayment thickness that will make the new floor match the height of floors in adjoining rooms. Cut the panels to size, and place them on the floor so the joints are staggered. Then attach the panels with screws driven through the underlayment and subfloor, and into the floor joists.

TOOLS & MATERIALS
- Basic carpentry tools ▌ Wood filler
- 1-inch ring-shank nails or galvanized screws
- Circular saw with plywood blade
- Underlayment ▌ Power drill-driver

1 To cut plywood underlayment, place the panel on scrap boards; mark the length on both edges; and snap a chalk line between the two marks. Make the cut using a circular saw. Be sure to set the blade depth so the saw cuts through the panel but doesn't hit the floor.

2 Start the second course of underlayment with a sheet that's shorter than the first, so the joints in the underlayment will be staggered. Maintain a uniform 1/8-in. expansion joint between sheets and along the room walls.

3 Underlayment panels should be attached to the floor joists, not just the flooring. Lay out where the joists fall, and snap chalk lines above each. Drive screws that are long enough to reach through all the layers on the flooring and at least 1 in. into the joists.

Types of Underlayment

Underlayment-grade plywood made from fir or pine is available in 4 x 8-foot sheets in thicknesses of $\frac{1}{4}$, $\frac{3}{8}$, $\frac{1}{2}$, $\frac{5}{8}$, and $\frac{3}{4}$ inch. Because it can expand when damp, plywood is not as good a choice for ceramic tiles as cement board.

Lauan plywood, a species of mahogany, is often used under resilient flooring. It is available in 4 x 8-foot sheets. The usual thickness for underlayment is $\frac{1}{4}$ inch.

Cement board is also called tile backer board. It is made of a sand-and-cement matrix reinforced with fiberglass mesh. It is usually available in 3 x 5-foot sheets in a thickness of $\frac{1}{2}$ inch. This is the preferred base for ceramic tile and stone floors in wet areas.

If the old flooring is not in good condition, remove it and smooth down the old underlayment before installing the new floor covering. If you can't remove the old floor covering, just apply the new underlayment over it.

UNDERLAYMENT OPTIONS

Floor Covering	Acceptable Underlayments
Resilient floor coverings	Old vinyl or linoleum flooring in sound condition Underlayment-grade plywood Lauan plywood
Wood parquet flooring	Old vinyl or linoleum floor in sound condition Underlayment-grade plywood Lauan plywood Hardboard
Laminate flooring	Any sound surface
Solid wood flooring	Underlayment-grade plywood
Ceramic tile and stone	Old ceramic tiles, if sound Concrete slab Cement board Underlayment-grade plywood

CREATING LAYOUT LINES

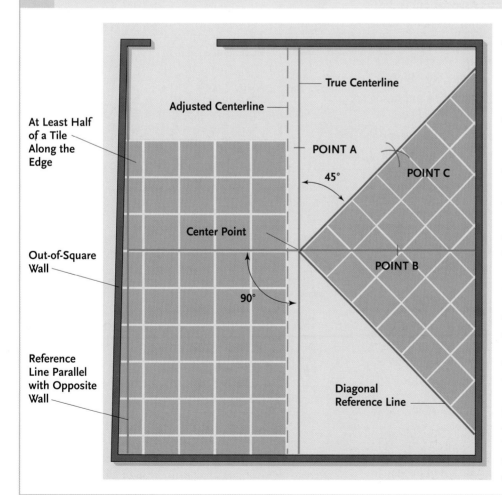

When installing any type of tile floor, it is best to create layout lines to guide the installation. For a standard layout, snap chalk lines in the middle of opposite walls. To create diagonal layout lines, measure out an equal distance along any two of the original perpendicular lines, and drive a nail at these points, marked **A** and **B** in the drawing. Hook the end of a measuring tape to each of the nails, and hold a pencil against the tape at a distance equal to that between the nails and the center point. Use the tape and pencil as a compass to scribe two sets of arcs on the floor. The arcs will intersect at point **C**.

Snap a diagonal line between the center and point **C**, extending the lines in each direction. Repeat the process for the other corners.

VINYL FLOOR TILES

Installing vinyl or resilient floor tiles is fairly simple and requires only a few tools. For a professional effect, though, you'll need to plan the layout and prepare the substrate properly.

Most resilient floor tiles come in 12-inch squares. Trim strips in various accent colors are available in ¼- to 6-inch widths. When ordering, figure the areas in square feet to be covered (length times width) and add 5 to 10 percent for waste.

Start with the Right Base

When you pick out a resilient flooring material, check the manufacturer's instructions for acceptable substrates. This will guide you as to the type of underlayment to put down and the corresponding adhesive. Here are some commonly acceptable substrates for resilient tile and sheet flooring and what to watch out for:

Plywood that bears the stamp "Underlayment Grade" (as rated by the American Plywood Association) is the best underlayment for resilient flooring. Use only material of ¼-inch or greater thickness. Lauan, a tropical hardwood, is also used, but make sure you get Type 1, with exterior-grade glue. All plywood should be firmly attached, with surface cracks and holes filled and sanded smooth.

Wood strip flooring will serve as an underlayment only if it is completely smooth, dry, free of wax, and has all joints filled. Even then, the wood strips can shrink and swell, so a better bet is to put down an underlayment of ½-inch underlayment-grade plywood or ¼-inch lauan plywood.

Old resilient tile, sheet flooring, and linoleum should be clean, free of wax, and tightly adhered with no curled edges or bubbles.

Ceramic tile must be clean and free of wax. If the surface is porous, make sure it is completely dry. Joints should be grouted full and leveled.

Concrete must be smooth and dry. Fill cracks and dimples with a latex underlayment compound.

Preparing the Layout

Set tiles working from the middle of the floor outward. Begin by finding the middle of each wall and snapping a chalk line between opposite walls. Use a framing square to make sure the intersection of the lines is square.

---

project

INSTALLING VINYL FLOOR TILES

Vinyl floor tiles come in almost an endless array of colors, patterns, and finishes. But all of these can be categorized into just two basic types: tiles that are laid in adhesive, such as those shown here, and self-sticking tiles that come with protective paper on their sticky side. To lay self-sticking tiles, first thoroughly clean your existing floor; snap some layout chalk lines; then peel off the paper, and press the tile down onto the floor. While there's no question that self-sticking tiles are easier to install, the traditional type, with separate adhesive, is considered by most to yield the more durable installation.

TOOLS & MATERIALS
- Framing square
- Chalk-line box
- Tape measure
- Utility knife
- Rolling pin or floor roller
- Resilient tiles
- Adhesive
- Solvent
- Notched trowel (notch size as specified by adhesive manufacturer)

smart tip

ALWAYS CHECK WITH THE MANUFACTURER WHEN SELECTING AN UNDERLAYMENT MATERIAL. TWO THAT MOST MANUFACTURERS REJECT:

- *PARTICLEBOARD BECAUSE IT SWELLS GREATLY WHEN WET. IF YOU HAVE PARTICLEBOARD ON THE FLOOR NOW, REMOVE IT OR COVER IT WITH UNDERLAYMENT-GRADE PLYWOOD.*
- *HARDBOARD BECAUSE SOME TILE MANUFACTURERS DO NOT CONSIDER IT A SUITABLE UNDERLAYMENT FOR THEIR PRODUCTS.*

1 After marking work lines on the floor, lay out the tiles dry to make sure your installation plans will work. Place the tiles against the work lines in all four directions.

2 Check the adhesive container to find out how long the adhesive can be exposed before it starts to dry. Then plan to install an area that you can comfortably get done in this period. Spread the adhesive in this area using a notched trowel held at a 45-deg. angle.

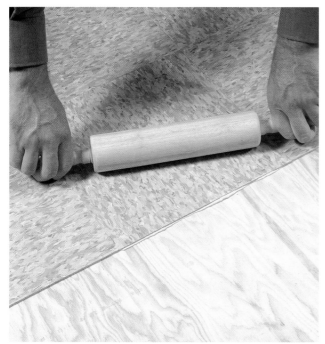

3 Carefully lower each tile into place to avoid smearing the adhesive. Press the tile down with your hands; then roll it smooth with a kitchen rolling pin or floor roller. If any adhesive squeezes up between tiles, wipe it up immediately with the solvent specified on the product container.

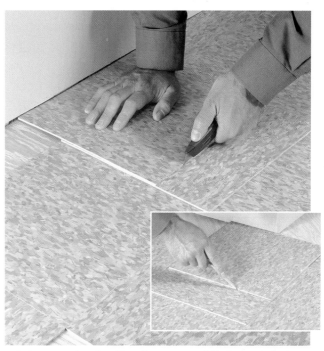

4 To cut a border tile, place a new full tile over the last full tile that has been installed. Then take another full tile and butt it against the wall. Cut along the edge of the top tile that's farthest away from the wall. To cut tiles for outside corners (inset), do the same thing, but on both sides of the corner.

INSTALLING VINYL SHEET FLOORING

Unlike laying vinyl tiles, installing vinyl sheet flooring requires some manipulation of large rolls of material. If you can find a big open place to work, the job will be easier. Many people use the garage floor.

Before you begin the installation process, create a scale drawing of the room on a piece of graph paper showing the exact outline of the flooring. A day or two before you begin laying the floor, cut the roll to approximate size, and put the cut section in the kitchen so it can acclimate to the room's temperature and humidity. Also, remove any shoe molding from around the kitchen baseboards. If you are careful removing it, you may be able to reuse it. Otherwise plan on buying and installing new molding when the floor is done.

Some sheet-vinyl products require no adhesive, some call for adhesive just around the perimeter, while still others demand spreading adhesive over the whole floor. The last method is the one shown here.

TOOLS & MATERIALS
- Linoleum roller (rent one from your flooring supplier)
- 6- or 12-foot-wide roll of resilient flooring
- Notched trowel ▮ Framing square
- Chalk-line box ▮ Tape measure
- Marker ▮ Utility knife
- Straightedge ▮ Seam roller
- Rolling pin ▮ Adhesive ▮ Solvent

UTILITY KNIFE BLADES DON'T COST VERY MUCH, ABOUT $1 FOR A PACKAGE OF 5. THIS MEANS THERE'S NO EXCUSE FOR NOT CHANGING BLADES FREQUENTLY WHEN CUTTING VINYL FLOORING. IF YOU TRY TO FORCE A DULL BLADE, IT CAN EASILY VEER OFF AND CUT VINYL YOU DON'T WANT CUT. CHANGE BLADES AFTER SIX CUTS.

1 Begin installing sheet vinyl by rough cutting the roll to approximate size. Use a sharp utility knife and a metal straightedge to make the cut. If you can find a place to work where you can roll all of the sheet flat, all of your cuts will be easier.

5 To apply vinyl sheet adhesive, roll half of the flooring back to the center of the room. Then spread the adhesive on the bare section of floor; and roll the flooring back to its original place. Repeat the same procedure for the other half of the floor.

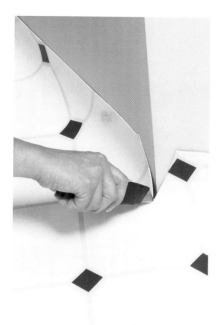

2 To cut around outside corners, slit the sheet margin down to the floor using a sharp utility knife. Be careful not to cut too far, or the cut mark will be visible on the finished floor.

3 To fit inside corners, cut diagonally through the sheet margin until you can get the vinyl to lie flat. Press the sheet gently down onto the floor on both sides of the cut.

4 To trim the vinyl along a wall, use a framing square to guide your cut. Leave a $1/8$-in.-wide gap between the flooring and the wall.

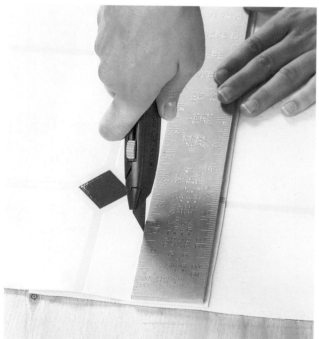

6 To make a seam cut, apply adhesive up to 2 in. from the edge of the bottom sheet. Then overlap the second sheet on top of the first by 2 in. Cut through both pieces, and remove the waste. Install the second sheet in adhesive, making sure to keep the seam between sheets tight.

7 Use a rented floor roller to force out any air bubbles that might have formed while the flooring was being installed. Work out from the center of the room toward the edges.

flooring options

FAR LEFT Mixing shapes of tiles adds visual interest to a floor design.

LEFT Real wood is still a popular kitchen flooring option.

ABOVE Set the tone for your kitchen with the flooring material and color you select. The natural stone tiles offer a fresh, clean look.

RIGHT Tile pavers provide a rustic, natural feeling to this family kitchen.

LEFT It looks like tile, but it is really vinyl sheet flooring. Most vinyl products have long-lasting, no-wax finishes.

BELOW Sophisticated designs are the latest trend from the manufacturers of vinyl sheet flooring.

CERAMIC TILE

Ceramic and stone floor tiles are installed much the same way as vinyl tile, described on page 196. But there are differences, and it's the differences that make tiling more difficult than setting a vinyl floor. Tile is set in thinset adhesive, and cutting tiles is more difficult than trimming vinyl products. (See "Cutting Tiles," opposite.) You must also grout the spaces between tiles, a step that takes some time and practice to get right. However, the results are well worth the extra effort and will provide a durable, long-lasting floor.

You can start your tile installation in a corner or from the center of the floor, using chalk lines as described on page 195. In either case, it is best to lay out the tiles in a dry run. Use tile spacers to indicate the width of the grout joint; if using mesh-backed tile sheets, you don't have to worry about joint spacing. Try to lay out the tiles to avoid narrow pieces of tile (less than 1 inch) abutting a wall. If this happens, adjust the layout.

If the corners in the room are not square or if you must install cut tiles around the perimeter of the room, make guide strips by temporarily nailing 1x2 or 1x4 battens to the underlayment. If you are tiling on concrete, weigh down the ends of the guides with heavy weights, such as a few stacked bricks. Place a strip parallel with each of two adjacent walls, with their leading edges positioned on the first joint line. Begin your installation here, and then go back and fill in the space between the first full row of tiles and the wall by cutting each tile to fit.

To make sure the strips are at right angles, use the 3-4-5 method. Measure 3 units (3 feet, if the room is big enough) from the corner along the guideline (or strip), and mark the spot. Measure out 4 units (4 feet) along the long guide line, and mark the spot. Now measure the diagonal between the two points. If the diagonal measures 5 units (5 feet), then the two guides are at right angles. If not, adjust the lines (or strips) as necessary.

Laying a Threshold

The transition from the tiled kitchen floor to an adjacent floor of a different material, and possibly different height, is made with a saddle, or threshold. Choose from among the following: trim pieces of tile that come with a molded edge, solid-surface material (cultured marble), metal, or hardwood. A hardwood threshold offers the chance to cut and shape the piece to blend floors of two different heights. Apply adhesive to the floor and bottom of the saddle. Then screw or nail the saddle in place. Conceal the screw or nailheads with putty or plugs. Allow space between the saddle and tile for a grout joint.

LEFT Ceramic tiles provide beautiful, long-lasting floors. Notice how the counter material complements the tiles.

CUTTING TILES

A snap cutter consists of a metal frame that holds the tile in position, a carbide blade or wheel to score the tile, and a lever to snap the tile along the score line. You can buy or rent snap cutters, but many tile dealers loan these tools to their customers for the duration of the project. If you do buy or rent one, make sure that it can handle the tiles with which you will be working. Some models will not cut thick, unglazed quarry tiles or pavers.

Tile nippers take small bites out of tiles. They are good for cutting out curves and other irregular shapes to fit

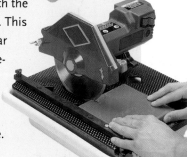

tiles around pipes or openings. The cuts will not be as smooth as cuts produced by the other tools, so plan on hiding the edges of these tiles under molding or some other type of trim.

A wet saw is a step up from both the tile nippers and the snap cutter. This rental tool is a stationary circular saw with a water-cooled carbide-grit blade. Don't use this tool on floor tiles coated with a slip-resistant abrasive grit, because the grit will dull the blade.

basic tile shapes and patterns

The basic floor tile measures 12 x 12 in. with a $\frac{1}{8}$-in. to $\frac{1}{4}$-in. grout joint.

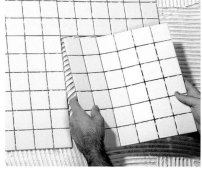

Sheet-mounted tile will look like individual mosaic tiles when installed.

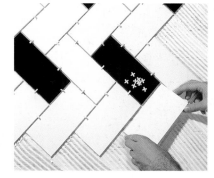

Rectangular tiles can be used to create basket-weave patterns.

Combining different shapes allows you to create a variety of patterns.

Hexagon-shaped tiles create an interlocked pattern.

Multicolor and multisize tiles are available in sheets.

LAYING CERAMIC FLOOR TILE

Ceramic floor tiles come in a wide variety of different shapes and colors. One of the primary differences is whether the tile is glazed or unglazed. The unglazed type shown here is a common choice for both bathrooms and kitchens. The reason is simple: most unglazed tiles provide better traction in wet conditions. To protect them from staining, a sealer is applied every year or two.

TOOLS & MATERIALS
■ Rubber float ■ Notched trowel ■ Pail
■ Sponge ■ Soft cloths ■ Hammer
■ Tile cutter ■ Tile nippers ■ Small brush
■ Jointing tool or toothbrush ■ Roller and pan
■ Tiles ■ Grout ■ Adhesive
■ Solvent ■ Sealant
■ 12-inch piece of 2x4 wrapped with carpet

1 Begin by laying out the floor and snapping chalk lines to guide your work. Then spread only as much adhesive as you can cover with tile before it dries. The container will specify the open time of the adhesive inside. Use a notched trowel held at a 45-deg. angle.

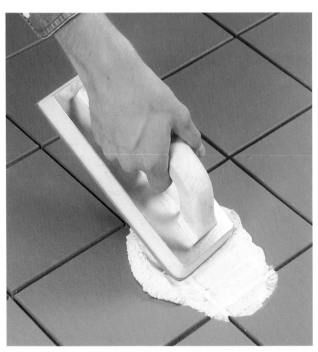

4 After the tile adhesive has cured, clean out the grout joints between all the tiles using a soft broom or a shop vac. Then mix the grout, and spread it into the joints using a float tool. Make sure the grout completely fills all the joints.

5 To remove the excess grout, drag the rubber float across the joints at a 45-deg. angle. Do not press too hard because this can pull grout out of the joint and require you to apply a second coat.

2 Press individual tiles into the adhesive, giving each a slight twist to make sure the back of the tile is completely covered with adhesive. Keep tiles and grout lines aligned as you work.

3 Make sure all the tiles are embedded completely in the adhesive by tapping them with a padded board and a hammer. Use the block every couple of courses, and make sure the block spans several tiles every time you strike it.

6 Clean off any remaining grout with a sponge and clean water. Work in a circular motion, and clean the sponge frequently. Also change the water as soon as it becomes completely cloudy. When the tiles are as clean as you can make them, let the surface dry. Then buff the tiles using a clean, soft cloth.

7 Seal unglazed tiles and grout with a transparent sealer. Use a roller to apply it, according to the manufacturer's instructions printed on the product container. Diagonal strokes force the sealer into the grout joints better. If your tiles are glazed, apply sealer only to the grout using a brush.

INSTALLING A LAMINATE FLOOR

Atypical laminate floor is installed as a floating system. This means that the boards or tiles are glued to one another but not attached to the floor. This allows the flooring to "float" without buckling or cracking as it expands and contracts with changes in temperature and humidity. To create a barrier between the floating floor and the immobile subfloor, you install a foam pad that is about ¼ in. thick.

TOOLS & MATERIALS
- Laminate flooring Spacers
- Foam underlayment padding Glue
- Hammer Installation block
- Plastic putty knife Strap clamps
- Circular saw or handsaw
- Chalk-line box

1 Make sure the existing flooring is in sound condition; then roll out the foam padding starting at one corner. If you are covering a concrete slab, most manufacturers require you to lay a polyethylene vapor barrier underneath the foam.

2 Assemble the first two or three rows of boards by spreading glue along the tongues (inset) and pushing the boards together. Install plastic spacers between the boards and the edges of the floor. The gaps created by these spacers give the floor room to expand with increases in temperature and humidity without buckling.

3 If you can't push a board in place using only your hands, then gently drive the boards together using a soft wood block. Don't strike the block too hard because this might cause damage to the tongue on the board. Remove any excess glue using a plastic putty knife.

THE LAYERS OF LAMINATE

Laminate flooring has two things going for it: it is easy to install and it can be made to look like anything, including wood, stone, ceramic tile, or any color of the rainbow. The inner fiberboard core provides dimensional stability and water resistance that make these products suitable for installation in a kitchen; the wear layers protect a decorative image. You can install laminate flooring over any substrate except carpeting. Simply make sure that the original flooring is clean and level. Most manufacturers require a foam padding under the floor. A glue-type installation is shown opposite, but some manufacturers also offer a glueless version where the individual components snap together.

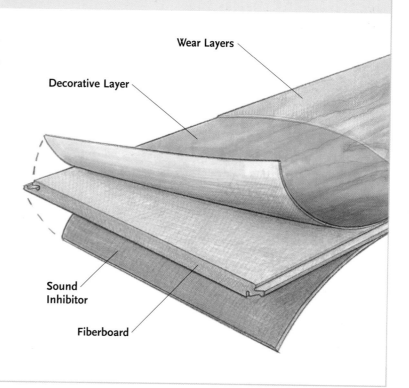

Wear Layers

Decorative Layer

Sound Inhibitor

Fiberboard

4 After you've installed three or four rows of boards, hold them with strap clamps, and let the glue set up for about an hour before continuing. As you progress across the floor, just lengthen the clamp straps.

5 To measure the perimeter boards that need cutting, first lay a full plank over the last installed board. Use a third board, pushed against the wall, to scribe the board that needs cutting. Make the cut using a circular saw and a fine-tooth blade.

INSTALLING WOOD STRIP FLOORING

These days many different wood species are used for flooring, generally as veneers glued over plywood panels. But traditionally, solid maple and oak were used for floors because the wood was so hard and the trees were so plentiful. Solid wood floors may be difficult and time-consuming to install, but they look wonderful and are very durable, often out-living the houses where they were installed.

TOOLS & MATERIALS
▪ 15-pound felt building paper ▪ Backsaw
▪ Chalk-line box ▪ Basic carpentry tools
▪ Electric drill with assorted bits
▪ Flooring and finishing nails ▪ Wood flooring
▪ Nail set ▪ Pry bar ▪ Rented nailing machine
▪ Circular saw or handsaw ▪ Dust mask

1 Start the job by removing the moldings along the floor. If you want to reuse these boards, then carefully pry them from the wall, and pull the nails out from the back side using locking pliers. Also be sure to label them on the back so you'll know where each came from.

5 Drive each board into the last row until the joint is tight. Then use a rented floor nailer to edge-nail the board. Place the tool over the tongue, and strike the plunger with a mallet. Nail the flooring at the frequency recommended by the manufacturer.

6 Some boards are warped and won't fit easily into the previous row. If these boards are very distorted, set them aside and cut shorter boards out of them later. But for modest problems, you can drive the board in place by tapping a wedge between the board and a block that's screwed to the floor.

2 Use a piece of scrap flooring as a guide to undercut doorway casing boards. Then lay 15-lb. felt paper across the entire floor, and staple it in place.

3 Snap a chalk line for the first board; then push the board against the perimeter spacer blocks. Drill pilot holes along the back edge, and face-nail the board.

4 Test fit several rows of boards. This allows you to plan for staggered joints as well as matching variations in the color between the boards.

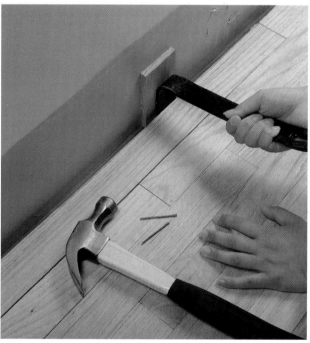

7 To fit boards that finish a row, hold the board up to the gap and put a spacer at the end next to the wall. Mark the board, and cut it to length using a miter saw or a circular saw.

8 To close up the joint between the last board and the wall, use a pry bar against a wood block to protect the wall. Hold the joint tight, using the pry bar if necessary, and drive nails along the back edge of the board. Cover the gap with baseboard and shoe moldings.

REFINISHING A WOOD FLOOR

Solid hardwood floors are one of the most attractive building materials available. So it makes good sense to repair ones that are damaged instead of replacing them. Probably the most common repair is refinishing the surface. At the end of this job, you're bound to love the results. But getting there can cause an incredible amount of dust. For this reason, make sure to seal any doorways and heat registers using heavy polyethylene plastic and duct tape.

You also have to protect yourself. There is no substitute for wearing a respirator equipped with dust-filtering canisters. A simple paper mask just isn't enough. The respirator is also required, this time with vapor canisters, for when you are applying the finish on the floor.

TOOLS & MATERIALS

- Hammer (or nail puller if necessary)
- Sharp wood chisel
- Drum sander ▌Edge sander
- Hand-held sander
- Medium-grit sanding belt and pad
- Fine-grit sanding belt and pad
- Hand-held floor scraper
- Vacuum ▌Rotary buffer
- Lamb's wool applicators
- Tack cloth ▌Polyurethane

TO REVIVE A POLYURETHANE FINISH OVER AN UNDAMAGED FLOOR, GO OVER THE FLOOR WITH A SANDING SCREEN. ATTACHED TO A ROTATING FLOOR POLISHER, THE SCREEN REMOVES THE OLD FINISH WITHOUT CUTTING INTO THE FLOOR AS TRADITIONAL SANDING WITH A DRUM SANDER DOES. DO NOT SCREEN FLOORS WITH WAX TOP COATS.

1 Check the surface of the floor for any raised nail-heads and lifted board edges. Either pull out the raised nails or set their heads below the surface and fill the holes. Use a sharp chisel to shave down any lifted edges.

5 Sand the entire floor at least twice, finishing up with a fine-grit abrasive. Completely remove all the sanding dust from the floor and room using a shop vac. Then stain the floor or start applying the first coat of polyurethane finish using a lamb's wool applicator.

2 Install a medium-grit belt on a rented drum sander, and go over the floor in the direction of the wood strips. Keep the tool moving to avoid damaging the floor.

3 Switch to a rented edge sander to remove the finish close to the walls. Be careful: this sander uses rotating disks that can create circular scratches on the boards.

4 Use a hand scraper to remove the finish from areas that the edge sander couldn't reach. The scraper is also a good tool for removing any scratches left from the edge sander.

6 Allow the first coat of finish to dry; then buff it using a rotary buffer with a steel-wool pad attached. Keep the buffer moving at all times, and work in the direction of the strips, not across the strips.

7 After buffing, clean all the dust and steel-wool particles off the floor using a floor vacuum. Then use a slightly damp cloth or a tack cloth to remove anything that's left behind by the vac. Apply at least one more coat of polyurethane, followed by buffing and vacuuming.

9 walls and ceilings

Now that you've done all the heavy construction work for your kitchen, it's time to turn your attention to the bare walls and ceilings. This is a rewarding phase of the project because you finally get to see how the paint colors and wallpaper patterns you've selected actually look on your walls and ceilings. But before you get started painting and papering, you must first repair any damage to the surfaces and make them as smooth as possible. The old saying is true: a good paint or wallcovering job depends on good prep work.

This chapter starts with the basics of repairing drywall, plaster, and wood surfaces and then takes you through painting and hanging wallcoverings. It concludes with techniques for adding true distinction to your new kitchen through the use of molding and trimwork.

WALL TREATMENTS

It's hard to beat the ease of a coat of paint for adding a fresh face to a kitchen. But there are other ways to finish off the walls, too, such as vinyl wallcovering and paneling. You can go with one, two, or all three of these options in several combinations.

Paint. Basically, there are two kinds of paint: latex, which is a water-based formulation, and oil-based products. You can buy latex and oil paint in at least four finishes: flat, eggshell, semigloss, and gloss. In general, stay away from flat paint in the kitchen because it is difficult to keep clean. The other finishes, or sheens, resist dirt better than flat paint and are easier to clean.

Latex is a term used to describe a variety of water-based paints. They are recommended for most interior surfaces, including walls, woodwork, and cabinets. Latex paints come in a huge assortment of colors, clean up with soap and water, and dry quickly.

Oil-based paint refers to products that use alkyd resins as the solvent. Manufacturers once used linseed or some other type of oil as the solvent, and the name stuck. They provide tough, long-lasting finishes. However, the convenience of latex products, along with government regulations limiting the amount of volatile organic compounds oil-based products produce, has forced their use to decline. This kind of paint is especially good for use over bare wood and surfaces that have been previously painted. If you plan to use it (or latex, for that matter) on new wallboard, you'll have to apply a primer first.

Wallcoverings. Vinyl wallcoverings and coordinated borders offer an easy, low-cost way to put style into your new kitchen. Practical because they are nonporous, stain resistant, and washable, vinyl coatings are available in a great variety of colors, textures, and patterns. Prepasted, pretrimmed rolls are the easiest for a novice to install.

OPPOSITE A bold color painted on the walls can help brighten up a small room.

RIGHT This patterned wallcovering complements the traditional design of this kitchen.

BELOW Wood paneling imparts a warm glow to this contemporary kitchen.

Just remember to remove any old wallpaper before applying new covering to walls.

Paneling. If you're looking for a simple way to camouflage a wall's imperfections, paneling is it. Today's paneling options include prefinished softwood- or hardwood-veneered plywood, simulated wood grain on plywood or hardboard, prehung wallpaper on plywood, simulated wood grain or decorative-finish panel board, tile board, or other decorative hardboard paneling, and solid pine or cedar-plank paneling. For a versatile look, apply wainscoting, which is paneling that goes halfway or three-quarters of the way up the wall. Top it off with chair-rail molding; paint or wallpaper the rest of the wall.

PREPARING DRYWALL FOR PAINTING

project

Paint may be an economical and durable finish, but every paint job is only as good as the surface preparation that took place beforehand. For drywall surfaces, this preparation usually involves just three things: drywall joint compound, sandpaper, and latex primer. The compound can repair just about any blemish; the sandpaper makes the compound smooth; and the primer hides the compound so the repairs don't show through the paint.

TOOLS & MATERIALS
- Basic carpentry tools ▮ Utility knife
- Drywall joint compound ▮ Putty knives
- Fiberglass joint tape
- Masking tape ▮ Sandpaper
- Power palm sander (optional)
- White shellac

1 Scrape off any construction debris that may be on the walls, including any cracked or flaking paint, which usually indicates some water damage. Check carefully for the source of the damage, and make any necessary repairs.

3 Torn paper and other shallow surface damage are best repaired with two or three thin coats of drywall joint compound. Use a 12-in. flexible taping knife to feather the edges of each coat. Sand lightly after each coat dries to provide the best surface for the next coat.

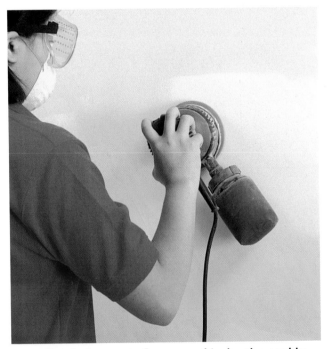

4 After the last coat of compound is dry, thoroughly sand every patch until it is smooth and even with the surrounding surfaces. To control the dust, use a palm sander with a dust collection system. Wear a dust mask and eye protection when you work.

2 Some wall and ceiling damage inevitably tears the paper on the outside of the drywall. To stop a tear, cut the paper using a sharp utility knife, and pull off the damaged piece.

5 Spot prime all of the drywall repairs using latex primer. For areas that have stubborn stains, including watermarks, prime using a white-pigmented shellac. Both of these primers dry very quickly, so you can move on to applying the topcoat of paint almost immediately.

● FIXING SMALL HOLES

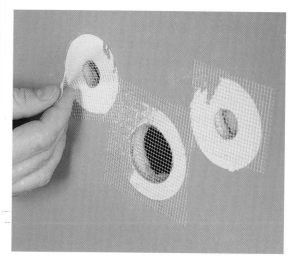

1. Once a hole goes all the way through the drywall panel and is larger than 1/2 to 3/4 inch in diameter, it won't hold the patching material you apply. To solve the problem, apply self-sticking fiberglass mesh tape over the hole, and press it firmly in place. The tape will keep the joint compound from falling into the hole.

2. Spread a thin layer of joint compound over the damaged area. Wait for it to dry completely before applying a second coat. You may need to spread on additional coats to completely repair the damage. As you work between coats, feather the patch onto the surrounding drywall. Sand to a smooth finish when the patch is complete, and apply a coat of primer.

PREPARING PLASTER FOR PAINTING

project

Traditional plaster isn't installed in many new homes these days, but there are still many old houses that have this premium finish. Serious plaster problems, such as big sagging sections of ceiling, are better left to an experienced plasterer. But smaller troubles, such as cracks in otherwise sound plaster, are easy to fix and require just a couple of common tools. Because sanding is involved, make sure to tape plastic sheeting over doorways and heat registers to keep dust from spreading around the house.

TOOLS & MATERIALS
▌Utility knife or can opener
▌6-inch and 12-inch drywall knives
▌Patching plaster
▌Fiberglass mesh drywall tape

1 To fix small plaster cracks, first clean out the crack and slightly undercut both sides with a sharp tool, such as a utility knife or a can opener. Brush any dust out of the crack; then fill it with patching plaster. When the plaster is dry, sand it smooth to the surrounding surface.

2 Fix wider cracks by cleaning them out first and then filling them with patching plaster. Let the plaster dry, and sand it smooth. Then cover the crack with self-sticking fiberglass mesh tape. Flatten the tape using your fingertips.

3 Cover the mesh tape with two or three coats of patching plaster. Feather the edges of each coat away from the tape to make a gradual transition to the rest of the wall. Sand each coat smooth before adding another.

PREPARING WOODWORK FOR PAINTING

project

The way to prepare wood trim for painting depends on the condition of the trim. If you are reusing old boards that have nicked or deeply scratched paint, you'll have to fill all holes and cracks with wood filler. Then sand the boards smooth so the filler won't be apparent when the boards are repainted, and clean up all the dust. If you are working on new boards, proceed as shown in these photos.

TOOLS & MATERIALS
▌ Hammer and nail set
▌ Putty knife
▌ Wood filler
▌ Caulk and caulking gun
▌ Primer
▌ Narrow paint brush

1 Set all nailheads below the surface of the trim boards with a hammer and nail set. Fill the depressions above the set nails with wood filler. If you plan to use a clear finish, choose a colored filler that matches the wood. If you plan to paint, any type of wood filler can be used.

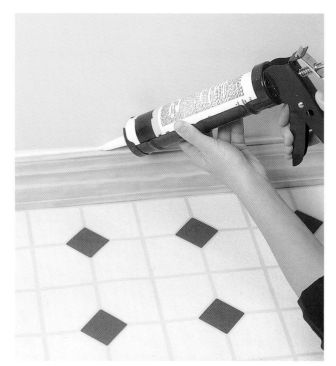

2 Once all the nailholes are filled, caulk all the joints between the trim boards and the walls and ceilings. Use latex caulk, and try to apply a smooth bead. Finish the caulk by running a wet finger over the bead.

3 After the caulking is done, apply a latex or alkyd primer. Use smooth brush strokes to achieve the best surface. After the primer is dry, lightly sand any rough areas. Then wipe up the dust, and apply a topcoat of paint.

PAINTING WALLS AND CEILINGS

project

For best results on new surfaces, use one coat of primer and two coats of paint. Before beginning work, protect wall or ceiling light fixtures with plastic trash bags and the floor with drop cloths. The typical painting sequence is to start with the ceiling, followed by the walls, and finish up with the trim. But if you are painting all of the surfaces the same color, do the trim before the walls.

TOOLS & MATERIALS
- Screwdriver ▌ 1½- or 2-inch sash brush
- Roller pan ▌ Roller with ¼-inch nap cover
- Paint shield ▌ Razor blade
- Masking tape (if necessary)
- Roller handle extension (optional)
- Drop cloths
- Wall and ceiling paint

1 It only takes a few minutes to remove the cover plates from electrical switch and receptacle boxes. But it makes the painting go much faster with less aggravation. Just be sure to turn off the power to all the circuits before taking off the covers.

2 Begin painting your kitchen by trimming around the ceiling using a sash brush. Don't worry if the paint overlaps the walls. It's easier to paint a finished trim line on a wall than on the ceiling.

3 A roller is the best tool for painting a ceiling. It distributes the paint evenly over a large area and it's much quicker than a brush. If you'd like to roll the ceiling by standing on the floor, just use an extension on the roller.

SORTING OUT WOOD FINISHES

Wood/Finish	Undercoat
Bare wood, penetrating oil	Penetrating oil; one or more coats
Bare wood, clear finish	Stain (if desired); two coats clear surface finish
Bare wood, paint finish	Latex wood primer or white shellac
Painted wood, paint finish	Spot-prime filled areas with latex wood primer or white shellac

painting tips

To get a clean job, remove any knobs from doors and cabinets before painting. Unless you need to paint large surfaces, use a small sash brush (1½ to 2 inches wide) to paint all wood. Paint the edges of doors first, ending with the larger surfaces. Use a paint shield while painting baseboards.

When painting a window sash, allow the paint to cover about 1/16 inch of glass to help seal the juncture between the glazing and the wood. Don't worry if paint slops over onto the glass. Go back after the paint dries, and scrape any spills off of the glass with a razor blade. Protect tile surfaces with painter's tape.

4 When the ceiling paint is dry, start with the walls by cutting in a trim line along the ceiling. Use a sash brush, and try to maintain smooth strokes. Keep in mind that the finished line doesn't have to be perfect. It may look rough when you are working just a foot away. But from the floor it will look much better.

5 Once you have painted the perimeter of the walls and around any windows and doors, start on the center of the wall. Use a roller, and apply the paint in a zigzag motion. Finish off the section with strokes that are straight up and down.

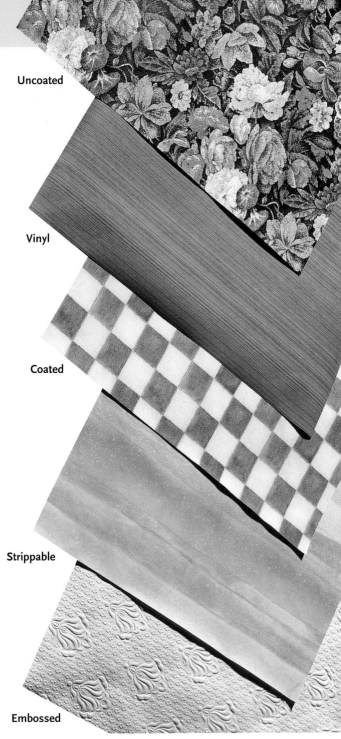

Uncoated

Vinyl

Coated

Strippable

Embossed

WALLCOVERING BASICS

Wallcovering includes a wide range of products, from traditional paper to treated fabrics and fabric-backed vinyl, paper-backed grass cloths, and even more exotic variations. For kitchens, look for a covering that withstands scuffs and cleans easily, such as solid vinyl, though vinyl-coated paper might be suitable for an eating area.

Preparing for a Project

Most wallcoverings now come prepasted, but some types still must be pasted strip by strip as they go up. If you have a choice, choose the prepasted paper. Installation is easier, and there is less of a chance of problems developing. Both types must be applied to a clean, smooth surface. Cover unfinished drywall with a wallcovering primer/sealer. If your kitchen's walls are already papered and the covering is still sound, you can probably scuff the surface with sandpaper to promote adhesion and apply a new wallcovering right over it. Check this with your wallcovering dealer before making a decision. It's frequently necessary to apply a wallcovering primer/sealer or to strip an old covering completely.

Planning the Job

Wallcovering is sold in rolls of various widths. Because patterned coverings must be matched side to side along the edges of the strips, there may be a fair amount of waste in trimming to keep the pattern repeating properly. To estimate material needs, determine the number of square feet in the area to be covered (less openings like windows, doors, and any wall space taken up by cabinets), then divide by 30—a number derived by subtracting the likely wastage from the standard 36 square feet in a roll. Round up to the nearest whole number for ordering standard rolls. If you're buying other than standard 36-square-foot rolls, consult your dealer about how many you need.

The repeating pattern in wallcovering also requires careful planning of where the covering job should start and end. Theoretically, you can start the first strip anywhere as long as the pattern lines up as you apply each strip. But it is often best to begin in an inconspicuous corner, say behind a door. That way any mismatch that comes when you try to align the pattern from the last sheet with the one from the first strip will be less noticeable.

Cutting Wallcovering

Because wallcovering comes in rolls, it must always be cut to fit the height of the wall. Always use sharp cutting tools. To cut a piece of wallcovering to length, add about 2 inches to the wall height to allow for overlap at the top and bottom. This lets you adjust a sheet to match the pattern. You will trim to fit exactly once it is on the wall.

Long cuts on wallcovering should be marked at both ends, measuring from the edge that will meet the piece already on the wall. Long cuts are usually made to fit the covering into corners.

USING WALLPAPER PASTE

project

These days most wallcoverings come prepasted. To install them, just dip the pieces in a tub of water to activate the adhesive; then hang them on the wall. However, some papers need paste applied to the back. Paste comes in two forms: a ready-mixed liquid and in a dry powder form that has to be mixed with water. The choice depends on personal preference. Experienced wallpaper hangers often pick the powered form so they can mix the paste to the consistency they like.

TOOLS & MATERIALS
▌ Pasting brush
▌ Clean, flat work table
▌ Wallpaper paste
▌ Wallpaper

1 Paste is available in premixed liquid form or in powder form that has to be mixed with water. If you mix your own, add the powder to the water, while stirring continuously, until the mix reaches a viscous consistency.

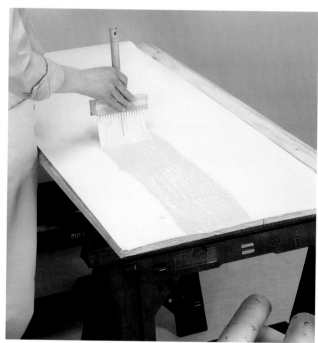

2 Roll the paper out onto a clean, flat worktable and spread the paste on the back side using a pasting brush. Start at the middle, and work toward both sides. The best way to keep most of the paste off the table is to align two edges of the paper with the edges of the table.

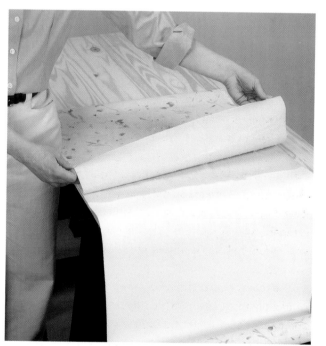

3 Fold the pasted section of the strip onto itself, a process that is called booking, and paste the remaining section of paper as shown in step 2. Take care when folding and moving the paper to avoid tearing it.

HANGING WALLPAPER

There are several common sense keys to successful wallpaper hanging. Work with a sharp utility knife; change the blade after just a couple of cuts. Try to keep your worktable clean and free of paste or adhesive. Make sure the outside of each strip of paper is cleaned with a damp sponge before you hang another piece in place. And handle the paper gently.

TOOLS & MATERIALS
- 48-inch level ▌Tape measure
- Utility knife with extra blades ▌Scissors
- Long straightedge ▌6-inch taping knife
- Smoothing brush ▌Sponge
- Seam roller ▌Seam adhesive
- Prepasted wallpaper
- Wallpaper trough

1 To establish a starting line, take a sample piece of the new paper and hold it against the wall with one end folded ½ in. past the inside corner. Mark where the straight end of the paper falls on the wall.

2 Use a 4-ft. level to mark a starting line on the wall. Draw the line from the floor to the ceiling, making sure that the line is exactly plumb along its entire length.

3 Cut a piece of prepasted paper to length; then roll it up loosely; and lower it into a tub of lukewarm water. Slowly pull the paper out of the tub, and spread it across a clean worktable. If you pull the paper out too quickly, the water may not have time to completely activate all the paste.

ABOVE Vinyl wallcoverings make a good choice for kitchen walls. There are numerous colors and patterns from which to choose, and the paper itself is easy to keep clean. Consider a complementary border treatment.

4 Fold the wet paper onto itself from both directions. This is called booking the paper and makes it easier to carry and install than trying to work with a long, unwieldy strip of wet paper.

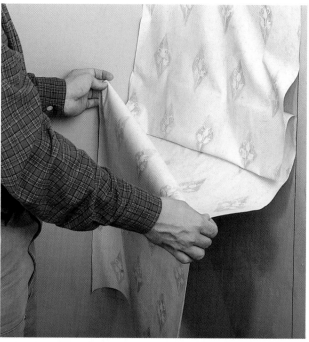

5 After the paper sets up according to the manufacturer's directions, carry it to the wall; peel away the top section; and press it against the wall. Make sure that one edge of the piece turns the corner slightly. Handle the paper carefully to avoid tearing it.

(continued on page 226)

(continued from page 225)

6 Align the strip with the plumb line that is drawn on the wall. Start the strip slightly away from the line, and gently push it over to the line. Leave excess paper at the top and bottom of the wall so that you can make the finished cuts.

7 Use a smoothing brush to remove any air bubbles from under the paper. Work from the center of the paper toward the edges in slow, firm strokes. But don't bear down so hard that you distort or tear the paper.

8 Trim the strip to length by first pressing a taping knife against the wall to create a sharp crease. Then cut along the edge of the knife using a sharp utility knife. Use the same technique to cut the top of the paper against the ceiling.

9 Hang the next strip on the wall, and make sure any pattern lines up properly. Keep in mind that the paste doesn't set up immediately. You have time to manipulate the paper, either to push it against the first strip or adjust the seam.

10 On pieces that overlap, use a sharp knife to cut through both strips at once. Discard the top piece; then lift the seam and pull out the other cut piece from underneath. Cutting both pieces like this creates a perfect seam.

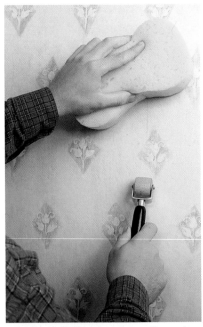

11 Roll the cut seams flat using a wallpaper roller. Use a damp sponge to wipe away any paste or adhesive from the surface. Also clean away any adhesive from the baseboard or the ceiling that may have rubbed off the paper.

PAPERING AROUND CORNERS

Corners, both inside and outside, are easy to paper. The only real trick is always drawing a new plumb line on the second wall. By hanging the first sheet on this wall so that it's plumb, and cutting the other side of it to match the piece that's already installed, all the ensuing pieces on the second wall will fit correctly, even if the corner itself is out of plumb.

TOOLS & MATERIALS
▌ 48-inch level ▌ Tape measure
▌ Long straightedge
▌ Utility knife with extra blades
▌ Scissors ▌ 6-inch taping knife
▌ Smoothing brush ▌ Sponge
▌ Seam roller ▌ Seam adhesive

PAPERING OUTSIDE CORNERS

FOR WRAPPING OUTSIDE CORNERS, FOLLOW THE SAME PROCEDURE YOU USED FOR INSIDE CORNERS, BUT ADD 1/2 INCH TO THE MEASUREMENT. PLACE THE PAPER IN POSITION, BUT BEFORE WRAPPING IT AROUND THE CORNER, MAKE SMALL SLITS IN THE WASTE PORTIONS OF THE PAPER NEAR THE CEILING AND THE BASEBOARD. THE CUTS WILL ALLOW YOU TO TURN THE CORNER WITHOUT WRINKLING OR TEARING THE PAPER. HANG THE REMAINDER OF THE CUT SHEET SO THAT IT OVERLAPS THE FIRST PORTION. IF THE CORNER IS OUT OF PLUMB, DRAW A NEW PLUMB LINE ON THE SECOND WALL OF THE CORNER, AND ALIGN THE STRIP WITH THAT FIRST.

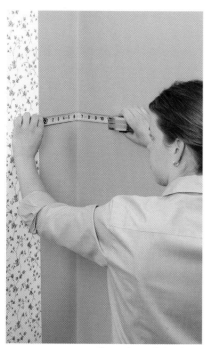

1 Measure to the edge of the last full sheet into the corner at the top, middle, and bottom of the wall. Cut the paper ⅛ in. wider than the widest measurement.

2 Hang the cut piece, and smooth it into place using a wallpaper brush. This piece should turn the corner slightly.

3 Draw a plumb line on the second wall that matches the width of the waste piece left when the first sheet was cut. Align this piece with the plumb line, and smooth it in place.

wallcovering options

ABOVE LEFT Wallcoverings enhance any room but work particularly well when used with simple cabinet designs and neutral finishes.

LEFT Bright colors provide a rich background when paired with white or neutral cabinets and appliances.

ABOVE LEFT Paper or paint? The pattern in the wallcovering complements the French country style.

ABOVE A painted finish is better suited for the casual feeling of this homey kitchen.

LEFT The formal feeling of this breakfast area is reflected in the wallcovering pattern and the floral border.

229

INSTALLING WOOD TRIM

The hardest part of installing wood trim is cutting the coped joints that are required where the trim meets an inside corner. A coping saw, with its thin blade, is the right tool for this job because it can easily follow a curved cut line. But getting used to the saw takes a little time. Most people who use these tools regularly install the blade with the teeth pointing toward the handle, so the cutting takes place on the pull stroke.

TOOLS & MATERIALS
▌ Molding ▌ Backsaw ▌ Combination square
▌ Miter box or power-miter saw
▌ Coping saw ▌ Utility knife or small chisel
▌ Round file and half-round files
▌ Power drill-driver and ⅟₁₆-inch bit
▌ Hammer and nail set ▌ Glue ▌ Sandpaper

1 Start installing the ceiling molding by pushing a full size piece into one corner. Nail the bottom edge into the wall studs and the top edge into the ceiling joists or blocking above. Set the nailheads below the surface, and fill the depressions with wood putty.

4 Once the coped cut is complete, use an assortment of files and rasps to clean up the cut. Test fit the coped cut periodically to check your progress. The first couple of joints will take a while, but later ones will move faster as your techniques improve.

5 When you are satisfied with the fit, spread glue on the coped cut, and push the coped board in place next to the uncoped board. Make sure the joint is tight; then nail the coped board to the wall and ceiling; set the nailheads; fill the depressions with putty; and sand the filler smooth.

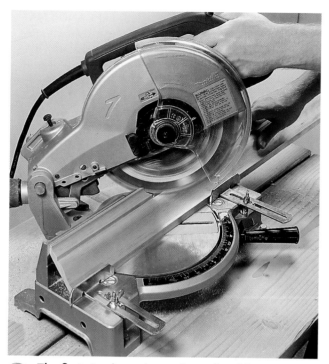

2 The first step in coping a piece of molding is to miter one end. Note how the board is installed in the miter box at a 45-deg. angle between the bottom and the fence.

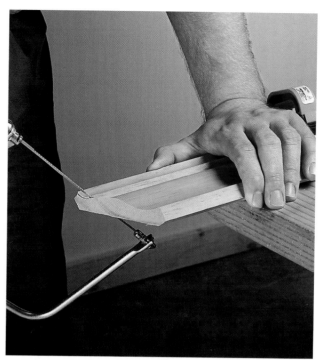

3 Use a coping saw to cut the molding profile along the mitered edge. Tip the saw toward the back of the board at about a 50-deg. angle, and follow the line formed by the miter and the outside surface of the board.

● UPGRADING BASE MOLDING

1.

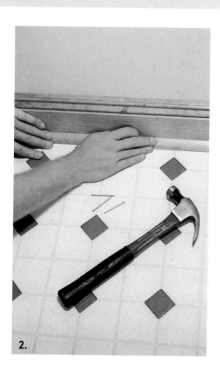

2.

To replace vinyl cove molding with real wood, first remove the vinyl. Insert a pry bar or screwdriver into the corner to peel a small section back. Once it is free and you can grip the vinyl, pull back as you work the pry bar behind the molding. Use a hand scraper to remove the old adhesive. Don't use chemical adhesive removers.

Attach the new molding to wall studs with finishing nails. Set the nails, and fill the holes with putty. You can install a simple one-piece molding or build up the profile with a decorative top bead and quarter-round installed along the floor.

trimwork options

FAR LEFT AND LEFT Define a style with the help of molding. The dentil molding at the far left and the decorative pilaster, left, set the tone for traditional kitchens.

BELOW The heavily carved crown molding complements these cabinets.

ABOVE Molding completes a room's design. The rope molding adds a distinctive touch to this cabinet.

RIGHT Top and bottom molding define this corner unit.

BELOW Baseboard molding protects and frames this half wall.

10 lifestyles

Today's kitchen is often the gathering place for family and friends, the spot where the kids do their homework, and your place to pay the bills, plan the family vacation, design a craft project, or have a heart-to-heart talk with a friend over a cup of coffee. All of that is in addition to the kitchen's traditional function as a place to prepare and serve food. This one room has become so important that prospective home buyers consider it a primary factor when shopping for a new home. But most homeowners undertake a kitchen remodeling project because their old kitchen does not suit the way they live or wish to live. In this chapter you will learn how to create the new kitchen—one that incorporates such homey touches as eating areas, snack bars, and a variety of special activity centers.

KITCHEN OPTIONS

The kitchen is a hot-ticket item in the real estate market today, and no wonder: more and more, family life is centered around this room. It's not unusual to find most of the family in the kitchen, even when they're not eating. It's the place to do homework, pay the bills, play games, and even entertain company.

The goal is to create a plan, using the latest design trends, that integrates the way you and your family actually live. A thoughtful look at your lifestyle will help you

discover whether you want the open design of a great room, which integrates areas for cooking, dining, and relaxing. If your approach is more formal, you may prefer the traditional arrangement that keeps the kitchen and its cooking clutter off-limits to dining and living areas. In this case, a small table or eating bar for casual family meals and snacks may suit you better.

Whether or not you go for the open-plan kitchen, you may still want to include activity centers in the remodeled kitchen's design. If you love to bake, sew, or create crafts, or you need a space to organize a home office,

ABOVE Open floor plans allow cooking and living areas to merge, creating an informal atmosphere.

ABOVE Connected spaces allow someone working in the kitchen to remain in contact with family or guests who are relaxing in the living area.

think of making a secondary work center part of the kitchen to accommodate one or more of these activities.

Whatever the scope of your new kitchen, be sure to incorporate barrier-free design elements. This simply means taking measures to make the space comfortably accessible to all who will need to use it, including those who walk, reach, and lean, or sit and wheel. Barrier-free design follows the same tenets as all good design: form follows function.

Great Rooms

Kitchens to live in have become popular in home design. The large rooms combine separate but open-to-one-an-

other spaces for cooking, dining, relaxing, and entertaining. Such spaces are often called great rooms. Families with young children, for example, will love a kitchen that is part of an open-room plan. This open design allows cooking parents to keep an eye on kids who may be watching TV.

Dinner guests tend to congregate here, too, because they like to stay in touch with the cook. This informal great-room arrangement suits casual contemporary lifestyles, as well as changing attitudes about food. For many families, cooking has evolved from a necessary chore to a creative event where everyone gets involved—guests as well as family.

ABOVE Room additions give you the chance to expand the kitchen work area and add extras, such as an eating area.

Getting Space

You can create a great room by building an addition to your home or by combining space from adjacent rooms. (See page 48.) If you choose the latter, make sure that you compensate for load-bearing walls you will remove, and be mindful of any other structural elements that may interfere with your design.

One benefit of combining two or more smaller spaces into one is that the sum of the parts is often greater than the whole. Not only is total floor space combined, so is light and ventilation. Traffic options and floor plans are opened up, too, and focal points such as worktables or counters can do multiple duty for different tasks.

When considering the floor plan, remember that the kitchen is the key element. Traffic must be diverted away from the work areas. One way to manage traffic is to incorporate an island or peninsula into the layout. An island will keep the kitchen open to other areas while closing off

the cooking zone to anyone who doesn't have to be there. A large island or peninsula with an eating bar also offers a handy place to set up a buffet, serve a snack, or let the kids do homework. An island also provides a convenient spot for guests to gather while dinner is in the works.

smart tip

IF A PENINSULA OR ISLAND SEPARATES THE KITCHEN WORK AREA FROM THE EATING OR LIVING AREA IN A GREAT ROOM, CONSIDER INSTALLING A 48-INCH-HIGH SNACK BAR ALONG THE DIVIDING LINE AND STANDARD HEIGHT COUNTERS EVERYWHERE ELSE. THE HIGH COUNTER WILL HELP KEEP DIRTY DISHES, POTS, AND PANS OUT OF SIGHT WHILE YOU ARE DINING.

Unifying Space

Because a great room is an open plan, you'll want a co-hesive decor to flow throughout the spaces. Coordinated fabrics and wallcoverings will help you do this, as will in-stalling the same flooring material throughout. Also, some manufacturers produce furniture-quality cabinet designs, as well as matching units to house media equip-ment, bookcases, desks, and the like, which can dress up the space with a custom-built appearance.

Even appliance manufacturers are great-room con-scious. When shopping for a typically noisy appliance, such as a dishwasher, range hood, or waste-disposal unit, ask about low-noise or noise-free models.

Lastly, take advantage of any scenic views you may have by installing lots of windows. If you have an adja-cent deck or patio, consider large patio doors.

RIGHT Peninsulas and islands help separate cooking centers from living areas.

BELOW Unify separate spaces by installing common finishes.

EATING AREAS

Most of us want a table or eating counter in the kitchen that's within easy reach of food-preparation and cleanup areas. If you live in a house that's more than 50 years old or in a newer "traditional" house, chances are you have a formal dining room that you rarely use. You may already have ideas about combining underused spaces like this to create one large room for cooking as well as enjoying meals.

Family Kitchen

The concept of the "heart of the home" or "family kitchen" recalls an earlier time when cooking was done over an open hearth and the entire family could gather to savor a good meal together. These days, removing the wall that separates a kitchen and dining room creates somewhat less than a great room but much more than a food prepa-ration laboratory. Though this kind of arrangement can make everyday meals especially convivial occasions, such togetherness may not be everyone's cup of tea.

If you do a lot of formal entertaining, prefer to be left alone while you cook, or just don't relish a meal served within sight of the pots and pans, consider pocket doors, sliding panels, or accordion-fold doors to close off the food-preparation area.

Table Talk

Your kitchen will need minimum clearances to accommo-date a table and chairs. In general, a family larger than five or six should look for sit-down space elsewhere. Still, you may want to provide an in-the-kitchen eating spot where you can serve snacks and off-hour meals to just a few people. In terms of dimensions, page 242 shows how to allocate the floor space you'll need for the furniture and for the people who sit around it.

ABOVE Formal dining areas are possible in great rooms. The area rug and chandelier create a defined area within the large open space.

LEFT Informal dining areas can consist of a table in the center of a room or a built-in table placed near dish and silverware storage.

BELOW Breakfast areas require nothing more than a table and lots of natural light.

SEATING ALLOWANCES

Because you must have room to sit down and get up, tables, chairs, and access room require a surprising amount of space. Figure on 12 to 15 square feet per person. A family of four will need at least 48 square feet of space for in-the-kitchen dining. To size a round table, figure that a 36-inch diameter table can seat four adults and a 48-incher will seat six. For a square or rectangular table, calculate 24 to 30 inches of table space for each person.

When planning space, you must pay attention to the distance between the table and any nearby walls and cabinets. A seated adult occupies a depth of about 20 inches from the edge of the table, but requires 12 to 16 inches more to pull back the chair and rise. This means you'll need about 36 inches of clearance between the wall and the edge of the table. You can get away with a minimum 28-inch clearance if you place chairs at angles to the wall. On any serving side, plan a 44-inch clearance to allow room to pass.

Also, as you plan a spot for your table, make sure that it doesn't intrude into the kitchen's work areas or interfere with traffic routes. Don't put the eating area too far away, however. The closer you are to cooking and cleanup centers, the easier serving and clearing will be.

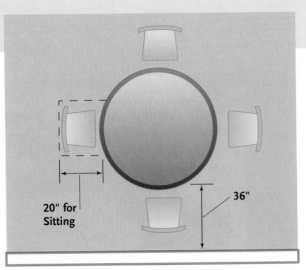

Allow space for diners to rise and sit down comfortably. Typical seating and push-back space is 36 in.

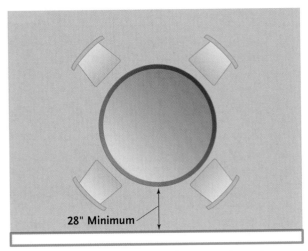

Gain space by arranging chairs at an angle to the wall. Here, seating and push-back space is only 28 in.

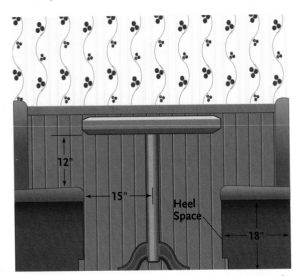

Booths save space. Be sure to leave a minimum of 12 in. between the bench and table for sliding room.

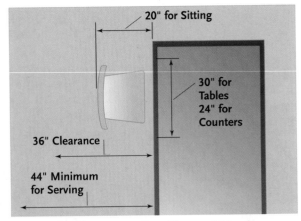

Required table space varies. Plan on 30 in. for a formal dining table and 24 in. at a counter.

Booths

Not enough room for a table and chairs? Take a tip from diners and restaurants, and plan a booth with bench or banquette seating. Booths conserve floor space because you don't need to slide chairs back. And if you box in the benches, provide heel space, and attach flip-up seats, you gain valuable storage for linens and other table items.

A kitchen alcove or bay window is a natural place for a booth, or you can back one up to an island, peninsula, or wall. Also, you can construct seating units with backs that are high enough to serve as walls of their own.

Plan 24 inches of table space for each person, with at least 15 inches of knee space underneath. This means that a family of four needs a table that's 48 inches long and 30 inches across. Because you slide into and out of a booth, the table can overhang the benches by 3 or 4 inches. Total floor space required for a four-person booth, then, would measure only 5 feet across, compared with a minimum of about 9 feet for a round or square table with chairs. (See the illustration on page 242.)

BELOW Gain storage space by installing booth seating with flip-up seats. Use the space to store table linens.

Counters

If you're planning to incorporate a peninsula or island in your new kitchen, you're probably already eyeing its potential as a counter for serving quick meals or snacks. What dimensions do you need for a good fit?

First, how many people do you hope to seat? Remember, each adult requires 24 inches of table space. This means a counter that's 72 inches long can accommodate three stools at most.

How high the top of the counter should be depends on the kind of seating you prefer. A 28- to 30-inch-high counter requires 18-inch-high chairs with 20 inches of knee space. If you make the counter the same height as any others in the kitchen (standard 36 inches), you'll need 24-inch-high stools and 14 inches of knee space. Go up to bar height—42 to 45 inches—and you'll need 30-inch-high stools with footrests.

One problem with snack bars is that everyone faces in the same direction making conversation difficult. Dining at a counter may be fine for breakfast or a quick lunch on the run, but you'll want a table for more sociable meals like dinner. Another problem is orientation. A counter that faces a blank wall is undesirable as an eating place, so try to orient yours facing into the kitchen or out a window.

ABOVE Place eating counters outside of the main work area of the kitchen but close enough to retain contact with the cook.

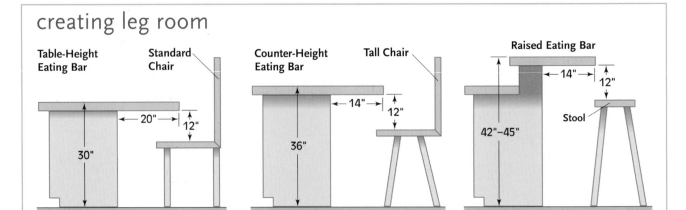

creating leg room

Table-Height Eating Bar — Standard Chair — 20" — 12" — 30"

Counter-Height Eating Bar — Tall Chair — 14" — 12" — 36"

Raised Eating Bar — 14" — 12" — Stool — 42"–45"

Based on the height of the eating surface, people sitting at standard-height tables need about 20 in. of space; those at higher counters require 14 in. Chair and stool heights range from 18 in. to about 30 in.

SECONDARY WORK CENTERS

If your new kitchen will be the hub of the household, it's going to be more than a place to cook and eat a meal. Depending on your family's needs, habits, and hobbies, you may want to incorporate a home office, gardening center, laundry, baking center, sewing and craft area, or entertainment bar into your design. Sometimes a corner or spare countertop will suffice.

Home Office

A desk-height surface with knee space provides a place in the kitchen to draw up lists, make phone calls, pay bills, leave messages for family members, look up recipes, and organize home management in dozens of other ways. This kind of planning center easily expands into a home office that can be used to do homework or run a cottage industry when you add a computer, printer, fax, and answering machine.

ABOVE Kitchen offices need not be large. The small work area above provides adequate space for making lists.

LEFT The larger space at left is big enough for a homework area or a convenient spot to pay bills.

Whether the space is as modest as a small countertop and a shelf for cookbooks or a complete work station with a full-size desk, file cabinets, and electronic equipment, decide on a spot early in the planning stage so that you can run any electric, telephone, and intercom wiring you need. Situate the area outside the kitchen's main work area, and provide adequate lighting for the kinds of activities you'll be doing there.

You may want to locate other electronic components in the office space, too. Your home's "command central"

can be as sophisticated as you can afford: it may include an intercom; a security system with separate controls for window, door, and smoke alarms; a programmable thermostat; timers; TV, DVD, and stereo equipment; and perhaps a closed-circuit-TV system for monitoring children's play areas.

Baking Center

Serious cooks, especially those who enjoy baking, will appreciate a well-appointed baking/mixing center. Allocate at least 36 inches of counter space near the oven or refrigerator—ideally between the two. To make mixing and kneading less tiring, drop the counter height 6 or 7 inches by using 30- or 32-inch-high base cabinets. Plan a countertop that is extra deep, too—30 inches or more—to provide plenty of room for rolling out dough. The surface should be heat- and moisture-proof.

A countertop made of smooth stone will provide a cool surface that keeps rolled-out dough from sticking, but a smooth laminate will work, too. You'll also want counter space for setting up a mixer or blender, laying out ingredients, and loading cookie sheets or baking pans on a cooling rack. Include good fluorescent under-cabinet lighting, so you're not working in your own shadow.

Give special thought to where you want the mixer. Some manufacturers offer mixer platforms that rise up out of a base cabinet, eliminating the need for awkward tugging and lifting to reach or replace the appliance before and after use. In addition, you'll want to keep small tools within hand's reach. Provide enough places to store the rolling pin, mixing bowls, and flour sifter, as well as cake, pie, muffin, and bread tins. Extra-deep cabinet drawers are handy for this use, as are carousel or slide-out trays. Items like cookie sheets and rectangular cake tins are best stored on edge in vertical compartments so that you don't have to stack them.

Lastly, consider all of the ingredients you want to keep on hand. Large pullout or tip-out bins are ideal for flour and sugar. Smaller containers can hold baking powder, nuts, raisins, vanilla, chocolate, and other spices and decorations.

TOP Drawer units, bookcases, and the like that match kitchen cabinets are available from a number of manufacturers.

LEFT Table-height surfaces are more convenient for kneading and rolling out dough than standard counters.

GARDENING CENTER

If you're an avid gardener, what better place to nurture new or ailing plants than a sunny kitchen window or greenhouse window unit? A full-scale kitchen gardening center might include an easy-to-clean counter for cutting and arranging flowers, starting seeds, and potting plants; a separate deep utility sink; a faucet attachment for watering; grow lights; and storage for pots, soil, plant food, and other supplies. Your center could also be as simple as a deep window sill surfaced with ceramic tile to stand up to water, or as extensive as an entire light-filled area dedicated to gardening.

Gardening centers require a waterproof surface for cutting and arranging flowers, and potting plants.

Laundry

If your current laundry facilities are in the basement, finding a place for a washer and dryer near your remodeled kitchen will save a lot of steps. There are a number of design criteria to keep in mind for a laundry center. A side-by-side pair of full-size appliances measures 48 to 58 inches wide. To conserve floor space you might consider stackable laundry machines, which are about half as wide as conventional machines but usually have smaller tubs. Full-size units are also 42 or 43 inches high, which is 6 to 7 inches taller than standard kitchen counter height, so you can't run a countertop over them. And because standard-size washers are usually top-loading, you can't put a dryer or cabinet above them.

If you want to fit laundry appliances under a counter, consider installing a set of front-loading stackable units side by side. The convenience of being able to do laundry while cooking dinner may more than compensate for

smart tip

PLAN FOR A BUILT-IN IRONING BOARD NEAR THE LAUNDRY AREA. IRONING-BOARD KITS COME IN CABINETS THAT ARE SURFACE-MOUNTED TO THE WALL OR FIT BETWEEN STUDS. MOST INCLUDE A BUILT-IN ELECTRICAL OUTLET.

LEFT Laundry areas placed near the kitchen can share some of the same finishes used in the main cooking area. A well-equipped laundry includes a counter for folding and sorting clothes, a sink, hanging rack, and cabinets for storage.

their smaller capacities. If you have a two-bowl sink, you can reserve one side for laundry when necessary. Don't forget a cabinet for storing detergent, fabric softener, and any other laundry supplies.

Sewing and Crafts

A few cupboards and drawers positioned well outside the work triangle near a peninsula, island, or table make an excellent station for sewing or crafting. A roll-top counter appliance garage with an electrical outlet might be just the thing to store a portable sewing machine so that you don't have to lift it onto a counter. Depending on the overall feeling in your kitchen, you might even keep some materials, such as dried flowers, raffia bows, or spools of thread, on open shelves or pegs so that they are available for a quick mend or a moment of inspiration.

Entertainment Bar

People who entertain a lot, especially in a great-room kitchen, will appreciate an area well stocked with glassware and equipped with trays and plates suitable for serving hors d'oeuvres and desserts. An area such as this can be quite simple: a short length of counter and cabinets, for example. However, a bar sink, a second dishwasher, an auxiliary refrigerator, and a warming drawer are helpful in this setting to keep pre- and post-meal clutter away from the main preparation and cleanup areas of the kitchen.

TOP A place to relax, such as a window seat, isn't a work center but it can be an important part of a new kitchen.

RIGHT Site entertainment bars near the living area but out of the way of anyone working in the kitchen.

SAFETY CONSIDERATIONS

More building codes govern the kitchen than any other room in the house. That's because so many accidents occur there. With that in mind, safety should reign as a primary factor in any kitchen remodel. The goal should be to lessen the chance of injury while increasing the performance of the room's layout, materials, fixtures, and appliances.

Take the following steps when designing for safety. And remember: you don't have to be very young or very old to suffer an injury in the kitchen. One of the most common Sunday morning hospital emergency room visits is by someone who has sliced open a hand while cutting a bagel.

Use Proper Lighting. Never work in a dim space. Good general lighting, supplemented with proper task lighting clearly focused on a work surface, without glare or harsh shadows, can vastly decrease your chance of injury while preparing a meal. In addition, good lighting should be adaptable to meet the needs of younger, as well as older, eyes.

Use Slip-Resistant Flooring. Falling with a hot casserole or sharp knife in your hand can have serious consequences. Choose a slip-resistant material for your floor, such as matte-finished wood or laminate, textured vinyl, or a soft-glazed ceramic tile indicated specifically for flooring. If you select tile, it helps to use a throw rug with a nonskid backing—especially around areas that get wet. Remember to inquire about the slip-resistance rating of any flooring material you may be considering for your new kitchen.

Keep a Fire Extinguisher Handy. A grease fire in the kitchen can spread rapidly. That's why it's so important to have a fire extinguisher within arm's reach of the ovens and cooktop. For maximum protection, there should be at least two extinguishers in any kitchen—one located in the cooking area and one stored in another part of the room. You want them to be handy; however,

BELOW Good lighting will help prevent accidents. Be sure your new kitchen has adequate general and task lighting.

smart tip

THE WORD *PASS* IS AN EASY WAY TO
REMEMBER THE PROPER WAY TO USE A
FIRE EXTINGUISHER.

*P*ULL THE PIN AT THE TOP OF THE
EXTINGUISHER THAT KEEPS THE HANDLE
FROM BEING ACCIDENTALLY PRESSED.

*A*IM THE NOZZLE OF THE EXTINGUISHER
TOWARD THE BASE OF THE FIRE.

*S*QUEEZE THE HANDLE TO DISCHARGE
THE EXTINGUISHER. STAND APPROXI-
MATELY 8 FEET AWAY FROM THE FIRE.

*S*WEEP THE NOZZLE BACK AND FORTH
AT THE BASE OF THE FIRE. AFTER THE FIRE
APPEARS TO BE OUT, WATCH IT CAREFULLY
BECAUSE IT MAY REIGNITE!

LEFT Create safe cooking areas. This cooktop has slightly staggered burners and all of the controls are in the front, making for a safe unit.

LEFT Well-organized storage not only makes the kitchen efficient, it helps make it a safe place to work as well.

you don't want fire extinguishers to fall into the hands of children. Install them high enough so that they are out of reach of curious youngsters.

Install GFCIs. Water and electricity don't mix. Make sure every electrical receptacle is grounded and protected with ground-fault circuit interrupters. These devices cut electrical current if there is a power surge or if moisture is present. Most building codes require them in any room where there is plumbing to protect homeowners against electrical shock.

Consider Lock-Out Options. New smart-home technology allows you to lock your range and ovens so that no one can use them while you are out of the house. The simple lock-out device can prevent burns, fires, or worse. You can choose between lock-out covers or a programmed lock-out system. Or you can install timers on all appliances you don't want in use when you can't supervise the cooking.

You might also consider designating one wall cabinet for storing cleansers and other toxic substances—drain cleaner, for example. Include a lock on the cabinet, and keep the key in a safe place.

Regulate Water Temperature. Install faucets with anti-scald devices. These units prevent temperatures from rising above preset limits. Another option is a programmable faucet that "remembers" temperature settings.

Design a Safe Cooktop. How many times have you been scalded reaching over a pot of boiling water or a hot element? Avoid this dangerous situation by selecting

staggered burners for your cooktop, or one straight row of burners.

If you can't find single burners, turn modular two-burner units sideways, placing them parallel with the front of the countertop. Never choose a unit with controls at the rear of the cooktop; controls should be along the side or in front.

Use Space Efficiently and Safely. You can have all the space in the world and still put family members in compromising situations. Avoid swinging doors. When placing appliances, think about how the traffic area will be affected when a door is open. Locate ovens and the microwave at a comfortable height that doesn't necessitate reaching in order to retrieve hot food. Make use of cabinet accessories to keep stored items organized and easy to reach.

Avoid sharp corners, especially at the end of a run of cabinetry or on the island or peninsula. If space is tight and you can't rearrange most elements, install a rounded end cabinet and choose a countertop material that will allow a bullnose edge.

UNIVERSAL DESIGN

Universal design addresses the needs of multigenerational households and people with special needs. As Baby Boomers bring home their aging parents while raising families of their own, it is not uncommon to have young children and grandparents living under one roof. Indeed, as our population ages it benefits everyone to think about ways to make the kitchen functional—and safe—for every member of the family. This section addresses all of these concerns.

Incorporating universal design into your remodeling is always smart, particularly if you plan to stay in your house as you grow older. Analyze your lifestyle and your family's needs now—and what you anticipate them to be in the future. Do you have young children? Do you expect to have an elderly parent living with you? Will you remain in the house after you retire? Planning to include some universal-design features in your new kitchen now will save you money later on, because it's more expensive to make changes to an existing plan.

According to the National Kitchen and Bath Association (NKBA), one of the most practical universal-design elements you can include is the installation of counters at varying heights, which allows you to perform some tasks (slicing vegetables, for example) while seated and others (such as rolling-out dough) while standing straight, not bending. Another idea that makes sense for any kitchen is a pullout counter near the cooktop and another at the oven. They provide handy landing places for hot pots, pans, and dishes.

Designs for Everyone

Some items to incorporate in your design include appliances with digital displays, which are easier to read and fairly standard on today's appliances; placing wall-mounted outlets and switches at the universal reach range of 15 and 42 inches from the floor; reserving a base cabinet for storing dishes, making dinnerware easier to reach; installing wrist-blade-style faucets that don't require grabbing or twisting; and buying a side-by-side style refrigerator, which places most foods at accessible heights. Compact work areas eliminate wasted steps.

It might also be worthwhile to investigate some of the smart-home technology available. This includes devices that allow you to call home from any phone to turn on the lights, heat the oven, raise the thermostat, or program dinner to start cooking. Of course, this sophisticated technology is expensive and may be more practical for new construction; some things are too complicated to retrofit into an existing home.

It seems that new technological advances are brought to the marketplace almost every week. The key is to look at universally designed features and match them to your home and situation. Don't forget: the goal is to make your life easier—and safer. If adding any of these features will destroy your budget or drastically change your concept of the room, don't use them, but be sure to retain any features that can save your family pain or injury.

LEFT Counter heights should suit those who work in the kitchen. This raised dishwasher makes loading and unloading easy.

Accessible Design

Accessible design normally means that a home—or in this case a kitchen—is barrier free. It also indicates that the room complies with design guidelines for disabled people found in government regulations such as the American National Standards Institute's A117.1 (ANSI A117.1-1986). There are a number of guidelines governing accessible design. Their goal is to provide design criteria for someone who uses a wheelchair to get around.

If a disabled person in your family will use the new kitchen, design appropriate clearances. A standard wheelchair occupies 10 square feet and has a turning diameter of 5 feet. Doorways must be at least 32 inches wide, and aisles must be a minimum of 42 inches wide, according to the NKBA.

A lowered cooktop with an angled nonfogging mirror installed above the surface lets someone seated see what's cooking. If you don't like the look of an open space below the cooktop, install retractable doors that open to accommodate the wheelchair and close for a finished look. Induction cooktops feature automatic shutoffs and cool-to-the-touch cooking surfaces, and they are easy to keep clean.

Low, shallow base cabinets outfitted with pullout and slide-out bins and trays, carousel shelves, and lazy Susans maximize accessibility, as do lower counter heights—30 to 31½ inches as opposed to the standard 36 inches. Light-colored countertops with a contrasting edge treatment that clearly defines where the surface ends are recommended for people with impaired vision.

Many American cabinet manufacturers have introduced a line of specially designed cabinets and accessories that accommodate everyone in the family, including those with special needs.

You might also want to consider having a second microwave near the kitchen table. The cabinet you choose to house it should have a drop-down door strong enough to hold hot dishes.

ABOVE Provide leg room for those who work at counters while seated. Note the opening next to the small sink.

KITCHEN DESIGN GUIDELINES

Here are some guidelines for making your kitchen efficient and functional under any circumstances:

▌ Design a floor plan that incorporates wide aisles (at least 42 inches) around the work area. Also, plan 60-inch-diameter turning circles at strategic places.

▌ Make doorways a minimum of 32 inches wide to accommodate wheelchairs and walkers. Avoid swinging doors and specify pocket or sliding types whenever possible. If you must use swinging doors, levers are easier to use than doorknobs.

▌ Plan lots of counter space near the food-preparation and cleanup areas. This space will allow the quick release of hands from heavy pots and objects.

▌ Install a variety of counter heights in addition to the standard 36 inches to serve different needs. A 32-inch-high counter with leg room below provides workspace for someone in a wheelchair and can serve double duty as a baking center, which calls for the same height. A 42-inch-high eating bar can provide a place for a person with back pain to work without bending over. Another flexible counter option is a slide-out surface, similar to a breadboard, with reinforced tracks capable of bearing extra weight.

▌ Install wall cabinets lower on the wall and with shallow shelves so that they can be reached easily by most people.

▌ Equip base cabinets with convenient pullout bins

Pullout cutting boards provide more work surface, and they are at a convenient height for someone in a wheelchair.

Contrasting colors along the edges of counters and tables help make these areas visible to those who have poor eyesight.

and swivel trays. Mixer platforms that rise up out of a base cabinet can be used for any heavy item.

▌ Make sure that electrical outlets and TV and phone jacks are no less than 15 inches from the floor. Light switches should be 42 inches from the floor—6 inches lower on the wall than standard installations.

▌ Try out the controls and knobs when shopping for appliances to ensure easy manipulation. Labels should be easy to read.

▌ If possible, buy cooking units with front-mounted knobs, which are easier to reach. However, they may be unsafe for use where there are young children.

▌ Be sure the cooktop has staggered burners, allowing the cook to gain access to the back without reaching over hot pots in the front.

▌ Install wall ovens and cooktops at heights geared to the specific needs of the cooks in your kitchen. Also, there are special 30-inch-high slide-in ranges that are designed for use by someone in a wheelchair but are convenient for anyone to use.

▌ As for a refrigerator, choose a side-by-side model for universal access, or use a modular unit that allows custom placement of individual units at locations most suited to specific workers and their tasks.

▌ Install a single-lever faucet with a programmed temperature-control valve. These faucets are easy to use and protect against scalding.

▌ Attach brass rails below the edge of the countertop to serve as grab bars. Grab bars should be 1½ inches in diameter.

KNEE SPACE

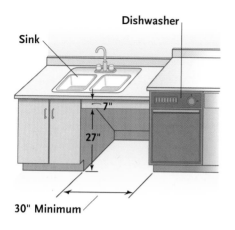

Sink

Dishwasher

7"

27"

30" Minimum

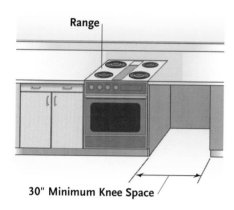

Range

30" Minimum Knee Space

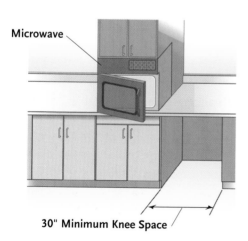

Microwave

30" Minimum Knee Space

Adequate knee space is a basic criterion for universal design. If providing leg room under a sink, be sure to cover pipes to protect users from burns. Openings next to ranges, dishwashers, and microwaves make these appliances accessible to everyone.

ABOVE Drawer storage makes retrieving pots and pans easy for someone in a wheelchair. Storing items where you use them is the most efficient type of storage.

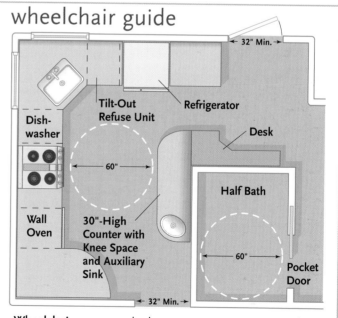

wheelchair guide

32" Min.

Tilt-Out Refuse Unit

Refrigerator

Dish-washer

Desk

60"

Half Bath

Wall Oven

30"-High Counter with Knee Space and Auxiliary Sink

60"

Pocket Door

32" Min.

Wheelchair users need adequate space to turn around, lower-than-normal counters, and leg room under fixtures and appliances.

11 money matters

The dreams you have for your new kitchen can quickly disappear when it comes time to sit down and add up the price of new cabinets, appliances, fixtures, and other materials. For a large project such as a kitchen remodeling, there are a number of financing options available. Sometimes, financing a new kitchen is simply a matter of compromise, knowing what you need and choosing to wait for what you'd like.

Believe it or not, professional advice from an architect or certified kitchen designer can help trim the fat from the tab, too. These trained professionals know more than one way to solve a problem. A contractor can also help you save money by suggesting economical shortcuts or alternatives in building techniques and materials.

CREATING A BUDGET

Kitchen remodeling costs can run from a few thousand dollars to a hundred thousand or more. Where your project falls in this broad spectrum depends on the most basic question: how much can you afford?

A major kitchen remodeling is one of the better home improvement investments. At the time of resale, it can return 75 to 90 percent of the amount invested. But you should also consider how much you want to spend in relation to the total value of your home. Budget advisers suggest that this figure should be no more than about 10 to 15 percent.

Allocating Costs

Before you solicit bids from architects or contractors, you should determine a preliminary budget. After you've worked out a rough plan, visit several kitchen showrooms in your area. Choose some cabinet styles you like, and ask the dealer to give you a ballpark figure for what you have in mind. Then go to appliance and plumbing suppliers. Choose two or three models of each piece of equipment you'll need, and jot down the price and list of features each model has. At a building-supply dealer, do the same for flooring and countertop materials, as well as any windows, doors, and skylights you'd like. A visit to an electrical supplier and a lighting showroom will give you an idea of those costs.

Next, make up lists of various possible equipment combinations and the prices. Add up the totals. Double each estimate to account for additional materials and labor if someone will be doing all or part of the work for you, and you'll have an approximation of what the project will cost.

Getting Bids

Once you have a rough estimate that falls within your budget, you're ready to proceed with soliciting bids. This can only be done when you, an architect, or a kitchen designer have prepared final building plans.

Request bids from at least two but preferably three contractors to get the best possible price. Provide each bidder with a complete set of plans. You can expect to wait two to four weeks to receive your bids. A contractor needs to assess the project properly, based on plans, to draw up all anticipated costs.

The usual method of bidding on remodel-

LEFT Estimating costs for a kitchen makeover can be tricky. Collect estimates from material suppliers before soliciting bids.

ABOVE Sources of financing for a kitchen remodel like this include personal savings, loans, and the equity in your house.

ing projects and new construction is fixed-price bidding, rather than cost-plus estimates. With a fixed-price bid, the contractor studies your construction plans, estimates the costs to do the work, adds in his overhead and profit, and comes up with a price for the job.

Once the contract is signed, the contractor is obligated to perform the work specified in the contract for the agreed-on sum. If, however, you decide to make changes after you have signed the contract, then the contractor is given a chance to adjust the final price. Stay away from cost-plus estimates, where you agree to pay the contractor any costs he incurs plus a profit margin. That kind of estimate is too open-ended for a large project like a complete kitchen renovation.

You may receive widely varying bids. The most expensive does not guarantee the best work. That contractor may have high overhead, or the job may come at a busy time, which may involve hiring extra workers or paying overtime. Conversely, a low bid could be submitted by someone who needs the work at the moment or who will do some of the work personally. If you feel that a bid is out of line, ask the contractor for a reason. Often, relatively small changes in your design or requirements can produce significant savings.

FINANCING YOUR PROJECT

Many families can't afford to pay cash for a major remodeling. If you've lived in your home for a number of years, the money for a new kitchen could come from the equity you've built up as a result of appreciation and mortgage amortization. Refinancing an old mortgage spreads the cost over 15 to 30 years—and the interest on the mortgage is tax deductible.

Personal and home-equity loans are two other sources of cash. Shop carefully for interest rates. Home-equity loans are generally based on the equity you've built in your house. They typically have lower interest rates and longer terms than personal loans. There are two types: home-equity lines of credit and lump-sum loans. With a line of credit, you receive—and pay interest on— the money you use. The advantage of a line of credit is that you can draw money gradually, and pay for the project as it proceeds. As its name implies, a lump-sum loan is disbursed in its entirety at one time, so you start paying interest on the whole principal from day one.

WORKING WITH PROFESSIONALS

There are many options for implementing your design ideas. You could hire designers and contractors to do all of the work for you. Or you could do all or part of the work yourself. But even if you plan on doing much of the work, you may still need the services of professionals. Some communities insist that registered architects draw up the plans for major renovations or additions.

Architects

An architect's job is to prepare floor plans and specifications for the construction phase. You can also hire an architect to supervise the entire job, from planning through construction. When hiring an architect, you'll sign a contract that sets forth the services to be performed and the fees to be paid. If you've hired your architect to work on your project from start to finish, expect to pay somewhere between 10 and 20 percent of the total construction cost. Architects charge a flat fee for preparing floor plans and working drawings.

Kitchen Designers

Kitchen designers plan out the functional details of a kitchen and often work in conjunction with cabinet dealers or design-and-build firms. If you plan to purchase your cabinets from one of these sources, the design fee will be included in the price of the cabinetry package. If you plan to buy the cabinets from another source, you can negotiate a flat fee with a designer for just the design work.

When choosing a kitchen designer, look for the initials CKD after his or her name. These letters indicate that the designer has been tested and certified by the National Kitchen and Bath Association (NKBA).

Contractors

When it comes time to start construction, you'll have to decide who's going to do the work. You can hire a general contractor, who will take the entire job from start to finish. Or you can hire individual contractors, such as a plumber, an electrician, a carpenter, and the like, to do separate parts of the job until the kitchen is done.

General Contractors. A general contractor takes responsibility for all construction phases of your job. He or she will supply the labor and materials, schedule and coordinate the various trades, contract with and pay sub-

ABOVE Planning and organization lead to a well-run project that produces the kind of results you want.

contractors, obtain any necessary building permits, arrange for required inspections at different stages of the work, and generally see that your plan is brought to fruition.

Ask for bids from several contractors. (Three is a good number.) Be sure you give them all the same information to work with if you want to compare their quotes legitimately.

Be certain that the contractor you choose is an established member of the business community in your area. Ask for references. Find out whether they were satisfied with the contractor's performance in terms of both quality and schedule. You'll also want to know that your contractor is in good financial shape, because any default on materials or subcontractor payments may end up as a lien on your home. Talk to local building trade suppliers (lumberyards, concrete companies) to find out whether your contractor has a good reputation within the industry. You can also check with the local Better Business Bureau or Chamber of Commerce to see whether there are customer complaints on file.

Subcontractors. If you hire a general contractor, he or she will hire and manage the subcontractors, who are members of individual trades. If you act as your own contractor, you must hire, schedule, and supervise the subs.

Doing It Yourself

If you decide to do some of the work yourself, plan on working at the beginning or end of the construction process. This way you can move at your own pace without holding up the subcontractors you've hired, which could increase the expense. For instance, do some of the demolition work, such as removing old cabinets and appliances, or some of the preparatory work, such as installing and taping drywall. Finishing work you should consider might include painting and wallpapering, staining, or laying down vinyl tiles. Even some new kinds of hardwood flooring are designed for do-it-yourself installation.

If something is beyond your reach, either due to lack of funds or lack of experience, put it off until you can handle it. Try to remodel the kitchen in stages. The project will take less of a bite out of your pocket this way, and in the end you'll get the results you really want.

● WHAT EVERY CONTRACT SHOULD CONTAIN

You have the right to a specific and binding contract. The more detailed, the better. Get specifics on every part of the project and on every product purchased. It is the details that will save you in the long run. Every contract should include basic items, such as:

- The contractor's name and proper company name, as listed on the business license
- The company's address, telephone and fax number
- The company's contractor license number if applicable (Some states don't require contractor licensing. If this is the case, find out the company's business license and verify it.)
- Details of what the contractor will and will not do during the project, such as daily cleanup around the site, final cleanup, security measures to be taken during the demolition phase, and so on
- A detailed list of all materials and products to be used, including the size, color, model, and brand name of every specific product (If you have written specifications, you'll need two signatures to change them—yours and the contractor's.)
- The approximate start and completion dates of the project (You might ask for estimated completion dates for various stages; for example, one-third, halfway, and two-thirds through the process.)
- Your signature required on all plans before work begins (This prevents last-minute surprises.)
- Notification of your right of recision
- Procedures for handling changes in the scope of the work during the course of the project (Change orders should require both your signature and the contractor's.)
- A listing and full description of warranties that cover materials and workmanship for the entire project
- A binding arbitration clause in case of a disagreement (Arbitration enables both parties to resolve disputes quickly and effectively without litigation.)
- A provision for the contractor's statements and waivers of liens to be provided to you prior to final payment

Include anything else that needs to be spelled out clearly. Remember: if it isn't in writing, it does not exist legally.

This list of manufacturers and associations is meant to be a general guide to additional industry and product-related sources. It is not intended as a listing of products and manufacturers represented by the photographs in this book.

Andersen Corporation
100 Fourth Ave. North
Bayport, MN 55003-1096
888-888-7020
www.andersencorp.com
The Andersen Corporation is a major window manufacturer that offers a full range of residential window and skylight sizes and styles.

Armstrong World Industries
Attn: Customer Response Center
P.O. Box 3001
Lancaster, PA 17604
800-233-3823
www.armstrong.com
Armstrong World Industries is a manufacturer of cabinets, flooring, and ceiling materials.

Faber
P.O. Box 435
Wayland, MA 01778
508-358-5353
www.faberonline.com
Faber specializes in range hoods in many shapes and sizes. The company offers information on selecting and sizing ventilation systems.

Frigidaire
P.O. Box 212378
Martinez, GA 30917
800-374-4432
www.frigidaire.com
Frigidaire is a manufacturer of many home appliances, including ranges, cooktops, range hoods, dishwashers, washers, and dryers.

General Electric
GE Customer Relations
P.O. Box 22108
Memphis, TN 38122
800-626-2000
www.geappliances.com
General Electric produces a wide variety of appliances, including refrigerators, dishwashers, and ovens.

Jenn-Air
Maytag Customer Service
240 Edwards St.
Cleveland, TN 37311
800-688-1100
www.jennair.com
Jenn-Air is a part of the Maytag Corporation that offers a wide range of kitchen appliances.

Kohler
444 Highland Dr.
Kohler, Wisconsin 53044
920-457-4441 x 77839
www.kohlerco.com
Kohler is a major manufacturer of kitchen and bath fixtures. They offer a wide variety of kitchen sinks, faucets, and kitchen accessories.

KraftMaid Cabinetry, Inc.
P.O. Box 1055
Middlefield, OH 44062
888-562-7744
www.kraftmaid.com
Kraftmaid Cabinetry manufactures an extensive line of built-to-order cabinets. The company offers a variety of finishes and storage options.

National Association of Remodeling Industry(NARI)
780 Lee St., Ste. 200
Des Plaines, IL 60016
800-611-6274
www.nari.org
NARI offers homeowners help in selecting and working with professional remodeling contractors.

National Kitchen and Bath Association (NKBA)
687 Willow Grove St.
Hackettstown, NJ 07840
www.nkba.org
800-843-6522
NKBA, a national trade organization, offers remodeling information to professionals and homeowners.

Rejuvenation
Sales and Service
2550 NW Nicolai St.
Portland, OR 97210
888-401-1900
www.rejuvenation.com
Rejuvenation is a manufacturer of lighting fixtures that range from vintage to modern designs.

Sears Cabinet Refacing
Sears National Customer Relations
3333 Beverly Rd.
Hoffman Estates, IL 60179
800-469-4663
www.sears.com
Sears Home Service division provides cabinet refacing and other contractor services for the entire house.

Sub-Zero Freezer Company
P.O. Box 44130
Madison, WI 53744-4130
800-222-7820
www.subzero.com
Sub-Zero makes built-in refrigerators and freezers for both home and industrial use. They are available in many different styles.

Thermador
5551 McFadden Ave.
Huntington Beach, CA 92649
800-656-9226
www.thermador.com
Thermador offers a broad line of kitchen appliances, including built-in ovens, electric and gas cooktops, and traditional ranges.

Tile Council of America, Inc.
100 Clemson Research Blvd.
Anderson, SC 29625
864-646-8453
www.tileusa.com
TCA is committed to improving the tile-installation industry. They offer literature on selecting and installing tile.

Velux-America, Inc.
450 Old Brickyard Rd.
P.O. Box 5001
Greenwood, SC 29648
800-888-3589
www.velux.com
Velux is an international manufacturer of skylights, roof windows, and solar energy systems.

Wellborn Cabinet, Inc.
P.O. Box 1210
Ashland, AL 36251
1-800-366-8040
www.wellborn.com
Wellborn Cabinet sells a wide variety of kitchen, bath, and entertainment cabinetry in a variety of styles, finishes, and price ranges.

Wilsonart International
P.O. Box 6110
Temple, TX 76503-6110
800-433-3222
www.wilsonart.com
Wilsonart is a manufacturer of solid-surfacing materials, laminates, and adhesives for cabinets, countertops, floors, and fixtures.

Wolf Appliance Company, LLC
P.O. Box 44848
Madison, WI 53744
800-222-7820
www.wolfappliance.com
Wolf, a division of Sub-Zero, offers professional-style cooking appliances, including ranges, cooktops, ovens, grills, and warming drawers.

York Wallcoverings, Inc.
750 Linden Ave.
York, PA 17404
800-375-9675
www.yorkwall.com
York Wallcoverings offers an extensive line of wallpapers and borders, as well as advice and decorating tips.

Accent lighting Lighting that emphasizes a particular area or object.

Ambient lighting Lighting that illuminates an area or room.

Appliance garage Countertop storage for small appliances.

Baking center An area near an oven(s) and a refrigerator that contains a countertop for rolling out dough, and storage for baking supplies and utensils.

Backsplash The finish material that covers the wall behind a countertop. The backsplash can be attached to the countertop or separate from it.

Base cabinet A cabinet that rests on the floor and supports a countertop.

Bearing wall A wall that supports the structure above it. Joists rest on the top plate of a bearing wall. See *Joist.*

Building codes The legal standards and methods that must be followed during any construction project.

Butcher block A counter or tabletop material composed of strips of hardwood, often rock maple, laminated together and sealed against moisture.

Carousel shelves Revolving shelves that are usually installed in corner cabinets.

Caulking Any one of a number of compounds used to fill cracks and seams.

Chalk line A device used to mark a straight line on a surface. Stretch the chalk-covered cord taut just above the surface. Pull the cord up in the center and release to leave a chalk mark on the surface.

Chair rail A decorative wall molding installed midway between the floor and ceiling. Traditionally, chair rails protected walls from damage from chair backs.

Circuit The electrical path that connects one or more outlets (receptacles) and/or lighting fixtures to a single circuit breaker or fuse.

Circuit breaker A device that closes an electrical circuit when demand exceeds safe limits.

Cleanup center The area of a kitchen where the sink, waste-disposal unit, trash compactor, dishwasher, and related accessories are grouped for easy access and efficient use.

Convection oven An oven in which heat is circulated by a small fan rather than radiated from a burner or element.

Cooking center The kitchen area where the cooktop or range, oven(s), food preparation surfaces, appliances, and utensils are grouped.

Coped joint Two pieces of molding that are joined by cutting the end of one with a coping saw to fit over the contours of the other.

Copper tubing Seamless tubing that is 99.9 percent copper.

Countertop The work surface of a counter, island, or peninsula, usually 36 inches high. Common countertop materials include plastic laminate, ceramic tile, slate, and solid surfacing.

Cove lights Lights that reflect upward, sometimes located on top of wall cabinets.

Crown molding A decorative molding usually installed where the wall and ceiling meet.

Drywall Sheets of gypsum sandwiched between backing paper and a smooth-finish front surface paper. Also called wallboard and, improperly, Sheetrock (a trade name).

Ductwork Sheet-metal passages that carry heated or cooled air, or exhaust air in a ventilation system.

Exhaust fans A fan used in a ventilation system that pulls air from a kitchen.

Fish tape A long, flexible metal tape used to pull wires through existing walls.

Floating floor A floor material that is glued together on it's tongue-and-groove edges but is not attached to the subfloor.

Fluorescent lights A type of light containing a phosphor that attracts ultraviolet light and then converts it into visible light.

Framed cabinets Cabinets with a full frame across the face of the cabinet box.

Frameless cabinets European-style cabinets without a face frame.

Framing The skeleton structure of the studs and joists that support walls, ceilings, and floors. See *Joist, Stud.*

Furring Strips of wood attached to a wall to provide support and attachment points for a covering such as hardboard paneling.

Gardening center A kitchen area used for cutting, arranging, and planting flowers.

General lighting Light that illuminates the entire room.

GFCI Stands for ground-fault circuit interrupter. A type of electrical receptacle that reacts to an abnormal condition in a fraction of a second.

Great rooms Open spaces where cooking, dining, and areas for relaxing flow into one another.

Grout A mixture of Portland cement and water—and sometimes sand—used to fill the gaps between ceramic tiles.

Halogen lights High-tech incandescent lights that require special fixtures.

Home equity loans A loan that is based on the equity you have in your house. Home equity loans generally have longer terms and lower interest than personal loans.

Header A horizontal structural member used to span an opening in the framing, such as for a window or door, and to transfer the structural load across the opening.

Incandescent lights Lights that heat a tungsten filament to incandescence in order to give off light.

Island A base cabinet and countertop unit that stands independent from walls, so that there is access from all four sides.

Jamb The vertical (side) and horizontal (top) pieces that cover the wall thickness in a door or window opening.

Joint compound The plaster material used to fill small holes and seams in drywall.

Joint tape Paper or synthetic mesh tape about 3 inches wide that is used to reinforce joint compound that is used on the seams between drywall panels.

Joist A floor or ceiling support member that rests on the top plates of bearing walls.

Kitchen fans Fans that remove grease, moisture, smoke, and heat from the kitchen.

Knockdown cabinets Cabinets that are shipped flat and assembled on the building site.

Laminate floors Floors whose structural core is covered with a plastic laminate wear layer.

Lazy Susan Axis-mounted shelves that revolve. Also called carousel shelves.

Low-voltage lights Lights that operate on 12 to 50 volts rather than the standard 120 volts.

Magnetic-induction cooktops Cooktops that transfer energy from under the surface directly to the cooking vessel without heating the burner.

Microwave oven A quick-cooking appliance that uses high-frequency electromagnetic radiation to cook food.

NKBA National Kitchen and Bath Association, an educational trade organization of the kitchen industry that, among other things, tests and certifies kitchen designers.

Nonbearing wall An interior wall that provides no structural support for any portion of the house.

Pantry A storage room or large cabinet for packaged foods.

Particleboard A material composed of wood chips and coarse fibers bonded with adhesive into large sheets from $1/2$ to $1 1/2$ inches thick. It is commonly used as the support for countertops and for cabinet construction.

Partition wall A wall built to separate certain parts of the kitchen, for example, a dining area from the work area.

Patching plaster A type of plaster mix used to fill holes and cracks prior to painting.

Peninsula A countertop, with or without a base cabinet, that is connected at one end to a wall or another countertop and extends outward, providing access on three sides.

Plastic laminate A hard-surface, thin material made from melamine under high pressure and used for the finished surfaces of countertops, cabinets, flooring, and furniture.

Plaster A pastelike material used on ceilings and walls that hardens as it dries.

Rail A horizontal member that runs between two vertical supports, such as the rails on a cabinet or door.

Range hood A ventilator set above a cooktop or the burners of a range.

Recessed light fixtures Light fixtures that are installed into ceilings, soffits, or cabinets and are flush with the surrounding area.

Refacing Replacing the doors and drawers on cabinets and covering the face frames with a matching material.

Roof windows A skylight that also serves as a way to exit a building in an emergency.

Secondary work center An area of the kitchen where extra activity is done, such as laundry or baking.

Semi-custom cabinets Cabinets that are available in specific sizes but with a wide variety of options.

Sheetrock See *Drywall*.

Shim A thin wedge-like insert used to adjust the spacing between adjacent materials.

Shutoff valves Supply valves that control the flow of water or gas to specific fixtures or appliances.

Sliders Sliding doors are made up of large, framed glass panels. In most cases, one door slides and the other is stationary.

Skylight A roof-mounted window that allows natural light into a building.

Soffit A short wall or filler piece between the top front edge of a wall cabinet and the ceiling above it.

Solid-surface countertop A countertop material made of acrylic

plastic and fine-ground synthetic particles, sometimes made to look like natural stone.

Stiles The vertical parts of a framework, such as a sash or a door.

Stock cabinets Cabinets that are in stock or available quickly when ordered from a retail outlet.

Stud A vertical framing member of a wall.

Sunrooms Also known as a solarium, a sunny room that has many windows or is enclosed by glass panels for maximum sunlight.

Task lighting Light aimed directly onto a work area, such as a sink or a cooktop.

Track lighting Lights that are attached to the ceiling by a track and can be easily moved and adjusted.

Traffic pattern The pattern of movement people use in a kitchen.

Under-cabinet light fixtures Light fixtures that are installed on the undersides of cabinets for task lighting.

Underlayment Sheet material—usually plywood—placed over a subfloor to provide a smooth, even surface for new flooring.

Vapor retarder A material used to prevent water vapor from moving from one area into another or into a building material.

Ventilation The process of removing or supplying air to a certain space.

Wainscoting Paneling that extends 36 to 42 inches or so upward from the floor level, over the finished wall surface. It is often finished with a horizontal strip of molding mounted at the proper height and protruding enough to prevent the top of a chair back from touching a wall surface.

Wall cabinet A cabinet, usually 12 inches deep, that's mounted on the wall a minimum of 15 inches above a countertop.

Wallboard See *Drywall*.

Work triangle The area bounded by the lines that connect the sink, range, and refrigerator. In theory, the sum of the lines in the triangle should not exceed 26 feet.

index

index

METRIC EQUIVALENTS

Length

1 inch	25.4mm
1 foot	0.3048m
1 yard	0.9144m
1 mile	1.61km

Area

1 square inch	645mm^2
1 square foot	0.0929m^2
1 square yard	0.8361m^2
1 acre	4046.86m^2
1 square mile	2.59km^2

Volume

1 cubic inch	16.3870cm^3
1 cubic foot	0.03m^3
1 cubic yard	0.77m^3

Common Lumber Equivalents

Sizes: Metric cross sections are so close to their U.S. sizes, as noted below, that for most purposes they may be considered equivalents.

Dimensional lumber	1 x 2	19 x 38mm
	1 x 4	19 x 89mm
	2 x 2	38 x 38mm
	2 x 4	38 x 89mm
	2 x 6	38 x 140mm
	2 x 8	38 x 184mm
	2 x 10	38 x 235mm
	2 x 12	38 x 286mm
Sheet sizes	4 x 8 ft.	1200 x 2400mm
	4 x 10 ft.	1200 x 3000mm
Sheet thicknesses	¼ in.	6mm
	⅜ in.	9mm
	½ in.	12mm
	¾ in.	19 mm
Stud/joist spacing	16 in. o.c.	400mm o.c.
	24 in. o.c.	600mm o.c.

Capacity

1 fluid ounce	29.57mL
1 pint	473.18mL
1 quart	0.95L
1 gallon	3.79L

Weight

1 ounce	28.35g
1 pound	0.45kg

Temperature

Fahrenheit = Celsius x 1.8 + 32
Celsius = Fahrenheit - 32 x 5⁄9

Nail Size & Length

Penny Size	Nail Length
2d	1"
3d	1¼"
4d	1½"
5d	1¾"
6d	2"
7d	2¼"
8d	2½"
9d	2¾"
10d	3"
12d	3¼"
16d	3½"